Anthropological Papers
Museum of Anthropology, University of Michigan
Number 91

Ethnobiology at the Millennium
Past Promise and Future Prospects

Edited by
Richard I. Ford

Ann Arbor, Michigan
2001

Printed in the United States of America
ISBN 0-915703-50-5

Cover design by Katherine Clahassey

The University of Michigan Museum of Anthropology currently publishes three
monograph series: Anthropological Papers, Memoirs, and Technical Reports, as well as an
electronic series in CD-ROM form. For a complete catalog, write to Museum of
Anthropology Publications, 4009 Museums Building, Ann Arbor, MI 48109-1079.

Library of Congress Cataloging-in-Publication Data

Ethnobiology at the millennium : past promise and future prospects / edited by Richard I.
Ford.
    p. cm. -- (Anthropological papers ; no. 91)
  Includes bibliographical references.
  ISBN 0-915703-50-5 (alk. paper)
    1. Ethnobiology--Congresses. I. Ford, Richard I. II. Anthropological papers
(University of Michigan. Museum of Anthropology) ; no. 91.

GN2 .M5 no. 91
[GN476.7]
306.4'5--dc21

The paper used in this publication meets the requirements of the ANSI Standard Z39.48-
1984 (Permanence of Paper)

Contents

List of tables, iv

CHAPTER 1.   *Introduction: Ethnobiology at the Crossroads, 1*
      RICHARD I. FORD

CHAPTER 2.   *Potentials of Zooarchaeology for Better Understanding of the Human Past, 11*
      ELIZABETH S. WING

CHAPTER 3.   *Ancient Seeds: Their Role in Understanding South Asia and Its Past, 21*
      STEVEN A. WEBER

CHAPTER 4.   *One Possible Future of Paleoethnobotany, 35*
      PAUL E. MINNIS

CHAPTER 5.   *Looking Back Through Time: Southwestern U.S. Archaeobotany at the New Millennium, 49*
      KAREN R. ADAMS

CHAPTER 6.   *An Ethnozoological Perspective on the Ethnobiological Enterprise, 101*
      EUGENE S. HUNN

CHAPTER 7.   *Linguistic Ethnobiology: Amerindian Oak Nomenclature, 111*
      CECIL H. BROWN

CHAPTER 8.   *In the Field with People, Plants and Animals: A Look at Methods, 149*
      CATHERINE S. FOWLER

CHAPTER 9.   *Pieces into Patterns: Botany of British Columbia Cultures and Influences of Society of Ethnobiology Members, 163*
      NANCY J. TURNER

CHAPTER 10. *Comments, 175*
      EUGENE N. ANDERSON

Tables

1.1. Distribution of articles by subject, *Journal of Ethnobiology*, 3

5.1. Some Southwestern archaeobotanical syntheses, 60
5.2. Evaluating macrofossils and pollen for ethnobotanical significance, 68
5.3. Systematic framework for describing modern and ancient grass (Poaceae) caryopses (grains), 70
5.4. Southwestern archaeobotanists, listed in alphabetical order, 75
5.5. Literature likely to contain Southwestern U.S. archaeobotanical reports by individuals in Table 5.4a, 76

6.1. Species and number of scientific papers published per species, 102
6.2. Relative emphasis on the ethnobotanical and ethnozoological domains, 103

7.1. Inventory of oak-naming systems in Native American languages, 121
7.2. Basic descriptive statistics organizing data of Table 7.1, 124
7.3. Culture area averages, 125
7.4. Averages relating to variables of AGR and ACN, 126
7.5. Association between AGR and GOT, 127
7.6. Association between AGR and BOT, 127
7.7. Association between ACN and BOT, 127
7.8. Association between AGR and SAT, 127
7.9. Association between ACN and SAT, 127
7.10. Association between AGR and ACN, 127

Introduction

Ethnobiology at a Crossroads

Richard I. Ford, University of Michigan

Ethnobiology is a relatively young field. First defined by Edward Castetter in 1935, it did not develop into an integrated discipline until the linguistic examination of living organisms became part of anthropology. Continuing an older tradition, those who engaged in systematics provided descriptions of plant and animal uses but did not give an integrated approach to ethnobiology and did not approach the biological relationships between a particular culture and all living organisms as a unified field. Following the lead of those that engaged in the classification of life forms, an ecological perspective in anthropology provided finally the theoretical means to integrate all practical organisms with the natural environment and cultural groups. Despite such a brief historical overview, ethnobiology at the millennium is at a crossroads.

The essays in this volume were presented at the annual meeting of the Society of Ethnobiology in Ann Arbor, Michigan, on March 30, 2000. All the participants are former presidents of the Society or, in one case, a former editor. These American leaders in the field present historical trends in various aspects of the field and the future promise of the discipline. Two past presidents are not included because they did not attend the meeting. Dr. Steve Emslie, who was a founder of the Society, is no longer conducting research in the field. Dr. Amideo Rea was unable to attend and elected not to submit a paper. In their place, Dr. Eugene Hunn, who was editor of the *Journal of Ethnobiology*, provided a special paper.

The 1890s witnessed an explosion of papers in ethno-science fields. Harshberger (1896) defined "ethno-botany" in 1895 as a separate field. Papers addressing this perspective appeared less than a year later (Fewkes 1896). The term was quickly adopted by anthropologists, graduate students in anthropology (Barrows 1900), and botanists. In the same decade papers from a field that would be called ethnozoology appeared as well. Stearns published about primitive (shell) money as "ethno-conchology" (Stearns 1889). Mearns (1896) wrote about birds at Hopi. Already in both fields scientists recorded the uses of plants or animals and their aboriginal names. At this time the fields were almost exclusively American observers of nature and American Indian cultures.

It is certain now that Harshberger did not intend to apply "ethno-botany" to ethnographic studies. His own work was based upon identifying plants from southwest Colorado and southeast Utah that were exhibited at the Chicago World's Fair. Archaeologists began to save plants from dry shelters and to have botanists identify them. By the 1930s archaeologists were encouraged to save plant remains from elsewhere and to submit them to the newly created Ethnobotanical Laboratory at the University of Michigan (Ford 1994). This field was later called archaeobotany or paleoethnobotany and has become an important component of ethnobiology. Three of the essays in this volume acknowledge the importance this subfield has in the discipline (Karen Adams, Paul Minnis, Steven Weber).

The identification of animal remains from archaeological sites has a different history. In Europe paleontologists identified archaeological bones. In the United States these were initially submitted to zoologists to identify and later a specialty was developed in American archaeology to identify, and to interpret these bones. Zooarchaeology has been incorporated into ethnobiology and is represented in this volume by Elizabeth Wing.

Linguistic Studies

Ethnobiology has benefited from the linguistic study of plants and animals and the way cultures use cognition and its linguistic attributes to express ethnobiology. Cecil Brown and Eugene Hunn present detailed studies about this aspect of the discipline in their papers. Catherine Fowler relates the importance of linguistic methods in ethnobiology to the evolution of her research in the Great Basin. All remind us of the importance of linguistics in the larger enterprise to understand other cultures.

The first researchers into plant and animal uses by people usually recorded native names for them. However, these were rarely systematized or analyzed for their meaning within the culture. Both have changed as folk taxonomy and ethnosystematics have become mainstays of ethnobiology.

Ecology

One reason that a unified ethnobiology did not emerge until relatively recent time is because the theoretical concept of the ecosystem developed long after scientists were observing the uses of biological organisms in other cultures. Description alone was acceptable. With the ecosystem concept, humans became recognized as active

TABLE 1.1. Distribution of articles by subject, *Journal of Ethnobiology.*

Volume / Subject	1	2	3	4	5	6	7	8	9	10	11	12	13	14	15	16	17	18	19	Total
Ethnobotany	6	3	4	2	3	3		1	2	3	4	1	3	5	4	1	5	1	2	53
Ethnozoology	1		1	1	1	3	1	1		1	2	1		2		2		1	1	19
Paleo-ethnobotany	4	1	3	3	2	1	2	2	1	2			3	1	1	1	2	2	2	33
Classification	2	3	1	1			4	1							2	1	1	1	2	19
History			1	1	2			1		3								1		9
Conservation						3					1	1	1	1			1	1	3	12
Palynology	1		1			1	1					1								5
Nutrition	4	1		1	1	1				1										9
Zooarchaeology	1	2	2		1	3	4		1	2		3		1	2	2				23
Phytoliths	1																			1
Cognition	1					2								1	2		1			7
Ethnoecology		1			1			1	2		2				1		2		1	11
Pharmacology						1	2	2	1		1	1		1				2	1	12
USA-Contemporary									1								1			2
IPR											1	1								2
Molecular													1							1

participants in the environment. Anthropologists and field biologists now had to be cognizant of the impact humans had on populations of organisms and the landscape as a whole. Ethnobiology shifted from being a record of passive cultural activities to a discipline where active interactions determined the structure of the landscape, the size of populations of organisms, and the very survival and well-being of people. Within an ecological paradigm, ethnobiology is meaningful for theoretical discourses and for solving contemporary environmental problems.

Recent Trends

The Society of Ethnobiology and its *Journal of Ethnobiology* are critical for the development of ethnobiology as a discipline. Nancy Turner (this volume) acknowledges the importance of the Society to her career. Many ethnobiologists have had similar experiences and made influential professional friendships. The annual meeting has become a primary professional "must" for most practicing ethnobiologists, certainly those in anthropology.

By reviewing the contents of the journal we can track the trends in the field as they have changed over the 20 years of its publication. Table 1.1 documents that traditional ethnobotany (53 articles) and its closely associated field, ethnopharmacology

(12 articles), remain predominant within the field. Similarly, articles about another close relative, paleoethnobotany, are regularly published in the journal. The number (33) increases further if we include palynology (5) and phytolith (1) analyses to the archaeobotanical studies that appear in the journal. Linguistic classifications of plants and animals, and theoretical discussions about what they mean, are prominent in the journal (19 articles) and the profession as a whole. If we consider linguistic studies to include studies of perception and cognition as well (7 articles), the journal distinguishes itself as a venue to demonstrate another approach to ethnobiology. Ethnozoology has a presence in the field with articles appearing regularly. However, animals are most apparent in the identifications of excavated remains by zooarchaeologists and the high frequency of articles in that subfield in the journal (23). A review of the journal reveals other trends as well. There has been an increase in the number of non-American authors. More attention has been devoted to ethnoecology and conservation as trends that have brought the field closer to conservation biology and restoration ecology.

Non-North American Ethnobiology

At one time American ethnobotanists dominated the profession and the literature reporting on the interaction of cultures with their plant world. This has changed. Presently, there are more ethnobotanists in India than in the United States. Ethnobotany is rapidly expanding in China, sub-Saharan Africa, and countries of the former Soviet Union. On a worldwide basis, non-American authors publish the majority of the literature in ethnobotany. An ecologically based ethnobiology is rapidly emerging in these areas as well. Ethnobiology is truly international and has been greatly enriched in knowledge and multicultural worldview as a consequence.

Molecular Biology

The way we identify and analyze archaeological biological remains is changing with the addition of "molecular archaeology" to the arsenal of interpretative methods. Ancient DNA and chemical discoveries of former agricultural land, the original color of charred maize, and the diets of herd animals are complementing the morphometric techniques that have long been staples of paleoethnobotany and zooarchaeology. While traditional laboratory techniques are indispensable for understanding adaptations of prehistoric cultures and their plants and animals, molecular procedures are more exacting to answer questions of origin of domesticates, the history of plant and animal movements, and the genetic consequences of prehistoric management practices. To find answers to many previously intractable questions, molecular archaeology is indispensable.

Aboriginal Management

In the past, scientifically trained managers made decisions about resources without regard to native people. Native people were rarely consulted because the assumption was that they were living in equilibrium in the environment. Ethnobiologists have recorded many examples of native people managing individual plants, populations of plants and animals, and entire communities. California was an early training ground for this change in attitude (cf. Anderson 1993). As more native people have been observed and taken seriously for their role in sustaining resources and landscapes, similar patterns have been recognized and will continue to emerge in the literature from around the world (cf. Atran et al. 1999).

Conservation Biology

Management by local people is but one dimension of conservation biology. Ethnobiologists are contributing information about past ecosystems through the identification of archaeological plant and animal remains. They are revealing dynamic landscapes that have changed for natural and cultural reasons. This information is essential for the reconstruction of ecosystems.

Contemporary Western Societies

There is a lingering belief that ethnobiology only studies primitive people or non-Western cultures. Such a perception has changed in anthropology. The subjects of ethnobiology are no longer the cultural residue of colonialism. Instead, postmodern communities have their ethnobiology. Our neighbors are just as perceptive about their lawns, houseplants, holiday decorations and food preferences as are distant cultures (cf. Ford 1979). These recent directions in ethnobiology are just as likely to be found in nontraditional loci as well. Literature in landscape architecture or cognitive psychology holds enormous insights that open new vistas for ethnobiological interpretation despite the source being our own country.

Furthermore, issues of interpretative ethnobiology—race, gender, class, ethnicity—are enlightened by the study of complex, postmodern societies, the United States the most obvious of them. The future will witness a plethora of studies of Western complex societies using long-established field research methods developed through the traditional study of ethnobiology in non-Western cultures.

Applied Ethnobiology

Ethnobiology has important practical applications. No longer is it an isolated field of hybrid scientists but it has become indispensable for addressing societal problems. In the future, ethnobiology's outreach will be appreciated even more. Native resource disputes headed to the courts will require expert testimony from witnesses with ethnobiological research experience. Western society will make use of ethnobiology in seeking natural products for cures as alternatives to Western medicinal practices: ethnobotanists have transferable knowledge. Finally, environmental education can benefit from research about traditional management practices. At present these highlight the applied end of ethnobiology but the relevant uses of ethnobiology will expand much further in the future.

Consultation in Native Legal Cases

For over a century ethnobiologists have been observing and recording indigenous uses of natural resources. In the United States there has been an extensive research effort in conjunction with Native Americans covering topics of plant and animal use, traditional agricultural practices, and resource management practices. As Native American communities and tribes seek to control their land and natural resources, they are using the courts for redress. Ethnobiologists are assisting them by providing documentation to support their claims and giving expert witness testimony to reinforce these cases. The land-damage case brought by the Zuni Nation against the federal government exemplifies how ethnobiology can be vital to the successful resolution of these grievances (Ford 1998).

Medicinal Products

Until recently the quest for healthful natural plant cures was a one-way street. Ethnobotanists would discover them while doing fieldwork and then share them with pharmaceutical companies. On the one hand the welcome mat in some communities was abruptly withdrawn when locals believed that the ethnobotanists were getting rich at the expense of the native consultants, even though the majority of the products never made it to any market. One the other hand, native rights activists and professional sympathizers have been critical of this customary practice in the hope to protect indigenous intellectual knowledge and to allow traditional societies to determine how such knowledge should be disseminated. Presently some groups, and in the future more, are requesting ethnobotanists to conduct surveys of their medicinal knowledge to determine if any are efficacious and potentially useful for a wider segment of humankind. They are contracting with the ethnobotanists or requesting assistance from ethnobotanists in a quest to discover medicinal plants, and as a by-product to preserve local knowledge. Kelly Bannister and Nancy Turner work cooperatively with the Secwepemc (Suswap) in Canada in the field and laboratory (Bannister 2000). The difference between past ethnobiological practices and the future is that the native people will set the agenda and determine the consequences of any newly discovered information.

Environmental Education

The "greening" of the world is accompanied by recognition that native people know much more about the landscape and its care than Western people have acknowledged in the past. Now that legacy is being developed in curricula in American schools, at nature centers, and for public education in some state and national parks. Ethnobiology has a critical role in this trend. So vital is this information that employment opportunities are opening for graduates with background in ethnobiology regardless of their professional specialty. The contributions of ethnobiology are quickly being communicated to new adherents through science curricular reforms, local ecology projects, and continuing education classes.

Conclusion: Crossroads for the New Millennium

The old ethnobiology, which concerned the uses of plants and animals in "primitive" cultures, is only history now. Ethnobiology has gone in many directions since 1935 both as separate fields and as a whole. Today the discipline has ecology to provide a unifying paradigm of lifeways that are holistic to all cultures. It is a significant advance over the separate ethno-somethings of Western science. Hunn (1990) has effectively accomplished the union of ecology with cognitive and linguistic studies and his work stands as a model for the present.

As we stand at the millennium, however, ethnobiology is at a crossroads. A tension is revealed when one reads works in the field (or subfields) written by biologists, in contrast to anthropologists. There is a difference between those who work within established rubrics of a discipline and those who work in close association with traditional people, such as ethnoecology as defined by Nazarea (1999).

Ethnobiology has not developed significantly with new theories for some time but it has exploded in applied directions, a trend that will continue further in the future. The center of gravity of interest and need has shifted from North America to other countries in Latin America, Africa, Asia, and China where cadres of indigenous ethnobotanists are addressing local concerns.

The methods of analyses are changing. This could not be more apparent than in the archaeological fields of paleoethnobotany and zooarchaeology. Chemical and molecular methods are complementing more tradition microscopic procedures. These will only continue and these fields will have stronger self-identities and confidence in new explanations developed through biological science. Ethnographic analogy will be important for understanding the processes of genetic variation and phenotypic change as a consequence of human manipulation and not as a source of usage alone as was once the case.

These are exciting times for ethnobiology. All aspects of the field are erected upon the directions described eloquently in the essays here but none can wager a prediction where we will be in the next decade, not a century, since changes are occurring so rapidly. At the crossroads we can tell where we have been, as these essays do, and also point to possible directions to travel next, as these essays do as well.

References Cited

Anderson, Kat
1993 Native Californians as ancient and contemporary cultivators. In: Before the Wilderness: Environmental Management by California Indians, edited by Thomas C. Blackburn and Kat Anderson, pp. 151-74. Menlo Park, CA: Bellena Press Publications.

Atran, S., D. Medin, E. Lynch, V. Vapnarsky, E. Ucan Ek', and P. Sousa
1999 Folkecology and commons management in the Maya lowlands. Proceedings of the National Academy of Sciences U.S.A. 96: 7598-7609.

Bannister, Kelly
2000 Chemistry Rooted in Cultural Knowledge: Unearthing the Link Between Antimicrobial Properties and Traditional Knowledge in Food and Medicinal Plant Resources of the Secwepemc (Shuswap) Aboriginal Nation. Doctoral dissertation, University of British Columbia. Vancouver.

Barrows, David P.
1900 The Ethno-Botany of the Coahuilla Indians of Southern California. Chicago: University of Chicago Press.

Castetter, Edward F.
1935 Uncultivated native plants used as sources of food. Ethnobiological Studies in the American Southwest, I; University of New Mexico Bulletin No. 266, Biological Series 4.1. Albuquerque.
1944 The domain of ethnobiology. American Naturalist 78(775): 158-70. Lancaster.

Fewkes, J. Walter
1896 A contribution to ethno-botany. American Anthropologist o.s. (1): 14-21.

Ford, Richard I.
1979 Human uses of plants: don't walk on the grass! Ethnobotany in Middle America. In: Plants, People and Environment, edited by Peter B. Kaufman and J. Donald LaCroix, pp. 281-88. New York: Macmillan.
1994 Ethnobotany: historic diversity and synthesis. In: The Nature and Status of Ethnobotany, 2nd ed., edited by Richard I. Ford, pp 33-49. Anthropology Papers 67, Museum of Anthropology, University of Michigan. Ann Arbor.
1999 Ethnoecology serving the community: a case study from Zuni Pueblo, New Mexico. In: Ethnoecology, Situated Knowledge/Located Lives, edited by Virginia D. Nazarea, pp. 71-87. Tucson: University of Arizona Press.

Harshberger, John
1896 Purposes of ethnobotany. Botanical Gazette 21(3): 146-54.

Hunn, Eugene S.
1990 Nch'I-Wana "The Big River": Columbia River Indians and Their Land. Seattle: University of Washington Press.

Mearns, Edger A.
1896 Ornithological vocabulary of the Moki Indians. American Anthropologist o.s. 9 (12): 391-403.

Minnis, Paul E. (editor)
2000 Ethnobotany: A Reader. Norman: University of Oklahoma Press.

Nazarea, Virgina D.
1999 Introduction. In: Ethnoecology, Situated Knowledge/Located Lives, edited by Virginia D. Nazarea, pp. 3-20. Tucson: University of Arizona Press.

Stearns, Robert E.C.
1889 Ethno-conchology: a study of primitive money. U.S. National Museum Annual Report 1887: 297-334.

2

Potentials of Zooarchaeology for Better Understanding of the Human Past

Elizabeth S. Wing, Florida Museum of Natural History

Introduction

The great increase in the numbers of people concerned with the study of animal remains excavated from archaeological sites has resulted in rapid development of this discipline. The recognition of the insights gained from research on subfossil animal remains is more widely accepted by archaeologists as well as those engaged in zooarchaeological research. Zooarchaeology has contributed to the central mission of archaeology through repeated demonstrations of the value of this research to a general understanding of the human condition. Though the importance of zooarchaeology still has to be trumpeted and optimum methods in research encouraged, much progress has been made.

Zooarchaeology in the twenty-first century can build on the foundation laid by the twentieth century. At its base is the general acceptance of the importance of sound analysis of the animal remains from archaeological sites. Continually more refined methods for interpreting the remains will enhance the subfield. Greater sophistication in zooarchaeological research and the potential for answering ever more interesting questions comes with the progress that has been made.

Rapid Development of Zooarchaeology in the Past Fifty Years

Since its beginnings, when the species associated with archaeological sites were simply listed without systematic recovery, quantification, or analysis, the subfield of zooarchaeology has seen great strides (Reitz and Wing 1999; Smith 1976). Archaeologists and zooarchaeologists alike realized that the animal remains represented the refuse from former meals and thus prehistoric subsistence became the focus of many zooarchaeological investigations. In other areas such as Europe and the Near East the initial focus of zooarchaeological research was investigation of the origins and spread of domestic stock (Davis 1987; Zeuner 1963). Thus zooarchaeologists with backgrounds in archaeology, paleontology, zoology, and veterinary science have undertaken research on faunal remains bringing to the field different but related perspectives. As more people with different approaches are involved in zooarchaeological research, this subfield is enriched and better able to make important contributions to our understanding of past human conditions.

With this rapid development has come a growing awareness of people as a keystone species embedded in the ecosystem. Evidence for the direct and indirect effects of preindustrial human activities on animal populations are becoming more clearly documented all the time (Peacock 1998a). In the Southeast, the sizes of Atlantic croaker have declined (Hales and Reitz 1992). Similarly, Caribbean reef fishes and other territorial species such as the land crabs and topsnails declined in size through time (Wing, in press). These size declines and population changes can be demonstrated as early as A.D. 500 in the Caribbean. Intensive hunting, fishing, and gathering pressure in which the larger individuals in the population were targeted resulted in these size changes. Other human activities such as land-clearing and agriculture has had unintended consequences of either improving ecological conditions for some species or destroying conditions for others. Many species are attracted to ecotones and garden plots making garden hunting possible (Linares 1976). Other species such as some species of freshwater unionid mussels require clear water and can not tolerate silt that erodes from cleared land. Siltation-sensitive mussels that once lived in the Tennessee and Cumberland rivers began to show population decline as early as the Archaic period. This decline accelerated during the Woodland and Mississippian periods as the result of greater land-clearing, and resulting turbid water carrying heavy loads of silt made the riverine conditions unfavorable for these species (Peacock 1998b).

Though we may think of humans as dominant in the ecosystem, zooarchaeological studies have shown the importance of animals in shaping human cultural evolution. The clearest example of this is animal domestication and cultural accommodation to domestic stock (Davis 1987; Zeuner 1963). On a basic level domestic animals need to be provided with food, and their movements controlled. Further cultural institutions that arose from animal husbandry are scheduling of castration, breeding, herding to new pastures, slaughtering, and ritual in which animals are the key players.

Faunal assemblages associated with archaeological sites are intermediate in time between fossil and modern ones. As such they provide an objective view of changing baselines as memories disappear. Zooarchaeological data can help us better understand changing biodiversity, the history of overexploitation, extinction events, extirpation of species, and the effects of animal introductions (Steadman 1995). The part played by people in the demise of the megafauna of North America is still debated (Martin and Klein 1984). However, little doubt concerns the eradication of the moas (Dinornithiformes) hunted by the Maori in New Zealand (Trotter and McCulloch 1984; Crosby 1986; Diamond 2000; Holdaway and Jacomb 2000). The indirect effect of land-clearing and introduced domestic dogs may have contributed to their rapid extinction. The moas were not the only species to become extinct during the first five hundred years of human occupation of the island. Several other flightless birds and the giant eagle (*Harpagornis moorei*) all became extinct, changing the face of the island's fauna and the economy of the people living there. With the extinction of the large terrestrial birds, the Maori turned their attention to resources of the sea for subsistence. Europeans following Captain Cook's voyage to New Zealand in 1769 initiated a profitable sealing and whaling industry. Europeans not only took sea mammals, but brought with them their entire barnyard complex as well as wild plants, animals, and disease organisms. Sheep that now out-number people graze where moa populations once trod. During the slightly more than seven hundred years of human colonization of New Zealand baselines of animal resources sought for food or profit have changed several times.

Changes in Zooarchaeology Responsible for This Development

The past fifty years has seen an enormous growth in archaeology and recognition of the importance of ancillary fields such as zooarchaeology in the understanding of archaeological deposits and the human behavior that they represent. This growth in zooarchaeology was brought about by the combined efforts of increased numbers of people working in this subfield and using improved methods in their research.

The combined research efforts of more zooarchaeologists working with diverse faunal samples have both provided a large and varied database and exposed zooarchaeologists to a wide range of research problems.

The application of improved methods allows a more accurate representation of the composition of the deposits (Reitz and Wing 1999). An important methodological change is the recovery of adequate samples by sieving the deposit with fine gauge screen. In some cases recovery with fine gauge sieves will yield nothing not already recovered with coarse gauge screen. This may be either because of poor preservation or the deposit of only larger skeletal elements as in some butchering situations. In most refuse from living floors one might expect remains of small commensal animals in addition to discarded inedible food waste. Similarly all deposits will not provide what would normally be considered an adequate sample. When preservation is poor or samples are inadequate in size or biased by recovery strategies, interpretations are limited and need special caution.

Improvements in taphonomy have allowed a more informed understanding of how people disposed of animal remains. The recognition of the losses and additions to deposits that occur over time adds an important dimension to the changing nature of the landscape.

Expanded taxonomic scope and more accurate identification with more comprehensive comparative collections have offered new challenges for zooarchaeological research. The more holistic approach, in which all animal classes represented in a deposit are identified, can provide information about many facets of the lives of the occupants of the site. For example, evidence for the stabling of horses at the General Accident site during the Roman period in York is strengthened by the presence of flies associated with horses and plants from local pastures as well as distant ones, in addition to the skeletal remains of horses (Hall and Kenwood 1990:400-404). The particular combination of plants and animals is replicated in several other Roman period sites in England suggesting a pattern of animal husbandry with respect to horses. Identification of broad taxonomic categories and understanding of their natural history usually requires the close cooperation of specialists.

Biological principles and techniques derived from other disciplines must be adopted for zooarchaeological research with care. In addition to careful and accurate identifications it is important to know the biology of the animals identified in order to understand the implications of their presence in a deposit. For example, the presence of European rats of the genus *Rattus* in an American site indicates an historic deposit or contamination of a prehistoric one. Similarly, correlation between seasons and incremental growth structures in hard clams (*Mercenaria* spp.) must be established for each location before season of death can be ascribed (Jones and Quitmyer 1996). In the southern part of their range, warm summer water temperatures limit growth while in the northern parts of their range the cold winter temperatures limit growth. Therefore it is important to know the limiting factors imposed by the local environment. In this research, stable isotopes of oxygen are used to establish water temperature changes with fast and slow growth increments. Stable isotopes can also provide important information about diet in the past. Isotopes of carbon give different results when collagen or mineral components of bone are analyzed. The carbon isotope signatures of collagen provide information about the protein portion of the diet and the bone apatite values reflect the whole diet (Ambrose and Norr 1993). All of these studies are based on experiments designed to understand both the potentials and limitations of the new techniques so they can be accurately applied.

Future Directions and Challenges

Any projections into the future have to be grounded in what we know about the present unless we are true prophets. Perhaps all one can really say is that zooarchaeology seems to be on the right course and to suggest some directions that may help to continue the productive growth and development of the subfield. Two different approaches are profitable. One is for a more holistic approach integrating different types of data from a single site or integrating data of one kind for a series of sites within a broad geographic area. The other approach is to return to old collections with carefully designed projects that avoid conflicts of collection biases to glean the great amount of information they contain.

The holistic approach attempts to integrate the data from different classes of remains from a site or complex of sites. For example, the archaeobotanist may find a decline in the fuel wood quality and a corresponding increase in wood of second growth trees. In the same site the zooarchaeologist may encounter an increase in the relative abundance of rodents and a decrease in the size of territorial fishes and snails. These floral and faunal changes are associated with an increase in the size and number of sites. These findings suggest overexploitation of resources, both wood and fisheries, resulting in population changes of tree species and other environmental changes more suitable for rodent population growth, all driven by human population pressures. The question then is what cultural changes did people make to overcome the decline in resources. Bioarchaeological evidence points to increased fishing off shore and suggests intensification of horticulture based on second growth, which in turn implies land-clearing. These changes are accompanied by artifactual changes related to economic ones? These data are more difficult to integrate than may be imagined. It requires that the archaeobotanical and zooarchaeological information be coordinated, rather than relegated to Appendix Y and Z of the site report. Not only must there be a will to integrate information but also the opportunity to do so through close collaboration.

Part of the success of an integrated approach is due to the principal investigator (often but not always the archaeologist) and the specialists working together from the inception of the archaeological project. In this way all the specialists can insure that material is recovered in optimal fashion and everyone will be able to contribute to the research plan and set objectives.

This is not a new approach. A symposium presented at the meeting of the Society for American Archaeology, April 2000, was entitled "Integrating Plants, Animals, and People in Archaeological Interpretation" and was devoted to examples of successful integration of diverse data sets. Each paper illustrated enhanced understanding of the past by such an integrated approach. The fact that the topic is being discussed demonstrates concern about this issue and provides a forum for exchanging ideas about solutions to an integrated approach that so rarely achieves its full potential. Patty Jo Watson, the discussant for the symposium, pointed out that good communication and coordination between all members of an archaeological team are essential for promoting integration of the classes of the data gleaned from a site to achieve more than the sum of their parts of the excavated remains. This requires a full-time commitment, but the more comprehensive results warrant the effort.

Another form of integration is tracing the presence of an organism or group of organisms through time over a whole region. John Guilday (1958) surveyed changes in the prehistoric distribution of the opossum in eastern North America based on data from archaeological sites. An example of broader scope is the survey of wild and domestic animals from very closely dated post-Neolithic contexts from sites in the Khabur drainage system of northern Mesopotamia (Zeder 1994). Through this approach, Zeder reveals variation in the adoption of domestic stock and discusses the social and environmental factors controlling the observed differences.

These surveys of changes in distribution of species through time and space are now possible with the accumulation of data and the power of computers. A large project initiated by Illinois State Museum and known as Faunmap uses late Quaternary data to document the distributions of mammals in the United States (Graham et al. 1994). Only those data from paleontological or archaeological strata with secure radiocarbon dates are included. A new initiative following the procedures established by the Faunmap Working Group has now been undertaken for Europe and Mexico using the relational database management software Paradox.

The data from many zooarchaeological collections are being computerized for data management purposes using programs such as Paradox or Access. Sophisticated computer users can convert data from one software program to another. These databases could form the basis for a program similar to Faunmap and include both vertebrates and invertebrates identified from archaeological sites. Another tool, geographic information systems (GIS), can be used to plot archaeological sites through time. Such a database would allow an investigator to plot the changing distributions of animals, the impact of introduced animals on native fauna, the effects of human activity such as agriculture and land-clearing on animal population, and many other intriguing problems.

Morphometrics is another analytical tool enabled by new technology. Again, the computer makes it so much easier to analyze measurements gleaned from large samples. Changes in the sizes of animals have important implications for environmental change as well as changes resulting from hunting pressure and animal domestication.

Biochemical techniques involving DNA and stable isotopes are much better understood and their applications are becoming more widespread (Ambrose and Norr 1993). Animal domestication is a particularly important area for DNA studies. DNA studies have provided new insights into the complex history of dog domestication (Vilà et al). As one can see from the nine authors of the study of the ancestry of dogs, these studies are not lightly undertaken, but require complex scientific equipment and procedures as well as collections of tissues pertinent for the study. Despite these difficulties, the information they yield cannot be found by other means.

Old collections continue to be important for specific studies in which the old recovery methods do not bias the assemblage. Older collections are particularly useful for studying the distributions of the larger animals, those that do not have to be recovered with fine gauge screen. Other topics that lend themselves well to analysis with older collections are size change through time (provided the small end of the range would not be lost with the recovery strategy used), extinction, extirpation, production of bone tools, and primary contributors to the meat portion of the diet. An excellent example of a reexamination of older collections is the study by Melinda Zeder and Brian Hesse (2000) of the early domestication of goats (*Capra hircus*) in the Zagros mountains. This study is particularly notable for the detailed metrical analysis of a large skeletal sample (37 specimens) of modern wild goats from the Near East. This sample included a range of ages, both sexes, and individuals from different habitats, thereby providing patterns of size influenced by different environmental conditions. The comparative material provided a baseline for the analysis of the archaeological remains of goats from sites that bracket the transition from hunting to herding. This meticulous research based on specimens excavated decades ago clearly demonstrates the application of new methods such as the use of relatively large comparative collections, measurements of individuals of all ages, and the attention to environmental factors affecting size. The result is a better understanding of the details of the domestication of this important herd animal.

An issue that affects all zooarchaeology is preservation of archaeological sites worldwide. In the face of population growth and major landscape changes, archaeological sites are being lost at an alarming rate. The alleged bulldozing to prevent farmland flooding has destroyed a portion of the Gesher Benot Ya'aqov site on the banks of the Jordan River in northern Israel (Balter 2000). This is only one example of countless other sites destroyed directly or indirectly by people. It is incumbent upon archaeologists themselves to conserve sites by excavating only what can be analyzed, recovering material in optimum fashion, and making findings available to the public so that everyone has an interest in the cultural heritage and a stake in its preservation.

Acknowledgments

My thanks to Richard Ford for the invitation to present these thoughts at the twenty-third annual conference of the Society for Ethnobiology. I am, as always, grateful for discussions with friends and colleagues about the field of zooarchaeology. Those who have directly influenced my thinking are Lee Newsom, Evan Peacock, Irv Quitmyer, Betsy Reitz, Donna Ruhl, Sylvia Scudder, David Steadman, and David Webb.

References

Ambrose, S. H. and L. Norr.
1993 Experimental evidence for the relationship of the carbon isotope ratios of the whole diet and dietary protein to those of bone collagen and carbonate. In: Prehistoric Human Bone: Archaeology at the Molecular Level , edited by J. B. Lambert and G. Grupe, pp. 1-37. Berlin: Springer-Verlag.

Balter, M.
2000 Dredging at Israeli site prompts mudslinging. Science 287:205-6.

Crosby, A. W.
1986 Ecological Imperialism: The Biological Expansion of Europe, 900-1900. Cambridge: Cambridge University Press.

Davis, S. J. M.
1987 The Archaeology of Animals. New Haven, Conn.: Yale University Press.

Diamond, J.
2000 Blitzkrieg against the moas. Science 287:2170-71.

Graham, R. W., and E. L. Lundelius Jr.
1994 Faunmap: a database documenting Late Quaternary distributions of mammal species in the United States. Illinois State Museum Scientific Papers, Vol. 25, No. 1, pp. 1-287.

Guilday, J. E.
1958 The prehistoric distribution of the opossum. Journal of Mammalogy 39:39-43.

Hales, L. S., Jr., and E. J. Reitz
1992 Historical changes in age and growth of Atlantic croaker, *Micropogonias undulatus* (Perciformes: Sciaenidae). Journal of Archaeological Science 19(1):73-99.

Hall, A. R., and H. K. Kenwood
1992 Environmental evidence from the Colonia. The Archaeology of York.Vol. 14, Fasc. 6, pp. 289-434.

Holdaway, R. N., and C. Jacomb
2000 Rapid extinction of the moas (Aves: Dinornithiformes): model, test, and implications. Science 287:2250-54.

Jones, D. S. and I. R. Quitmyer.
1996 Marking time with bivalve shells: oxygen isotopes and season of annual increment formation. Palaios 11:340-46.

Linares, O. F.
1976 "Garden hunting" in the American tropics. Human Ecology 4(4):331-49.

Martin, P. S., and R. G. Klein (editors)
1984 Quaternary Extinctions: A Prehistoric Revolution. Tucson: University of Arizona Press.

Peacock, E.
1998a Historical and applied perspectives on prehsitoric land use in Eastern North America. Environment and History 4(1998):1-29.
1998b Fresh-water Mussels as Indicators of Prehistoric Human Environmental Impact in the Southeastern United States. Doctoral dissertation, University of Sheffield, U.K.

Reitz, E. J. and E. S. Wing.
1999 Zooarchaeology. Cambridge: Cambridge University Press.

Smith, B. D.
1976 "Twitching": a minor ailment affecting human paleoecological research. In: Cultural Change and Continuity: Essays in Honor of James Bennett Griffin, edited by C. E. Cleland, pp. 275-92. New York: Academic Press.

Steadman, D. W.
1995 Prehistoric extinctions of Pacific Island birds: biodiversity meets zooarchaeology. Science 267(5201):1123-31.

Trotter, M. M., and B. McCulloch.
1984 Moas, men, and middens. Pp. 708-727 In: Quaternary Extinctions: A Prehistoric Revolution, edited by P. S. Martin and R. G. Klein, pp. 708-27. Tucson: University of Arizona Press.

Vilà, C., Savolainen, P., Maldonado, J. E., Amorim, I. R. Rice, J. E., Honeycutt, R. L., Crandall, K. A., Lundeberg, J., and R. K. Wayne.
1997 Multiple and ancient origins of the domestic dog. *Science* 276(5319):1687-89.

Wing, E. S.
In press The sustainability of resources used by Native Americans on five Caribbean Islands. In: Archaeozoology of Oceanic Islands, edited by A. Anderson and F. Leach. International Journal of Osteoarchaeology.

Zeder, M. A.
1994 After the revolution: Post-Neolithic subsistence in Northern Mesopotamia. American Anthropologist 96(1):97-126.

Zeder, M. A., and B. Hesse.
2000 The initial domestication of goats (*Capra hircus*) in the Zagros mountains 10,000 years ago. Science 287:2254-57.

Zeuner, F. E.
1963 The History of Domestic Animals. New York: Harper and Row.

3

Ancient Seeds
Their Role in Understanding South Asia and Its Past

Steven A. Weber, Washington State University

Introduction

It now has been 23 years since the first ethnobiology conference and 19 years since the *Journal of Ethnobiology* was first published. These developments were in part a response to increasing academic diversification of long-established scientific realms, in part due to a desire to bring together a diverse group of scholars working in the fields of anthropology and biology. Back then I described ethnobiologists as scholars interested in the interrelationship between living organisms and human culture, whether prehistoric, historic or contemporary (Weber 1986). I still believe that this creative integration of ideas and data from many different sources is what is leading to a better understanding of natural and cultural processes, and it is this aspect of our research that unifies us as an interdisciplinary field.

As the first president of the Society of Ethnobiology I have seen this organization grow and mature from its inception. Similarly, I have observed my own subdiscipline of ethnobiology, paleoethnobotany, evolve into a more dynamic enterprise for understanding past societies. This is especially true in South Asia where I have been working for the past 17 years. Like ethnobiology as a whole, paleoethnobotany takes an interdisciplinary approach, but in this case it combines botany and archaeology. Plant remains from archaeological sites can and do provide crucial clues to understanding specific societies, as well as insights into the human-plant interrelationship in general.

For the millennium meeting of the Society, Dick Ford has graciously provided a forum to explore ethnobiology and its future. My contribution to this endeavor will be to examine the historical development of the practice of paleoethnobotany in South Asia and in so doing explore the significance and future promise of this avenue of research.

Why Ancient Seeds?

In South Asia as elsewhere, paleoethnobotany is best seen as a subspecialty of archaeology that is concerned with the recovery and identification of plant remains from archaeological sites for the purpose of reconstructing ancient environments and diets, inferring how plants were obtained and used, and describing and explaining changes in plant occurrence, environment, and agricultural strategies over time (see Ford 1979; Pearsall 1989; Hastorf and Popper 1988; Gremillion 1997). Seeds, wood charcoal, plant impressions, pollen, phytoliths and residue remains on artifacts, are all important parts of the archaeobotanical record that contribute to paleoethnobotanical research. Each type of remain is derived from different parts of the plant, accumulates and preserves differently in the archaeological record, and requires different techniques of study. Different scholars often specialize in their analysis (Pearsall 1989; Fuller, in press). While the bulk of my experience and expertise is with seeds, like many practicing paleoethnobotanists, I am familiar with most forms of archaeobotanical data. I also consider this avenue of research an integral part of archaeology.

Archaeological seeds are the most common form of archaeobotanical data found in South Asia (Weber 1992). They represent the bulk of the archaeobotanical record because good preservation from charring has left a large numbers of seeds that were easily recovered and identified. Since seeds are my area of interest and because they have been collected for a longer period of time, from more archaeological sites, and with greater interest than any other form of plant remains, this paper will focus on this particular category of analysis.

A Historical Perspective

South Asia is a large region incorporating many distinct cultures, environments and histories. Most research involving the collection and analysis of seeds has been done in present day Pakistan and India. This is an area with a complex layering of foreign and indigenous influences in political, religious, socioeconomic, and linguistic arenas as well as in scholarly pursuits. The history of the development of archaeobotanical data collection and analysis in these countries is not that different from other regions of the world, the main difference being the late arrival of archaeobotanical ideas and techniques, and the slow rate of their adoption. Based on the methods of collection and use, and our growing understanding of the archaeological seed data, four general periods of South Asian paleoethobotany are identifiable, each being closely associated with a developmental stage of South Asian archaeology. The discussion of each period, especially the later two, are based on many of my own experiences, observations and interactions. For a more complete historical review of archaeobotany in India see Dorian Fuller's (in press) recent definitive paper on the subject. The idea for these four periods comes from this work.

Grab It and Bag It

Prior to the 1960s, archaeologists working in South Asia were basically concerned with artifact typology and the development of technology through time (Allchin and Allchin 1982:3). Knowledge was slowly building of a number of prehistoric and proto-historic civilizations, including the initial recognition of the Indus Civilization (see: Possehl 1990). It was also a time when many large-scale excavations were being conducted, often under British supervision. When an excavator of one of these sites noticed plant material, it might be collected and sent to a botanist for identification (e.g., Vats 1940; MacKay 1938; Marshall 1931). Most of these finds represented unusual circumstances when the conditions were just right for seed preservation to occur (for example, inside pots or sealed pits, and in occasional pockets of charred debris). Botanists generally had little understanding of archaeological method and theory, and had little interest in interpreting the significance of these finds. They were simply asked to identify the recovered seeds taxonomically.

This stage, which I like to call the "grab it and bag it" stage, has never really ended, since the practice still goes on, though to a much lesser extent than in the past. The result of such "analysis" was a list of species found at a particular site, usually without reference to provenience or context. Data collected in this manner and during this period includes charred grains from no more than ten sites found throughout the subcontinent, but these sites are some of the most important in the Indus Civilization and findings from these sites have greatly influenced ideas about domestication, agriculture and urbanism. Not surprisingly, the kinds of seeds being recovered were all large cereal grains of wheat, barley, melon, sesame, dates and peas. These scant archaeobotanical assemblages are all that remain from these early excavations at sites like Harappa and Mohenjo-daro (see Wheeler 1953). During this period, most descriptions about the usage of plants in the past were based on perceptions of what should be there or what was most likely to have been used, rather than actual observations from the archaeological record. There was too little actual archaeobotanical evidence to make testable statements about any prehistoric culture.

The Involved Botanist

The 1960s and 1970s saw an increased pace of excavating and writing about past cultures of South Asia. As archaeologists focused on cultural historical theories and became more interested in the totality of these cultures, there was a shift towards incorporating more disciplines in the understanding of archaeological sites (Allchin and Allchin 1982:3). As more archaeobotanical material was being recovered, there developed a need for specialists to make sense of it. Hence the second stage can best be referred to as "the involved botanist" phase. Although these botanists were becoming skilled in the analysis of wood charcoal, archaeological seeds and pollen, they were not trained or knowledgeable in the practice of archaeology. By this point, over twenty different plant species had been identified, with archaeobotanical remains being collected from dozens of sites. Still, all archaeological plant material came from accidental finds of large easily visible grains. Based on species known to be present, attempts were made to identify shifts in plant use, towards domesticates or crop plants. Wood charcoal data implied that the environment had changed little over the last few thousand years, so change in plant usage was judged to reflect influence from neighboring regions (Fuller, in press). The involved botanists were basically using archaeobotanical material and knowledge of modern cropping strategies to identify local and regional agricultural systems of past cultures.

It was during the end of this period that I was first exposed to archaeology and paleoethnobotany, although my work and training at this time had taken place in the American Southwest. In India, Dr. Vishnu-Mittre, a man I later worked with in the 1980s, was beginning to make a major contribution in the application and understanding of archaeobotany in South Asia. He was not only making lists of identified species (Vishnu-Mittre 1961, 1968, 1974), but he used these data to produce one of the first syntheses on the origins and development of agriculture and the environment of prehistoric South Asia (Fuller, in press). This and other early writings on the development of agriculture were made with little reference to, or even interest in, the context of the archaeobotanical material or the associated cultural material. Cultural factors that might have influenced the occurrence or disappearance of individual species were rarely discussed. Emphasis remained focused on identification over interpretation. This was in contrast to work in North America and Europe which was already turning toward interdisciplinary research with a more systematic approach to analysis and a growing interest in interpretation. Clearly, advances were being made in archaeobotany, but they were slow to catch on in this region of the world.

The Professional

The demand for botanists experienced in the analysis of archaeobotanical material eventually led to the formation of a small group of skilled professionals who specialized in archaeological plant remains, particularly the identification of archaeo-logical seeds. With more involvement in the excavation and a greater understanding of the archaeological material, these "professionals" differed from those of the pre-vious period. The growth of this stage corresponds to a variety of changes in South Asian archaeology, including the introduction of processual archaeology and its emphasis on explanation. Archaeologists working here were now interested in cul-tural ecology and on how agriculture and its origins influenced culture and culture change. Work coming out of Deccan College in this period, under the direction of H. D. Sankalia, showed that a genuine interest in archaeological plant remains was part and parcel of the development of Indian archaeology.

By the early 1980s, South Asian archaeology was finally looking upon archaeo-botany as a contributor to problem-oriented research. A small group of full-time archaeobotanists, trained in both archaeology and botany, were moving away from simple identification of the plant material and more towards interpretation and model building. It is at this point we see the first efforts at systematically collecting soil from archaeological sites for the purpose of finding archaeobotanical material. While dry screening was being practiced, it was the introduction of flotation that most dramatically affected paleoethnobotanical research.

The "flotation revolution" which began in America during the late 1960s (Archer et al. 2000:33), didn't take hold in South Asia until the 1980s. There was a belief held by many archaeologists and archaeobotanists alike that such carbonized macrobotanical material as seeds would not preserve in the soils of South Asia with its destructive summer monsoon rains. Therefore, little initial effort was made at flotation, and when it was practiced it was with low volumes of soil leading to rela-tively small collections of seeds. Nevertheless, increasing amounts archaeobotanical material was being recovered, in part by the floating of soil, and in part because archaeologists were now looking for seeds as never before. With the work of Dr. Kajale at Deccan College, Drs. Saraswat, Sharma, Savithri and Vishnu-Mittre at Birbal Sahni Institute of Palaeobotany, and Drs. Chowdhury and Ghosh of the Dehra Dun Forest Research Institute, paleoethnobotanical research and the recovery of such archaeobotanical remains as seeds and wood charcoal had become truly entrenched in South Asian archaeology.

By the mid-1980s over 80 different plant species had been identified from nearly 70 pre-Iron Age (ca. 1000 B.C.) archaeological sites (Weber 1999). Most of this ma-terial still represents accidental finds with small numbers of any given species. Large cereal grains remained the dominant material although with the advent of flotation larger numbers of small grains like millets and a variety of weedy species were being recovered. A few archaeologists working in South Asia realized the true potential of flotation. One such archaeologist was Gregory Possehl, who early on incorporated paleoethnobotany into his research designs. He not only understood the potential for this avenue of research but he also was one of the first to use flota-tion at his excavations. More importantly to me was his invitation in 1982 to take charge of the archaeobotanical portion of his Rojdi excavation, a second millennium B.C.E. site in western India (Possehl and Raval 1989).

Prior to this point, I had remained a North American archaeologist with a strong interest in botany. In 1978 Steve Emslie and I had formed the Center for Western Studies, Inc. We saw that with the rise of processual archaeology and its emphasis on ecological models there would be a growing need for biological analysis of material from archaeological sites. We therefore founded an organization with expertise in all forms of biological analysis. As ethnobiologists we also realized there was a need for a forum in which articles of ethnobiological interest could be presented together. In the past, these articles had been scattered in specialist journals, archaeobiological data appearing in archaeological journals, plant-human material in plant journals, and so forth. We felt this hampered the accessibility of such articles to all researchers in ethnobiology, and that the integration and fruitful development of the field within which we had chosen to practice could only take place once it had formally established a journal. Therefore, with the formation of our corporation we began publishing the *Journal of Ethnobiology*. We invited a number of scholars to serve on the board, all of them known for their achievements and interests in ethnobiology, and whose diverse research objectives and accomplishments were essential if the journal was to reflect adequately and intelligently the rich variety of data and ideas which could be subsumed under ethnobiology (Weber 1986). A short time later we realized that the *Journal* needed its independence so we founded a non-profit organization (Society of Ethnobiology) whose primary purpose was to oversee the publication of the *Journal* and the organization of its annual conferences.

In 1983 I began my work at Rojdi. It wasn't long before I realized that many differences existed between what I had experienced in America and what was being practiced in South Asia. The politicization of archaeology was new to me, especially the influence of Indian nationalist politics on archaeological interpretation. Excavations involved large crews of local villagers. Contextual control of each excavation unit differed depending on the overseeing archaeologist and his or her experience and knowledge. An actively involved archaeobotanist was needed. Working under the supervision of Dr. Possehl and with the help of Dr. Vishnu-Mittre, I was able to develop a comprehensive sampling strategy and a well integrated research project. Comparative collections were built up and all analysis of recovered material was done locally since the Indian government would not allow any samples to be taken out of the country. I spent between three and seven months of each of the next five years working in India. By 1988 I had put together one of the largest archaeobotanical databases in South Asia with over 14,000 seeds, collected from 455 soil samples encompassing 2400 liters of floated soil (Weber 1991).

When you get large archaeobotanical assemblages and have an interest in comparing both the relative importance of different taxa present within a sample and the overall contents of different samples to one another, you need to summarize the data numerically. Although a growing trend toward quantification and statistical analysis of the archaeobotanical record is evident, only a limited number of scholars were using relative frequencies, ubiquity and ratios. Most work still remained focused on simple presence and absence.

With large numbers of systematically collected seeds now available from a limited number of sites and with many sites producing small collections of seeds, models were developed that challenged many of the preconceived ideas about how agriculture and cropping strategies influenced culture and culture change (see Costantini 1981, 1983; Kajale 1977, 1988; Saraswat 1986). Models appeared suggesting that there was a shift to multicropping during the Indus Civilization (Jarrige 1985; Meadow 1989), that the introduction of new species from other regions, including Africa, played a prominent role in changing the settlement system (Possehl 1986), and that the shift towards more localized cultural units and away from urban complexes was associated with, or even stimulated by, a "revolution" in agricultural resources and techniques (Jarrige 1985; Possehl 1986; Meadow 1989). Further, just as archaeologists were becoming more aware of depositional and postdepositional processes, so were these new professional archaeobotanists thinking about the effects of formation processes on archaeological plant data (Thomas 1983, 1989). Archaeobotanical variability within sites and between sites was finally being examined, though on a limited basis (Weber 1992).

By the end of the 1980s, archaeobotanists working here were paying more attention to the context of recovery, and how the material might have been carbonized and how it had reached that location. The complete plant assemblage—and not just crop plants and domesticates—became of interest, including species of seeds known to be weeds and the types of associated chaff (e.g., Lone et al. 1993). While archaeobotany was still not functioning on the order of what could be seen in Europe or America, tremendous growth had been achieved. Archaeologists were finally becoming aware of the true potential of what good archaeobotanical research could contribute to their projects.

The Specialist

In the 1990s, there has been continued flotation, quantification and a growing archaeobotanical database. As postprocessual approaches began to influence archaeology so too were they impacting paleoethnobotanical research in South Asia. With more self critique, less strict ecological models, and a real concern for understanding seed preservation, a greater variety of archaeobotanical approaches were appearing. Paleoethnobotanists were now beginning to explore how various social processes affected the occurrence of specific plants in the archaeobotanical record. Fuller (in press) argues for more understanding of crop processing. Ethnoarchaeological studies are now taking on special importance as efforts are made to document the processing sequence (see Reddy 1997). Studies of living societies and their cropping, harvesting and processing practices are helping make sense of archaeological seed assemblages. New studies focusing on archaeobotanical taphonomy, crop process-ing and the potential contribution of dung-burning activities are evident.

Other milestones of the 1990s include wood charcoal, pollen and phytolith analy-ses. Large, quantifiable collections of wood charcoal make this line of research pos-sible and valuable. With pollen studies and tentative efforts to extract phytoliths from soil, new plants are being identified, in turn changing our view of agriculture, the environment and its impact on culture change. Large excavations are finally incorporating many different types of archaeobotanical work with their accompany-ing scholars. There are more well-trained paleoethnobotanists, with backgrounds in both anthropology and biology, than ever before working in South Asia. Because of the variety of paleoethnobotanical research being practiced, involving such a di-verse group of experts, we are now in the period of "the specialist."

I have seen in the last ten years an increasing awareness of the benefits of archaeobotanical research and a greater desire to have a fully incorporated paleoethnobotanical project associated with an excavation. With flotation becoming a more common practice in South Asia, archaeologists are having trouble finding enough qualified archaeobotanists to work on their projects. In 1996, the Director General of Archaeology in Pakistan tried to address this problem by inviting me to come and establish a paleoethnobotanical research facility. In 1997, under the direc-tion of the Fulbright program, I established such a facility at the Pakistan Institute of Archaeological Training and Research and was involved in the training of faculty and staff from several universities and institutions. Clearly, the analysis of archaeo-logical seeds has finally come of age in South Asia.

New Directions and the Future

In the year 2000 "the specialist" lives on, but with a new twist. Paleoethnobotanists working in this region are beginning to question and examine existing procedures and databases as never before. A real desire exists to make the data comparable between sites and throughout regions. Culture-wide syntheses are challenging exist-ing models of agriculture and its impact on culture change (see Weber 1999). While understanding the limitations of archaeobotanical data, paleoethnobotanical inter-pretation has become a more prominent component in archaeological explanation.

Efforts to understand and reconstruct agricultural practices and dietary systems in general are now being examined in terms of the rates of production and consump-tion as they relate to the catchment base of each site (see Fuller, in press; Weber 1991; Thomas 1983; Morrison 1994, 1996). Extending out of this are efforts to de-termine which plants and plant parts might be preserved and of these which might ulti-mately be recovered (e.g., Reddy 1994). The integration of archaeological and archaeobotanical data with an understanding of taphonomic processes is leading to models of plant use that emphasize dynamic change (Weber 1999; Morrison 1996).

So where does all this bring us and where are we heading? First I have a number of real concerns about the growing archaeological seed database in this region of the world. Problems with identification and quantification are evident. Not only are seeds misidentified, but the material is not being properly documented. There is a real need for a more standardized approach to describing, presenting (in drawings or photographs) and publishing one's results. In the mid 1980s, Dr. Kajale and I discussed this need to bring together archaeobotanists working in South Asia. Up to now the logistics of such a task have proved too difficult to surmount, yet after nearly twenty years and more of paleoethnobotanists entering the South Asian scene, this is even more important than ever. Further complicating the issue of interpretation, as Fuller (in press) points out, is that plant products and by-products may reflect different human activities and are impacted differently during the formation process of the archaeological record, which means that quantification and the use of statistical analysis also need to be more closely scrutinized. Making matters worse are inconsistent methods of excavation and collection of both material culture and archaeobotanical remains. Efforts to quantify archaeobotanical data from different sites for comparative purposes need to be closely watched. In the end, more communication and discussion is needed among paleoethnobotanists and with archaeologists, if regional or culture-wide models are to be accurately constructed.

Where I see paleoethnobotany going and where I hope it will continue to go is first toward the continued collection of meaningful archaeobotanical data. South Asia is still radically behind most other regions of the world in terms of the size and quality of the existing archaeobotanical record. When one considers the vast cultural and geographic make-up of this region, and then looks at how little we know about the human-plant interaction over the last six thousand years, one easily concludes that a lot of work needs to be done.

The second direction I would like paleoethnobotany to go is toward more experimental and ethnoarchaeological research. Since most archaeological seeds have been burned, an important consideration is the charring process. The use of fire and the process of hearth use and cleaning are customs that vary in different societies but greatly affect the plant remains that are recovered (Fuller, in press). We need greater understanding of the charring process and meaning of seed remains in a particular soil sample. One avenue of research is more detailed experiments regarding hearth use. Different fuels and different hearth functions will undoubtably lead to different archaeobotanical finds. The impact of burning dung as fuel is still not well understood even though it is widespread in South Asia. Through experimentation and ethnoarchaeology we can document the range of hearth designs and related functions. This is also a good approach for understanding crop processing activities and their relation to the archaeobotanical record. Today only a few crop-plant processing sequences have been studied, and most of these are for the large cereal grains.

It is true there has been an over-emphasis on cereal grains and crop plants in general while many other plant species present in archaeological assemblages have been ignored, pushed aside or even left out of the research strategy. Many of these "minor" plants can provide important information about past cultural activities. For example, weed seeds are helping our understanding of the stages of crop processing, the ecology, cultivation strategies and weeding practices (Hillman 1981; Fuller, in press). There is considerable growth potential in this avenue of study and there are probably more immediate gains for South Asian archaeology here than in new methods of analysis such as the extraction of ancient genetic material.

Most archaeologists in South Asia now know that paleoethnobotany has more to offer than simply recording a species recovered during the excavation process. With a greater understanding and interest in the natural and cultural processes leading to the archaeobotanical record, a more theoretical discipline has emerged. The analysis of ancient seeds has led to theoretical questions ranging from plant ecology to social issues regarding plant use, and incorporating biological, anthropological and archaeological theories. This interdisciplinary approach nicely exemplifies what ethnobiology is all about, contributing to our understanding of the interrelationship between living organisms and human culture.

I believe the future is bright for paleoethnobotany in South Asia as well as throughout the globe. We are beginning to see reanalysis of the existing data and a more detailed discussion. With a full range of scholars involved in debates about the archaeological seed record, paleoethnobotany is now an active participant in discussions about the past. Plants are an important part of our existence and paleoethnobotany is allowing us to understand it better, in more areas of the world, and at more points in our history, than ever before.

References Cited

Allchin, B., and R. Allchin
1982 The Rise of Civilization In India and Pakistan. Cambridge: Cambridge University Press.

Archer, S., C. Hastorf, J. Coil, E. Dean, R. Goddard, J. Near, M. Robinson, W. Whitehead and E. Wohlgemut
2000 Paleoethnobotany and archaeology 2000: the state of paleoethnobotany in the discipline. SAA Bulletin 18(3):34-38.

Costantini, L.
1981 Palaeoethnobotany at Pirak: a contribution to the 2nd millennium B.C. agriculture of the Sibi-Kacchi Plain, Pakistan, In: South Asian Archaeology, edited by H. Hartel, pp. 271-77. Berlin: Dietrich Reimer Verlag
1983 The beginning of agriculture in the Kachi Plain: the evidence of Mehrgarh. In: South Asian Archaeology, edited by B. Allchin, pp. 29-33. Cambridge: Cambridge University Press.

Ford, R.
1979 Paleoethnobotany in American archaeology. In: Advances in Archaeological Method and Theory, Vol. 2, edited by M. Schiffer, pp. 286-336. New York: Academic Press.

Fuller, D.
In press Fifty years of Archaeobotanical Studies in India: Laying a Solid Foundation. In: Indian Archaeology in Retrospect, Volume III. Archaeology and Interactive Disciplines. Manuscript in Press. New Delhi: Oxford and IBH.

Gremillion, K. J. (editor)
1997 People, Plants, and Landscapes, studies in Paleoethnobotany. Tuscaloosa: University of Alabama Press.

Hastorf, C. A., and V. S. Popper (editors)
1988 Current Paleoethnobotany. Chicago: University of Chicago Press.

Hillman, G. C.
1981 Reconstructing crop husbandry practices from charred remains of plants. In: Farming Practices in British Prehistory, edited by R. Mercer, pp. 123-62. Edinburgh: University Press.

Jarrige, J. F.
1985 Continuity and change in the North Kachi Plain at the beginning of the second millennium B.C. In: South Asian Archaeology, edited by J. Schotsmans and M. Taddei, pp. 35-68. Naples: IsMEO.

Kajale, M. D.
1977 Plant economy of Inamgoan. Man and Environment 1:64-66
1988 Plant economy. In: Excavations at Inamgaon, edited by M. Dhavalikar, H. Sankalia and Z. Ansari, pp. 727-821. Pune: Deccan College Postgraduate and Research Institute.

Lone, F. A., M. Khan, and G. M. Buth
1993 Palaeoethnobotany: Plants and Ancient Man in Kashmir. New Delhi: Oxford IBH Publishing Company.

MacKay, E.
1938 Further Excavations at Mohenjodaro. Government of India Press.

Marshal, J.
1931 Mohenjo-daro and the Indus Civilization. London: Arthur Probsthain.

Meadow, R. H.
1989 Continuity and change in the agriculture of the Greater Indus Valley: the palaeoethnobotanical and zooarchaeological evidence. In: Old Problems and New Perspectives in the Archaeology of South Asia, edited by J. M. Kenoyer, pp. 61-74. Wisconsin Archaeological Reports, 2. Madison.

Morrison, K.
1994 Intensification of production: archaeological approaches. Journal of Archaeological Method and Theory 1:111-59.
1996 Typological scheme and agricultural change: beyond Boserup in Precolonial South India. Current Anthropology 37(4):583-608

Pearsall, D. M.
1989 Paleoethnobotany: A Handbook of Procedures. New York: Academic Press.

Possehl, G. L.
1986 African Millets in South Asian Prehistory. In: Studies in the Archaeology of India and Pakistan, edited by J. Jacobson, pp. 237-56. New Delhi: Oxford IBH Publishing Company.
1990 Revolution in the Urban Revolution: the emergence of Indus urbanization. Annual Review of Anthropology 19:261-81.

Possehl, G. L., and M. H. Raval
1989 Harappan Civilization and Rojdi. New Delhi: Oxford IBH Publishing Company.

Reddy, S.
1994 Plant Usage and Subsistence Modeling: An Ethnographic Approach to the Late Harappan of Northwest India. Doctoral dissertation, University of Wisconsin. University Microfilms.
1997 If the threshing floor could talk: integration of agriculture and pastoralism during the Late Harappan in Gujarat, India. Journal of Anthropological Archaeology 16:162-87.
Saraswat, K.
1986 Ancient crop-economy of Harappans from Rohira, Punjab (c. 2000-1700 B.C.). The Palaeobotanist 35:32-38.

Thomas, K. D.
1983 Agricultural and subsistence systems of the third millennium B.C. in north-west Pakistan: a speculative outline. In: Integrating the Subsistence Economy, edited by M. Jones, pp. 279-313. BAR International Series 181. Oxford.
1989 Hierarchical approaches to the evolution of complex agricultural systems. In: The Beginnings of Agriculture, edited by A. Milles, D. Williams and N. Gardner, pp. 55-73. BAR International Series 496. Oxford.

Vishnu-Mittre
1961 Plant economy in ancient Navdatoli-Maheshwar. Technical Report on Archaeological Remains 2:13-52. Deccan College Publications.
1968 Inter-relationship between archaeology and plant sciences. Puratattva 1:4-15.
1974 Paleobotanical evidence in India. In: Evolutionary Studies in World Crops: Diversity and Change in the Indian Subcontinent, edited by J. Hutchinson, pp. 3-30. **city???** Cambridge University Press.

Vats, M. S.
1940 Excavations at Harappa. Delhi: Government of India Press.

Weber, S. A.

1986 The development of a society: an introduction to the special issue. Journal of Ethnobiology 6(1):iii-vi.

1991 Plants and Harappan Subsistence: An Example of Stability and Change from Rojdi. Boulder: Westview Press.

1992 South Asian Archaeobotanical Variability. In: South Asian Archaeology, edited by C. Jarrige, pp. 283-90. Monographs in World Archaeology No.14. Madison.

1998 Out of Africa: the initial impact of millets in South Asia. Current Anthropology. 39(2):267-74.

1999 Seeds of urbanism: paleoethnobotany and the Indus Civilization. Antiquity 73: 813-26.

Wheeler, M.

1953 The Indus Civilization. Cambridge: Cambridge University Press.

4

One Possible Future of Paleoethnobotany

Paul Minnis, University of Oklahoma

Introduction

For a paleoethnobotanist and archaeologist, looking to the future is an odd enterprise; by trade and inclination, after all, we look to the past, often millennia ago. Still, pondering the future of any discipline may help clarify its critical issues. Unlike most general considerations of paleoethnobotanical research, I will not focus on possible future methodological advances or theoretical improvements in prehistoric ethnobotany, although I am sure there will be many exciting ones. Rather, I will concentrate on other, mostly contextual, issues that I believe are relevant to paleoethnobotanical practice. We could well be missing some of the most important contributions that paleoethnobotany can make if we avoid these concerns.

The goals of prehistoric ethnobotanists in North America have changed over the past one hundred years. In the beginning, they focused on plant remains themselves: rarely-encountered oddities from the past. From the turn of the century to about 1960, a small group of dedicated scholars expanded the study of these remains. It would be most appropriate to recognize Melvin Gilmore and Volney Jones, to whom many of us owe an unrepayable professional and personal debt, and two of Jones' early students Richard Yarnell working in eastern North America, and Vorsila Bohrer working in the North American Southwest. In addition to these general practioners of prehistoric ethnobotany, botanical specialists analyzed specific taxa: most notably Kaplan with beans, Whittaker with cucurbits, Mangelsdorf with maize, and Cutler doing all three.

About forty years ago, archaeologists got environmental "religion." Natural environments and ecological theory were recognized as important for understanding the past; paleoethnobotanists became closer partners with their archaeological colleagues who increasingly embraced the business of human ecology with studies of how the interactions between prehistoric humans and their botanical environments shaped diet and settlement organization over the landscape. Techniques were also developed to recover plant remains efficiently. The widespread use of flotation, which is inexpensive and easily adapted to most research settings, increased exponentially the abundance and variety of plant remains from a greater number of archaeological sites (e.g., Pearsall 1968, 2000; Struever 1968; Watson 1976). It also has helped that more and more prehistoric ethnobotanists are also archaeologists who conduct their own field research. They can decide for themselves to deploy resources to ethnobotanical research rather than relying on the judgment of field archaeologists who, after all, have to juggle many different competing demands, only one of which is prehistoric ethnobotany.

Our research is in demand, and even more critically, archaeologists are routinely willing to pay for it. Paleoethnobotany in North America has arrived; for the past several decades we have been regularly invited guests at the table of archaeological research. The maturation of prehistoric ethnobotany can be seen in the fuller and more sophisticated body of literature now available, including overviews of methodological and interpretative issues (e.g., Ford 1979; Hastorf and Popper 1988; Miksicek 1987; Pearsall 1989, 2000) as well as collections of case studies (e.g., Gremillion 1997; Reitz, Newsom, and Scudder 1996).

More recently, prehistoric ethnobotanists have once again enlarged the scope of paleoethnobotany to include issues of agency, ideology, dialectics of change, gender, and differential power within and between groups, issues of concern to archaeologists, ethnologists, and other social scientists. The best known paleoethnobotanical volume in this genre is Hastorf's (1993) study of maize use with changing sociopolitical contexts in ancient Peru. Historical ecology (e.g., Crumley 1994) and landscape archaeology are two emergent frameworks that integrate environment and ecology with the social, political, historical, and cognitive dimensions of the human experience. Paleoethnobotanical research fits well with both.

One of the advantages of postmodern approaches (and, those unsympathetic with postmodernism might argue, one of the few advantages) is that they consciously and directly situate scholarly research within its political and ethical contexts. It is true as they argue that we do not simply uncover the past. Rather, the cultural setting of research and the researcher is an integral part of the interpretation of the past; interpretations of the past to some degree reflect the present. But we also do not simply reproduce the present in the past, as some of them suggest. Archaeologists can and do evaluate the appropriateness of competing ideas, theories, narratives, and models about the past, including prehistoric ethnobotanical ones.

If paleoethnobotanists in North America do not recognize theoretically how our work is embedded in its ethical and political context as the postmodernists keep reminding us, we recognize it in practice, having to deal at least tangentially with North American Graves Protection and Repatriation Act (NAGPRA) and other issues of tribal sovereignty. Archaeologists no longer are the sole guardians of the physical remains from the human past. Thus, we understand, or have been made to understand, that our research has implications for indigenous peoples whose ancestors created the prehistoric ethnobotanical record we study. As contentious as NAGPRA has been and as troubling as it continues to be for some archaeologists and paleoethnobotanists, having to deal with these issues has been positive in the long term. NAGPRA and other regulations have forced archaeologists to work with indigenous peoples. What has often been portrayed as only contentiousness between archaeologists and Native Americans is giving way in encouraging working relationships. Out of these associations can come alliances as both Native Americans and archaeologists recognize that their shared interest in and respect for the past binds them together in the face of much more politically and economically powerful forces that deny and destroy the past.

Much has been written on the special relationships between archaeologists and native peoples. Obscured in this discussion is the fact that prehistoric ethnobotany has value for many groups, not just researchers and local indigenous peoples. Here I argue that prehistoric ethnobotany has much benefit to constituencies beyond those commonly considered and that disciplines critical for dealing with modern environmental, demographic, and development issues are blissfully but unfortunately unaware of our potential contributions.

The Commonly Perceived Irrelevance of Paleoethnobotany

Before discussing the relevance of paleoethnobotany, let me begin with two recent personal experiences that illustrate our common dilemma. The first occurred recently while observing a planning session for a university-wide global environmental center. Representatives from approximately fifteen departments attended, and the two participating deans and organizers were sufficiently interested that they invited four accomplished and well regarded scholars from other institutions to offer their advice. So far, so good; we should be pleased anytime an institution becomes interested in environmental issues. But who was there and what they talked about should disturb us. Regrettably, as one could predict, only a token group of social scientists and scholars from the humanities was present among the many biologists, engineers, meteorologists, hydrologists, and public policy/development specialists.

While discussing global environmental problems one participant showed a slide of a Guatemalan peasant plowing a steep slope, and everyone immediately understood the speaker's point that fields have to be flat and that this farmer surely could not sustain this farming technique for any length of time. He may not be able to do so, and there is some evidence of soil erosion in the neighboring highlands of Chiapas (Collier

1975), but it did not occur to many participants that indigenous peoples throughout the world have perfected sustainable techniques for farming less than flat terrain...or muddy ground, or infertile soil, or high elevations, or a whole range of other locations considered marginal for industrialized agriculture. Such techniques do not always work, but there are enough examples through time to suggest we should pay attention to indigenous agroecological knowledge and techniques (e.g., Altieri 1995).

Such techniques however are not limited to indigenous peoples. Several months after the planning meeting I had my second experience, on a bus in Spain from Grenada to Cordoba. I watched with fascination as we passed hundreds of square kilometers of hill slopes planted in olives. Some of the slopes were steep and the ground under the olive trees was plowed, but erosion seemed minimal. I do not know how these farmers do it, but perhaps the speaker with the Guatemalan slides, his audience, and the rest of us should want to know.

At the planning session, when asked what role indigenous people have in environmental policy, the question met blank stares, though one of the invited scholars was gracious enough to provide a short response. I doubt that more than a few people in the room could conceive of how ethnobiology could possibly be related to modern environmental issues. People who should know, do not even know what they need to know about indigenous ecology.

If contemporary indigenous peoples were ignored at the planning session, then one can imagine how the planning session might view the relevance of ancient peoples to modern environmental and economic concerns. The whole event was discouraging but clearly illustrates a major concern for us.

The problem, however, is with us as well as with those outside of prehistoric ethnobotany. When is the last time paleoethnobotanists talked about how our studies were useful beyond our narrow scholarly communities?

An important future task for paleoethnobotany is clear; we must explain the value and benefits of prehistoric ethnobotany, even to those who do not think that they need to hear it. We can begin, of course, by pointing out that the vast majority of the human ecological experience is available only through study of the ancient past. If North America, as an example, was first occupied 15,000 years ago and standard written records did not begin in the region until about A.D. 1500 (just 500 years ago), then 96.7% of human experience is known only from the archaeological record or oral traditions. And even for the remaining 3.3%, much is not available via archival research. This calculation points to the potential, but does not explain the value of learning about the "other" 97% of human ecology in North America.

The Relevance of Prehistoric Ethnobotany

Let us begin by considering some benefits of our research. I suspect that in my research area of the American Southwest and northwest Mexico—a region faced with substantial human immigration of people sympathetic but unfamiliar with the local and all too easily disrupted biotic communities—a widespread appreciation of the long-term record human ecology stretching back into the ancient past and painstakingly reconstructed with the help of prehistoric ethnobotanists may well help build a political consensus to implement environmental and economic management that otherwise would not be palatable to the electorate. Showing prehistoric examples of how humans have affected their environments might offer concrete lessons not easily available elsewhere (Minnis 1999; Redman 1999).

The specific values or "relevancies" of paleoethnobotanical research I'll enumerate could be viewed as crudely instrumental or even vulgarly materialistic. And I plead guilty, but I have two major reasons for doing so. First, I think that all of us are sympathetic with the ideal that understanding the past has its own value. I see no reason defending this view here. Second, we must explain the value of our research to those in power and our colleagues. These are the individuals charged with implementing public policy and who are often ignorant of the fact that there is a long—a, very, very long—record of human environmental interaction in the areas of their interest. It is here that we need to inform our colleagues that prehistoric human ecologists have information vital for environmental conservation and development issues, real material issues.

I will very briefly outline two major relevancies of prehistoric ethnobotanical research: environmental conservation and agroecology.

Ecology, Anthropogenic and Otherwise

Let's first turn to environmental management and conservation. In order to maintain ecosystems, one must know what is to be maintained, and to do that it is necessary to understand the history of ecological dynamics. Paleoethnobotany can contribute to this goal in two ways. First, our data have been used to document past environmental conditions such as biogeography and biological community structure, but prehistoric ethnobotany is of special value for modeling a second aspect of environmental dynamics, anthropogenic ecology. The common assumption that indigenous peoples did not affect their environments is no longer tenable. In order to model environmental change, it is necessary, therefore, to understand the role of humans in ecology. A number of excellent works show the nature of anthropogenic ecology, even where we might least expect indigenous people, both past and present, to have significant impacts on their biotic environments. Fowler (2000) and Peacock and Turner (2000) are two recent examples cataloging a wide range of environmental manipulations by low density hunter-gatherers in western North America.

I will briefly describe one archaeological example, and since the essays in this volume are intended to be personal reflections, I will use a 1970s case study in which I participated. This example involves both environmental reconstruction and study of anthropogenic ecology.

The Mimbres River drainage in southwestern New Mexico flows approximately 70 kilometers north to south from the Mogollon mountains and ends in the sands of the southern New Mexican desert. While prehistoric peoples lived in the area for thousands of years, the region's archaeology is best known for the exquisite pottery produced during the Classic Mimbres period, A.D. 1000-1150. Despite the extensive damage to Mimbres sites due to looting for over a hundred years by those intent on recovering this pottery, research by a number of individuals and institutions have outlined the area's prehistory (Brody 1977; LeBlanc 1983; Nelson 1999). The research reported here came from work by the Mimbres Foundation in the 1970s and is more thoroughly documented in Minnis (1985).

Was the Mimbres environment in the past the same as today? In one instance, we can answer "no." The Mimbres River is now a fast moving, highly channeled waterway, but we have evidence that it was not this way in the past. Specialists in the analysis of biological remains recovered several organisms indicative of a slower moving, more ponded flow that are now absent or very uncommon in the Mimbres River valley today. The Mimbres Foundation zooarchaeologist recovered muskrat bones, while our palynologist identified much cattail pollen, and I recorded bulrush seeds and common reed fragments in flotation samples.

Evidence of prehistoric human impacts on the Mimbres environment was also present. We studied plant remains from the two time periods preceding and the two periods postdating the Classic Mimbres period, spanning a total time period from A.D. 200 to 1450. Each of these other time periods had a much lower population than the Classic Mimbres period. Analysis of the types of wood recovered mostly in hearths from a number of sites shows a shift. For three of the five time periods, the majority of woods used were hillside plants, generally pines (*Pinus*) and juniper (*Juniperus*). Wood from floodplain trees, mostly cottonwood (*Populus*) and willow (*Salix*) but also walnut (*Juglans*) and others, account for a significant minority of woods used. During the Early Pithouse period, A.D. 200-700, floodplain woods were not used as much, and this can be best explained by the fact that sites of this time period are father away from the floodplain.

Wood from floodplain plants are also little recovered from Classic Mimbres period sites, but distance cannot explain this deviation from the average, since sites of this time period are right next to the floodplain. Rather, the story is more complicated and interesting. Based on models of prehistoric human demography, agricultural field requirements, and spatial limitations of the best farming land, the drop in wood from floodplain plants is best explained thus: floodplain trees were removed to clear fields which were used to support a greatly increased population. This is an example then of anthropogenic deforestation of riparian woodlands.

The implications of this pattern go beyond an example of prehistoric anthropogenic ecology. As argued in more detail (Minnis 1985), I suggested that the Classic Mimbres system collapse at about A.D. 1130-1150 was due in no small measure to the expansion of the population during an unusually favorable time for agriculture when precipitation was not only more abundant but also more predictable than average. A return to a more normal precipitation regime at the end of the Classic Mimbres period left the people in a precarious situation, one that they were unable to sustain in the traditional ways. Whether this evidence of denuding of the floodplain gallery woodlands is but a single visible signal of more significant ecological damage by the prehistoric population is now unknown.

One of the problems with the study of anthropogenic ecology, including prehistoric ethnobotany, is that role of humans in ecological interactions are too often portrayed in simplistic terms. On one hand is the common and popular "Edenic" view that native peoples always lived in harmonious and sustained balance with their natural environment. On the other is the less common but still pervasive view that indigenous peoples often fouled their environments. Two recent, widely read books (Redman 1999 and Krech 1999) correctly counter the popular "Edenic" view, but unfortunately, they contribute to the common misconception that environmental management by indigenous peoples is always deleterious. Paleoethnobotanists are well situated to take a more holistic perspective recognizing that native people do actively manipulate their environments at differing scales of intensity and scale over varying lengths of time, yet such manipulations are *a priori* neither wise management on one hand nor environmental rape on the other.

Agrodiversity: Gone for Good?

The second issue is agriculture. The loss of crop diversity, both of crop species and cultigen diversity, has become a serious problem (Fowler and Mooney 1990; Nabhan 1989). The thousands of domesticated species and tens of thousands of crop varieties developed during the past ten thousand years of farming throughout the world are a vital legacy necessary for a sustainable food supply. Some of this diversity comes from North America where there were many native crops and cultigens, and efforts are being taken by governments and NGOs such as Native Seed/SEARCH to maintain this agrodiversity.

Does paleoethnobotany have a role to play here? What about prehistoric crops that no longer exist? There is an ever-growing record of North American crops domesticated in prehistory, and most no longer exist in their domesticated form being known only from the archaeological record. One of the major accomplishments of paleoethnobotanists in eastern North America, where this topic has been studied most thoroughly, is the documentation of a whole suite of such domesticates (Fritz 2000; Smith 1992). These include: the warty gourd/squash (*Cucurbita pepo ovifera*), sunflower (*Helianthus annuus macrocarpa*), a chenopod (*Chenopodium berlandieri "jonesianum"*), sumpweed (*Iva annua macrocarpa*), maygrass (*Phalaris caroliana*), little barley (*Hordeum pusillum*), and a knotweed (*Polygonum erectum*). Other plants probably were cultivated or highly managed (e.g., Hammett 2000).

Prehistoric native crops in eastern North America have been studied in greatest detail, but there is increasing information for western North America. Little barley

(*Hordeum pusillum*) and sunflower (*Helianthus annuus*) are the only species which appear to have been native crops in both eastern North America and western North America. Otherwise, the assemblages were separate. There is a growing corpus of indigenous crops from the American Southwest and northwest Mexico, although the economic base of this region's prehistoric farmers depended on Mesoamerican-derived crops (Ford 1981). Several historically known crops, such devil's claw (*Proboscidea parviflora*) and panic grass (*Panicum sonorum*), may have been cultivated prehistorically, but we lack evidence of their presence in prehistory (Nabhan and de Wet 1984; Nabhan et al. 1981).

The best example of a native cultigen in the American Southwest and northwest Mexico documented in the archaeological record is the century plant. Several species, including *Agave murpheyi*, probably were cultivated (Adams 1998). The Fishes and their collaborators (Fish et al. 1985) have demonstrated that this plant was cultivated extensively north of Tucson by the prehistoric Hohokam of the Sonoran Desert, and it now appears that cultivated agaves were widespread. For example, my colleague on a long-term archaeological project around the great site of Casas Grandes in northwestern Chihuahua, Mexico, Michael Whalen, and I have found evidence of prehistoric agave fields in northwestern Chihuahua (Whalen and Minnis 2001).

There are dozens of species that may have been domesticated or at least highly managed by prehistoric people in western North America. Here is a list of plants believed to have been managed by the people of American Southwest and northwest Mexico and the adjacent Great Basin, which I compiled (Minnis 1995) from a number of sources (Bohrer 1991; Fowler 1986; Minnis and Plog 1976; Nabhan 1985; Winter 1974; Winter and Hogan 1986; Yarnell 1965, 1977), and no doubt serious study would increase this list greatly. These plants include: *Cleome serrulata, Nicotiana attenuata, N. trigonophylla, N. rustica, Solanum jamesii, S. trifolum, Lycium pallidum, Physalis longifolia, P. hederaefolia, P. foetnens* var. *neomexicana, Rumex hymenosepalus, Ascelpias* spp., *Cirsium neomexicana, Condalia warnockii* var. *kearneyi, Opuntia* sp., *Sphaeralcea coccinea, Lepidium* spp., *Allium* spp., *Datura* spp., *Amaranthus powelli, A. lecocarpus, A. hypochondriacus, Datura* sp., *Mirabilis mutliflora, Helianthus* sp., *Chenopodium berlandieri, Atriplex argentea, Dichelostemma pulchella, Cyperus* sp., *Eragostis orcuttiana, Agropyron trachycaulum, Elymus* sp., *Rorippa curvisliqua, Echnochloa* sp., *Descurania* sp., *Sophia sp., Agave parryi,* and *Oryzopsis hymenoides.*

The rapidly expanding list of now-extinct crops may have practical utility. Could such plants be redomesticated or their genes used in the modern crop gene pool? These crops may now be extinct, but we know that their extant wild progenitors are amenable to domestication by the best evidence possible: people once domesticated them. Techniques for intraspecific and transspecific genetic manipulation are improving yearly. Given sufficient well preserved samples, is it far-fetched to think that genes from these ancient crops can be used?

Farming is more than crops. Prehistoric humans farmed much of North America for millennia, and, not surprisingly, they developed a wide range of techniques and strategies to grow crops under difficult circumstances (e.g., Denevan 1992; Doolittle 2000; Hurt 1987). In northeastern North America, archaeologists have found evidence of raised fields, and in the American Southwest and northwest Mexico where I work, techniques most easily seen in the archaeological record are water control features including irrigation, terracing, and rock mulching. Some of these techniques have found their way into the modern world and may have a wider applicability in the future. One example would be rock or lithic mulching (Lightfoot 1996) that utilizes a surface layer of gravel or small rocks to prevent erosion and reduce evaporation. Rock mulch was used in the prehistoric American Southwest and northwest Mexico in many areas. Similar techniques may be useful in hobby gardening in wealthy arid regions, such as the American Southwest, and be useful in subsistence economies of the less developed world.

Further Considerations

If paleoethnobotanists are to become more involved in the nonacademic implications of our work, then we must deal with a new set of ethical considerations that will make our research lives more complicated. Ethnobotanists working with living populations must address issues of intellectual property rights (e.g., Brush and Stabinsky 1996; Lewis 2000; Oldfield and Alcorn 1991; Orlove and Brush 1996; Redford and Mansour 1996; Snape 1996; Stevens 1997). No longer is it feasible, and it probably never was justified, to gather intellectual property from indigenous people as if it were free for the taking. The issue of intellectual property is especially important under two circumstances. The first is when such knowledge is recognized as proprietary; secret religious knowledge is a clear example. The second is when there is potential financial gain from the use of the traditional knowledge.

Paleoethnobotanists largely have not had to deal with these issues, but this may not continue. Until recently, prehistoric ethnobotanical data have rarely been considered proprietary by anyone other than the paleoethnobotanist. As Native American groups have greater say in archaeological research, both through doing the research themselves or by regulatory oversight, paleoethnobotanical research I suspect will find itself faced with more intense scrutiny. That paleoethnobotanists will also become involved, like our ethnological brethren, in arranging collaborative studies where indigenous peoples receive benefits from the research seems a remote concern us. But with new bioengineering techniques, it is not certain that archaeobotanical remains will remain "valueless" in the strictest monetary sense forever. Cultigens now extinct and knowable only through the archaeological record may have economic value in redomestication. It is less far-fetched to think so today than a decade or two ago. If so, then prehistoric ethnobotanists will need to face issues our ethnographic colleagues have been wrestling with for some time.

Conclusions

There is hope that paleoethnobotanical information may find its way to places where it is useful. Indigenous medical knowledge was in the not-too-distant past largely ignored and assumed to be irrational and unsuited for Western medicine. There is now, however, widespread recognition among the public and significant portions of the scientific and medical communities that indigenous healing knowledge is valuable. Could prehistoric ethnobotany follow a similar course?

Paleoethnobotany may well remain a quiet corner in the sometimes contentious world of science, but we should not take comfort in this thought. "Quiet" can mean irrelevant, and paleoethnobotany need not be so. I am not suggesting that the many lessons of paleoethnobotany are directly applicable to present day problems, that modern industrial and post-industrial nations are directly analogous to the prehistoric societies of the world, which often were small groups with subsistence economies tied closely to their local environments. However it is used, paleoethnobotanical research has a potential to contribute to the modern world. Arguing the greater relevance of prehistoric ethnobotany is not new, but the arguments need a louder and more focused voice. The future of paleoethnobotany in North America and elsewhere may be more difficult and challenging than in its seemingly prosaic past, but the rewards of our research may also be greater.

References Cited

Adams. K. A.
1998 How does the agave grow? Reproductive biology of a suspected ancient Arizona cultivar, *Agave murpheyi* Gibson. Desert Plants 14:11-20.

Altieri, M,
1995 Agroecology: the science of sustainable agriculture. Boulder: Westview Press.

Bohrer, V. L.
1991 Recently recognized cultivated and encouraged plants among the Hohokam. The Kiva: 56:227-35.

Brody. J. J.
1977 Mimbres Painted Pottery. Santa Fe: School of American Research Press.

Brush, S. B., and D. Stabinsky
1996 Valuing Local Knowledge: Indigenous People and Intellectual Property Rights. Washington, D.C., : Island Press.

Collier, G. A.
1975 Fields of the Tzotzil: The Ecological Bases of Tradition in Highland Chiapas. Austin: University of Texas Press.

Crumley, C. L.
1994 Historical Ecology: Cultural Knowledge and Changing Landscapes. Santa Fe: School of American Research Press.

Denevan, W. M,
1992 The pristine myth: the landscapes of native North America. Annals of the Association of American Geographers 82:369-385.

Doolittle, W. E.
2000 Cultivated Landscape of Native North America. Oxford: Oxford University Press.

Fish, S. K., P. R. Fish, C. Mikesicek, and J. Madsen
1985 Prehistoric *Agave* cultivation in southern Arizona. Desert Plants 7:107-13.

Ford, Richard I.
1979 Paleoethnobotany in America archaeology. Advances in Archaeological Method and Theory 2:285-336.
1981 Gardening and farming before A.D. 1000: patterns of prehistoric cultivation. Journal of Ethnobiology 1:6-27.

Fowler, C. S.
1986 Subsistence. In: Handbook of North American Indians, vol. 11: Great Basin, edited by W. D'Azevaedo, pp. 64-97. Washington, D.C.: Smithsonian Institution Press.
2000 "We live by them": native knowledge of biodiversity in the Great Basin of western North America. In: Biodiversity and Native America, edited by P. Minnis and W. Elisens, pp. 99-132. Norman: University of Oklahoma Press.

Fowler, C., and P. Mooney
1990 Shattering: Food, Policy, and the Loss of Generic Diversity. Tucson: University of Arizona Press.

Fritz, G. J.
2000 Levels of biodiversity in Eastern North America. In: Biodiversity and Native America, edited by P. E. Minnis and W. J. Elisens, pp. 223-47. Norman: University of Oklahoma Press.

Gremillion, K. J.
1997 People, Plants, and Landscape: Studies in Ethnobotany. Tuscaloosa: University of Alabama Press.

Hammett, J. C.
2000 Ethnohistory of aboriginal landscape in the southeastern United States. In: Biodiversity and Native America, edited by P. Minnis and W. Elisens, pp. 248-99. Norman: University of Oklahoma Press.

Hastorf, C. A.
1993 Agriculture and the Onset of Political Inequality before the Inka. New York: Cambridge University Press.

Hastorf, C. A., and V. S. Popper
1988 Current Paleoethnobotany: Analytic Methods and Cultural Interpretations of Archaeological Plant Remains. Chicago: University of Chicago Press.

Hurt, R. D.
1987 Indian Agriculture in America, Prehistory to the Present. Lawrence: University of Kansas Press.

Krech, S. III.
1999 The Ecological Indian, Myth and History. New York: W. W. Norton.

LeBlanc, S. A.
1983 Mimbres People: Ancient Pueblo Painters of the American Southwest. London: Thames and Hudson.

Lewis, W. H.
2000 Ethnopharmacology and the search for new therapeutics. In: Biodiversity and Native America, edited by P. E. Minnis and W. J. Elisens, pp. 74-96. Norman: University of Oklahoma Press.

Lightfoot, D. R.
1996 The nature, history, and distribution of lithic mulch agriculture: an ancient technique of dryland agriculture. Agricultural History Review 44:206-22.

Miksicek, C. H.
1987 Formation processes in the archaeobotanical record. Advances in Archaeological Method and Theory 10:211-47.

Minnis, P. E.
1985 Social Adaptation to Food Stress: A Prehistoric Southwestern Example. Chicago: University of Chicago Press.
1995 Extinction isn't always forever: biodiversity and prehistory. Plenary presentation at the annual meeting of the Society of Ethnobiology. Tucson.
1999 Sustainability: the long view from archaeology. New Mexico Journal of Science 23-41.

Minnis, P. E., and W. J. Elisens
2000 Biodiversity and Native America. Norman: University of Oklahoma Press.

Minnis, P. E., and S. E. Plog
1976 A study of the site specific distribution of *Agave parryi* in east central Arizona. The Kiva 41:299-308.

Nabhan, G. P.
1985 Native crop diversity in Aridoamerica: conservation of regional gene pools. Economic Botany 39:387-99.
1989 Enduring Seeds: Native America Agriculture and Wild Plant Conservation. San Francisco: North Point Press.

Nabhan, G. P., and J. M. J. de Wet
1984 *Panicum sonoraum* in Sonoran desert agriculture. Economic Botany 38:65-68.

Nabhan, G. P., A. Whiting, H. Dobyns, R. Hevley, and R. Euler
1981 Devil's claw domestication: evidence from southwestern Indian fields. Journal of Ethnobiology 1:135-64.

Nelson, M.C.
1999 Mimbres during the Twelfth Century: Abandonment, Continuity, and Reorganization. Tucson: University of Arizona Press.

Oldfield, M. L., and J. B. Alcorn
1991 Biodiversity: Culture, Conservation, and Ecodevelopment. Boulder: Westview Press.

Orlove, B.S., and S. B. Brush
1996 Anthropology and the conservation of biodiversity. Annual Reviews of Anthropology 25:329-52.

Peacock, S. L., and N. J. Turner
2000 "Just like a garden": traditional resource management and biodiversity conservation on the Interior Plateau of British Columbia. In: Biodiversity and Native America, edited by P. Minnis and W. Elisens, pp. 133-79. Norman: University of Oklahoma Press.

Pearsall, D. M.
1989 Paleoethnobotany: A Handbook of Procedures. San Diego: Academic Press.
2000 Paleoethnobotany: A Handbook of Procedures, second edition. San Diego: Academic Press.

Redford, K. H., and J. A. Mansour
1996 Traditional Peoples and Biodiversity Conservation in Large Tropical Landscapes. Arlington: American Verde Publications.

Redman, C. L.
1999 Human Impacts on Ancient Environments. Tucson: University of Arizona Press.

Reitz, E. J., L. A. Newsom, and S. J. Scudder
1996 Case Studies in Environmental Archaeology. New York: Plenum Press.

Smith, B. D.
1992 Rivers of Change: Essays on Early Agriculture in Eastern North America. Washington, D.C.: Smithsonian Institution Press.

Snapes, W. J., III
1996 Biodiversity and the Law. Washington, D.C.: Island Press.

Stahl, P. W.
1996 Holocene biodiversity: an archaeological perspective from the Americas. Annual Review of Anthropology 25:105-26.

Stevens, S.
1997 Conservation through Cultural Survival: Indigenous Peoples and Protected Areas. Washington, D.C.: Island Press.

Struever, Stuart
1968 Flotation techniques for the recovery of small-scale archaeological remains. American Antiquity 33:353-62.

Watson, P. J.
1977 In pursuit of prehistoric subsistence: a comparative account of some contemporary flotation techniques. Midcontinental Journal of Archaeology 1:77-100.

Whalen, M. E., and P. E. Minnis
2001 Casas Grandes and its hinterland: prehistoric regional organization in northwest Chihuahua. Tucson: University of Arizona Press.

Winter, J. C.
1974 Aboriginal Agriculture in the Southwest and Great Basin. Doctoral dissertation, University of Utah. Salt Lake City.

Winter, J. C., and P. F. Hogan
1986 Plant husbandry in the Great Basin and adjacent northern Colorado Plateau. In: Anthropology of the Desert West: Essays in Honor of Jesse D. Jennings, edited by C. J. Condie and D. D. Fowler, pp. 117-44. University of Utah Anthropological Paper no. 10. Salt Lake City.

Yarnell, R. I.
1965 Implications of distinctive flora on Pueblo ruins. American Anthropologist 67:662-74.

Yarnell, R. I.
1977 Native plant husbandry north of Mexico. In: Origin of Agriculture, edited by C. Reed, pp. 861-75. The Hague: Mouton Press.

-5-

Looking Back Through Time
Southwestern U.S. Archaeobotany at the New Millennium

Karen R. Adams, Crow Canyon Archaeological Center

Introduction

Archaeobotany is one of the few disciplines, along with archaeofaunal analysis, that allow ethnobiologists to look back through time. However that view is colored by tinted glasses, seen through a fog, and with a set of blinders thrown in for good measure. The people we are interested in have left us no written records of their interests in plants, or their changes to the landscape. The reality of what we do is to look at what I call the "black burned bits," which are essentially the remains of yesterday's dinners, discarded fuelwood, collapsed building timbers, clothing, tools, and ritual and medicinal needs. These bits are often, although not always, charred, but at times are in amazingly good shape for having spent the better part of the last millennium in the ground. We identify them on the basis of morphology and anatomy, which can be difficult. Once plant remains are identified, we bring to bear contextual information, ecological insights, the historic ethnographic record of plant use, statistical persuasion, and whatever else seems reasonable to interpret them. The variety of factors that influence the archaeobotanical record—including how and where people gathered and processed plants, inherent physical qualities of plant parts that forecast their ability to preserve in the soil for centuries, specific archaeological site preservation conditions, and all manner of investigator interests and procedures—can impact interpretation of a prehistoric plant record. Our fervent hope is that ancient plant use patterns by humans are so robust that these patterns can emerge despite the diverse range of past and present influences on this record. In these pages,

49

I follow in the footsteps of Vorsila Bohrer, who published a document in 1986 titled "Guideposts in Ethnobotany" (Bohrer 1986a) which focused on the American Southwest, and more recently of Christine Hastorf, who has provided us with a worldwide perspective (1999:55-103).

Strengths in the American Southwest

Four reasons why Southwestern archaeobotany has been so successful over the decades are superb preservation, intensified scale of recovery due to the era of contract archaeology, collaborative archaeologists, and a rich ethnographic record of plant use. The relatively arid Southwestern conditions, coupled with ancient preferences for living in caves and rockshelters, and for dumping daily trash into pits or unoccupied rooms of a community, have given us one of the best-preserved New World archaeological records of plant remains. Even open sites, exposed to day-in/day-out moisture fluctuations, often have pockets of exceptional preservation within them.

The sheer scale of archaeobotany in the American Southwest has increased dramatically, starting about thirty years ago, in part due to highway salvage projects, contract archaeology, and mineral extraction. Fairly thorough archaeological investigations have been conducted: (a) along many major highways in the Southwest, due to a wide variety of highway alterations; (b) in metropolitan areas, where explosive growth is responsible for significant landscape alterations, and (c) in the Four Corners region where oil and gas extraction has been intense.

As in other parts of the country, this proliferation has produced a trained corps of archaeologists familiar and comfortable with acquiring plant remains from sites. Large governmental projects in the 1970s, 1980s, and 1990s (e. g. Salmon Ruin, Dolores Archaeological Project, Trans Western Pipeline, La Plata Archaeological Project) have trained a whole generation of younger scholars in the routine acquisition of site sediments for the smaller plant remains (seeds, charcoal, pollen) often invisible to the naked eye (Bohrer 1986a). Many of these archaeologists are now in state and federal regulatory positions where they both appreciate and understand the value of archaeobotanical research, and are willing partners in expanding our knowledge of past plant use.

The ethnographic record, dating back to the late 1800s, has provided us with a rich record of human/plant relations, as well as commentary on human habits and activities that alter environments. This historic record is often referred to by archaeobotanists trying to craft explanations about past plant use and patterning at archaeological sites. Selection of modern groups considered likely descendants of a given prehistoric group, or selection of groups occupying the same or similar habitats, are two priorities in the choice of appropriate ethnographic analogs.

Highlights of Southwestern U.S. Archaeobotany

Subsistence

Depending on time period, an ancient dinner may have included corn, beans or squash, but most always likely included opportunistic plants (we might call them weeds) like goosefoot (*Chenopodium*), amaranth (*Amaranthus*), purslane (*Portulaca*), groundcherry (*Physalis*), more established plants like prickly pear (*Opuntia*) fruit, plus many other wild plants. The record of wild plant use in the prehistoric Southwest has been recently synthesized by Huckell and Toll (in press), while that of reliance on domesticated plants, both imported from Mexico and indigenous, has been summarized by Ford (1981, 1985) and more recently by Fish (in press).

A number of domesticates entered the Southwest from Mexico, summarized by Ford (1981, 1985), Wills (1988), Adams (1994), Fish (in press) and Huckell (in press). Two of the earliest were maize (*Zea mays* L.) and cultivated amaranth (*Amaranthus*). Based on direct dating of prehistoric remains, it seems that maize was being grown in the U.S.-Mexico borderlands region perhaps as early as 3500-4000 years ago (Hard and Roney 1998; Diehl 1999; Carpenter et al. 1999; Huckell et al. 1999). It was clearly well-established in the Southwest 3000 years ago (Adams 1994). Maize will be discussed in more detail below.

Cultivated forms of amaranth, identified because their seeds are commonly pale colored as well as black, were here by the Late Archaic. Based on scanning electron microscope observation of thin seed coats on charred specimens, an unidentified species of domesticated amaranth was present in northern Chihuahua by 1000 B.C. (Fritz et al. 1999). *Amaranthus cruentus*, identified via nonseed remains and dating to around 500 B.C., has been reported from Fresnal Shelter in New Mexico (Bohrer 1983; Tagg 1996). One of the grain amaranths (*Amaranthus hypochondriacus*, as *A. leucocarpus*) was first described from the late A.D. 1300's site of Tonto National Monument (Bohrer 1962:107-9), where uncharred fragmentary flowering heads, and both pale and dark seeds preserved. At that time, Bohrer (1962:108) suggested that a domesticated form "*could* have been cultivated" by the Hohokam in the earlier pre-Classic site of Snaketown, where quantities of charred *Amaranthus* seeds had originally been described as "wild rather than cultivated" because of their small size (Jones 1942). During reexamination of the Snaketown amaranth seeds, Miksicek (1987a) considered them cultivated, reporting them to be slightly larger and morphologically distinguishable in other ways from wild seeds. Cultivated amaranth seeds have also been reported from a small number of later southern Arizona Hohokam sites (Miksicek 1987a; Gasser and Kwiatkowski 1991a:441), and uncharred pale-seeded *Amaranthus hypochondriacus* was present in the post-A.D. 900 Pinaleno cotton cache in southeastern Arizona (Huckell 1993:183-84). A thorough review of the entire record of domesticated amaranths in the Southwest would be welcome. Since size may (Miksicek 1987a) or may not (Jones 1942; Sauer 1950) be a reliable way to delineate cultivated from wild amaranths, especially given effects of carbonization on seeds with a natural tendency to puff up or pop, this review should include an assessment of any morphological changes associated with charring, and illustrate other identification criteria (e.g. shape, seed-coat thickness) applicable to charred specimens that lack the critical pale color trait.

Other domesticates followed maize and amaranth from Mexico. Although it is difficult to distinguish wild from domesticated cucurbits based on rind fragments alone, *Cucurbita*-type rind fragments show up in early archaeological sites. Currently, the earliest dated squash identifiable to species (*Cucurbita pepo*) has been reported from 950 B.C. deposits at Sheep Camp Shelter in northern New Mexico (Simmons 1986), and from later caves in southern New Mexico (Cutler and Whitaker 1961). Fragments of non-wild bean (*Phaseolus*) cotyledons also show up in early agricultural sites, but provide challenges to identification. Domesticated common beans (*Phaseolus vulgaris*) are clearly present by 2000-2300 years ago in New Mexico (Kaplan 1956, 1965; Kaplan and Lynch 1999; Wills 1988). Tepary beans (*Phaseolus acutifolius*), thought by some to have been domesticated in the region of northern Mexico/southern Southwest (Nabhan and Felger 1978; Ford 1985), were likely in the Southwest early in the first centuries A.D., as were gourds (*Lagenaria*) (Cutler and Whitaker 1961). Some of the earliest cotton (*Gossypium*) dates to at least the third and fourth centuries A.D. in southern Arizona (Elson et al. 1995:228), though the production of cotton was primarily a Hohokam endeavor until after A.D. 1100 when it spread to the uplands (Huckell 1993). The presence of tobacco (*Nicotiana*) seeds have been reported from early agricultural sites in both Arizona and New Mexico (Miksicek and Gasser 1989; Hammett 1993; Huckell 1998:73-79), and although it seems reasonable that tobacco was being managed in these locations, the case for a domesticated form (*N. rustica*) needs strengthening.

A number of other crops came northward during yet another wave of introductions into the Southwest in the late prehistoric period, likely after A.D. 700. These included jackbeans (*Canavalia ensiformis*), lima beans (*Phaseolus lunatus*), and two other species of squash, the butternut (*C. moschata*) and cushaw (*Cucurbita argyrosperma*, formerly *C. mixta*) (Cutler and Whitaker 1961). The best present evidence suggests scarlet runner beans (*Phaseolus coccineus*) were introduced historically (Kaplan 1956:224), as was Hubbard squash (*Cucurbita maxima*) (Cutler and Whitaker 1961).

Maize Agriculture

As much as anywhere else in the United States, Southwestern archaeologists have filled the literature of the past fifty years with studies of, and opinions about, maize, while archaeobotanists have routinely counted row numbers and measured cupule (pockets where kernels are seated) widths (Adams 1994). The timing, location, and extent of the first commitments to maize agriculture, as well as the reasons for it, have all been the subject of debate (Wills 1996; Huckell 1995; Matson 1991), but the archaeobotanical record of maize agriculture is rarely used to test competing models of these early commitments. This dialogue has continued over the past decade in southern Arizona, where a number of Late Archaic sites with residential architecture, storage facilities, and abundant maize remains now date to the B.C. 800-A.D. 150 period (Mabry et al. 1997; Mabry 1998). Research in this region now suggests an earlier date for the serious adoption of agriculture in the Southwest (Huckell 1995; Mabry 1999), and archaeobotany has made major contributions to this story.

The literature talks about the varieties or races of maize present in the past, however, studies are sparse that examine the effect of growing season parameters (Adams et al. 1999) or charring (Brugge 1965; Stewart and Robertson 1971) on maize morphology, and whether these nongenetic factors significantly influence our ability to tell archaeological maize varieties apart. There are still few adequate morphological descriptions of maize races (see Adams et al. 1999). A number of other tasks pertinent to understanding maize in Southwestern prehistory previously pointed out by Bohrer (1986a) are as yet uncompleted.

Indigenous Domesticates

People of the prehistoric Southwest had relationships with wild plants that ranged from encouraged to cultivated, and to date the most work on potential indigenous domesticates has occurred in the Hohokam area (Bohrer 1991). The morphology of some parts leads us to believe they were domesticated in ancient times, for example little barley (*Hordeum pusillum*) (Bohrer 1984; Adams 1987a) and Mexican crucillo (*Condalia warnockii*) (Bohrer 1991). The unusual geographic distribution of agave (*Agave*) and cholla (*Opuntia*) plant parts in some locations suggests management of stands (Bohrer 1991; Fish et al. 1985, 1992a; Fish 1984a). Sonoran panic grass (*Panicum sonorum*) is thought to be an indigenous domesticate (Nabhan and de Wet 1984), and devil's claw (*Proboscidea parviflora*) is considered a historic domesticate, grown for its seed pod fibers as basketry material and for its edible seeds (Nabhan et al. 1981).

Supporting arguments remain to be developed for many other taxa suggested to have been locally cultivated or encouraged by the Hohokam. The same types of evidence utilized elsewhere, such as anatomical/morphological change, range extensions, and plausibility arguments (Smith 1992) should be considered. This effort could include the members of a cool-season complex of plants (*Chenopodium, Descurainia, Astragalus*, and *Phalaris*) (Bohrer 1991), and a number of other plants (*Lycium, Hoffmanseggia, Atriplex, Monolepis, Boerhaavia, Physalis*) listed as possibly manipulated in some way in prehistory (Fish and Nabhan 1991; Fish, in press). So far no one has taken a serious look at potential indigenous domesticates in either the Ancestral Puebloan or Mogollon culture areas, but efforts could be made for those wild plant resources (e.g. *Physalis, Stipa*) that are commonly recovered, some of which may have had established relationships with humans that went beyond simply the harvest of wild resources.

Extensive Use of Wild Plants

Detailed multisite and regional comparisons of flotation and macrofossil sample data are scarce. This is in part due to the difficulty of synthesizing a huge literature of archaeobotanical reports on archaeobotanical samples that have been acquired, processed and reported in diverse ways. Therefore, to date the extensive record of wild plant use in the Southwest has been broadly summarized by researchers, including a recent effort covering the entire Southwest (Huckell and Toll, in press).

In the Ancestral Puebloan (Anasazi) region, frequently identified resources include cheno-ams (*Chenopodium/Amaranthus*), ground cherry (*Physalis*), globemallow (*Sphaeralcea*), grasses (Poaceae) including ricegrass (*Stipa*), various members of the mustard (Brassicaceae) and sunflower (Asteraceae) families, purslane (*Portulaca*), and prickly pear and cholla (*Opuntia* spp.) cacti, among others (Brand 1994). Mogollon groups focused on similar resources (Minnis 1985; Huckell 1999). Based on perhaps the best currently summarized archaeobotanical record for a cultural area, the Hohokam gathered many of the same wild plants, along with saguaro (*Carnegiea*) and mesquite (*Prosopis*) fruit (Gasser 1982b; Gasser and Kwiatkowski 1991a, 1991b).

There is a short list of weedy annuals (cheno-ams, purslane, tansy mustard, globemallow) that appear throughout the Southwest through time. The inference is that disturbed ground, including agricultural fields, provided extensive areas for weedy plants that could be gathered both as greens and as seeds. There are also a number of well-established perennials (ricegrass, cacti, mesquite, pinyon and juniper) that contributed regularly to the diet. Diversification of resources with time is suggested for some locations in Arizona (Fry and Hall 1975; Sutton and Reinhard 1995; Gasser 1982a), New Mexico (Doebley 1976, 1981; Toll 1985) and Colorado (Stiger 1977, 1979). In other locations, for example the Hohokam region, diachronic variability was minor compared to spatial variability (Gasser and Kwiatkowski 1991a, 1991b).

Diet

What humans actually ate has been tracked generally via isotopic studies (Matson and Chisholm 1991; Chisholm and Matson 1994; Ezzo 1993; Martin 1999), and more specifically via the human coprolite record (e.g. Stiger 1977, 1979; Williams-Dean 1978; Minnis 1989; Sutton and Reinhard 1995). Carbon isotopic signatures in the Southwest are complicated by the availability of useful plants representing all three major photosynthetic pathways (C_3, C_4 and CAM). Coprolite studies do not always include analysis of possibly a major portion of the diet represented by greens (Bohrer 1986a). At present, however, the two types of analyses suggest maize was often a major subsistence resource, along with a diversity of other domesticates and wild plants. In the Grasshopper area of Arizona, a look at isotopes and trace elements suggested differences in diet due to time, space and gender (Ezzo 1993).

Nutrition

The nutritional components of prehistoric diets have been rarely considered, despite the fact that information on wild plant nutrient content is available (Ross 1941; Greenhouse 1979; Greenhouse et al. 1981; Calloway et al. 1974). One study has evaluated the nutritional value of presumed ancient plant and animal foods recovered in coprolites from southwestern Colorado and made inferences regarding disease, malnutrition and dietary deficiencies (Scott-Cummings 1991, 1995). The study suggested that diets were basically adequate, but likely at times experienced deficiencies of water soluble vitamins, iron, Vitamin C, and insufficient calories.

Material Culture and Environmental Insights

Fuels/Construction Timbers

People of the past developed fuelwood preferences and favored certain trees for construction timbers just as we might. In forested upland regions where conifers are common, juniper and pine (most likely pinyon) were often burned for fuel, as were smaller branches of a wide variety of shrubs and smaller trees. Juniper was an especially favored construction timber choice, likely for the same reasons we prefer it for fence posts and cedar closets. A recent effort to locate the source area of ancient construction timbers brought to Chaco Canyon included examining their chemistry and the chemistry of trees in locations where beams were likely harvested; initial results suggest that some insights into wood harvest behavior may be possible (Durand et al. 1999).

Even in the southern Arizona desert, where access to conifer wood was limited, the occasional piece shows up in an ancient community, in some cases likely carried down from the mountains as driftwood in floods. In the Sonoran Desert, people picked the legume trees such as mesquite (*Prosopis*) and acacia (*Acacia*) for fuels and foods, as well as many trees of riparian habitats such as willow (*Salix*), cottonwood (*Populus*), ash (*Fraxinus*) and sycamore (*Platanus*). A synthesis of wood use through time in the major cultural regions of the Southwest (Ancestral Puebloan, Mogollon, Hohokam) would be welcome.

Prehistoric Ecology

The Southwestern archaeobotanical record has provided us with a look at the ecology of some ancient plants and landscapes. For example, bugseed (*Corispermum*) was once considered historically introduced, but has since been clearly established via the archaeological record to have been there in prehistory (Betancourt et al. 1984). Other plants (*Mentzelia albicaulis, Portulaca spp., Cycloloma atriplicifolium, Kallstroemia* spp.*, Cucurbita foetidissima, Allium recurvatum, Tradescantia occidentalis*) now seeming to be locally extinct in some areas may well have been available in greater amounts in prehistory, due in part to intentional human actions (Bohrer 1978). Use of fire, to agriculturalists, may have been "as respected as the digging stick" (Bohrer 1992), and considered an important management tool to manipulate chaparral (Bohrer 1997; Adams 1998). A classic example of paleoenvironmental reconstruction was offered by Miksicek for the Hohokam in a region between the Gila and Salt Rivers (1984).

Palynologists have made some notable paleoecological contributions. The work by Bohrer at Snaketown in Arizona (1970, 1971) remains an outstanding example of archaeobotanical interpretation and paleoecological analysis in the American Southwest. She was the first to reconstruct plant communities visited by the Hohokam, and the first to utilize seed concentration indices to speculate on both successful riverine irrigation and episodes of irrigation crop failure. At Snaketown she interpreted cheno-am pollen in archaeological sites as reflecting human disturbance (Bohrer 1970), rather than as a direct measure of environmental conditions (Schoenwetter and Doerschlag 1971; Schoenwetter 1979). Later, along with others, she helped lay out a case for cultivation of cholla (*Opuntia*) cacti near ancient communities in both Arizona and New Mexico (Housley 1974; Bohrer 1986b, 1987; Fish 1984a; Gish 1987).

We already know quite a bit about prehistoric agriculturalists: for example, which crops were introduced from Mexico, the timing of their introduction, some of the indigenous domesticates and the possibility of others, and the geographical patterning of crops. In the northern Rio Grande, people have begun to realize the level of sophistication of field systems, including rock mulching systems and microtopographic water control (Anschuetz 1995). In southern Arizona, ancient farmers applied a variety of agricultural and wild plant gathering strategies to a diversified landscape that ranged from river bottom to lower mountain flanks (Fish et al. 1992b). A future challenge could focus more on how fields were laid out within field systems, looking for evidence of agricultural pollen types (Fish 1984a:129; Smith 1997).

An understanding of prehistoric ecology can be informed by a variety of modern studies, despite the potential effects of such historic forces as introduced non-native weed floras, domestic grazing animals, modern technologies for agriculture, and fire suppression. As a start, a general document such as "Biotic Communities of the American Southwest: United States and Mexico" (Brown 1982) introduces the Southwestern landscape, and provides lists of plants and animals associated with various modern plant/animal communities. Archaeobotanists must also utilize ecology and range-management literature for more specific data on individual species or locations, best exemplified by the publications of Bohrer (1992, 1997).

Southwestern archaeobotanists have made a number of direct contributions to baseline ecological information, in their efforts to understand ancient plant/landscape/pollen associations. For example, by carefully observing the reproductive biology of a living *Agave murpheyi* plant, the sequence of events involved in the production of clones has been outlined; in addition to baseline ecological data, such studies provide insight into previously unknown aspects of prehistoric *Agave* domestication (Adams and Adams 1998). Also in Arizona, a series of visits to modern landforms throughout a calendar year revealed that many of the weedy plants recovered from ancient Hohokam sites prefer to grow along the edges of modern agricultural fields, as opposed to other disturbed ground sites; this preference was likely shared in prehistory as well (Adams and Welch 1997). Repeated observations of plants and their preferred landforms not only inform us of the locations likely visited regularly by ancient gatherers, but also of the seasons when plant parts might be ripe, and of what other plant resources could have been simultaneously available (Adams and Welch 1994, 1997; Adams 1988).

Anthropogenic Ecology

People of the past altered their landscapes by such activities as clearing for agriculture, gathering wood for construction timbers or fuelwood, accidental or intentional use of fire, and repeated harvests of wild plants. For example, in Arizona, plant evidence suggests the people of the Queen Creek area manipulated vegetation by fire to clear fields and increase yields (Bohrer 1991, 1992), while farther north they burned chaparral to draw animals to new growth of shrubs such as mountain mahogany (Bohrer 1997; Adams 1998). Fish has looked specifically at Hohokam impacts on the Sonoran Desert environment, especially focusing on agricultural activity, irrigation systems, and use of fire (Fish 2000). Wood depletion in the ancient Southwest has been demonstrated in the Mimbres (Minnis 1978) and Ancestral Puebloan areas (Kohler and Matthews 1988; Kohler 1992; Dean 1969; Betancourt and Van Devender 1981). A range of studies of the ways ancient humans affected past landscapes at the ecosystem, plant population, and even individual plant level have been summarized by Adams (in press).

With perspective offered by the prehistoric record, we realize that some altered landscapes have yet to return to their state prior to intensive human use or occupation. For example, based on packrat midden studies (Betancourt and Van Devender 1981) and modeling the longterm effects of fuelwood harvests on pinyon/juniper woodlands (Samuels and Betancourt 1982), researchers feel that prehistoric wood harvesting at Chaco Canyon may have depleted a sparse forest of pine and juniper trees, a forest which has not returned since prehistoric abandonment of the canyon in the early twefth century. These same researchers also wonder if the historic invasion of pinyon/juniper woodland into southwestern grasslands is not so much an invasion, as a recovery of woodlands from heavy use by large prehistoric settlements (Samuels and Betancourt 1982; Betancourt et al. 1993).

Other Insights from the Archaeobotanical Record

Exceptions to the Norm

From time to time we are reminded that the archaeobotanical record we routinely recover often only provides a peek at past plant use, and likely a skewed one at that. This is illustrated at the Quemado Alegre site dating to A.D. 520 in west-central New Mexico, where a catastrophically burned pit structure preserved the original contents of over a dozen ceramic, gourd, and basketry vessels (Toll and McBride 1996a). This open site mimics caves or rock shelters in its ability to preserve ancient plant remains, with the added advantage that the vessels and baskets at Quemada Alegre were associated with artifacts in clearly defined activity areas. This assemblage not only linked plant remains with their contexts of use, but it offered some realistic perceptions of actual quantities of food materials in storage for a family at a given moment. Despite intense archaeological efforts to recover plant remains from numerous sites in west-central New Mexico, few reveal such insights as Quemada Alegre, which hints at what we might routinely be missing. The Quemada Alegre plant assemblage revealed that farming was a vital part of economic pursuits during a period when other area sites with poor preservation showed few signs of agricultural resources.

Economic Issues: Production, Processing, Consumption, Specialization

Other parts of the world have developed production and processing models, based on ethnographic observation and analysis of botanical samples gathered from traditional cereal processing (Hillman 1984; Jones 1984). In the Southwest, there has been little accomplished along these lines, in part because opportunities no longer exist to gather detailed data on plant production, harvesting and processing. However, there has been an attempt to recognize plant resource specialization in prehistory, based on the archaeobotanical record of Hohokam sites in the Sonoran Desert (Gasser and Miksicek 1985; Gasser and Kwiatkowski 1991b). For example, when the presence value of cotton (*Gossypium*) seeds exceeds 15-20%, increased production, possibly for exchange, may be implied. Other sites and regions within the Hohokam area were thought to have specialized in other resources.

In an effort to investigate resource specialization, trade, and redistribution, researchers attempted to distinguish production from consumption using archaeobotanical materials from the Hohokam Classic period in the Tucson Basin (Fish and Donaldson 1991). There, evidence pointed to differential production of cotton, corn and agave among archaeological sites located in situations with varying potential for successful floodplain agriculture. This project translated site-specific subsistence data into a framework of ancient economic relationships. In the Tonto Basin of Arizona, the record of pollen and charred remains indicated exchange of foods between large and small communities, all sharing similar subsistence bases, yet occupying different environmental situations (Fish 1998a). Finally, in the Phoenix Basin, the pollen record suggested two types of resource differentiation: a single structure within individual house groups often appeared to serve as a locus for food storage or preparation, and the platform mound precinct had the most abundant values for maize and other cultigens, signifying some level of social organization or control of foods in specialized structures (Fish 1989).

Political Questions

Elsewhere, Johannessen (1988, 1993) examined cultural and political change using plant remains from the American Bottom of the Mississippi River valley. Status among Moundville chiefdoms was partly reflected in plant remains (Welch and Scarry 1995). In the American Southwest, there are no good examples of the use of the archaeobotanical record to evaluate or contribute to political issues.

Medicinal and Ritual Use of Plants

It can be difficult to determine which plants ancient folks might have selected for medicinal or ritual/ceremonial uses. One problem is the principle of equifinality; that is, the same plants gathered for different reasons may leave similar looking records. For example, historically the Hopi have sought juniper (*Juniperus*) branches as firewood, to produce ash to protect newborns, to make tea for a variety of reasons, and to make a ceremonial body paint (Whiting 1966:62). Finding burned juniper charcoal and twigs in an archaeological hearth might reflect one or all of these activities, and interpreting the human behaviors that left the residue would be difficult.

On occasion, however, a clear instance of medicinal use of plants is revealed. An example of the medicinal use of Mormon tea (*Ephedra*), and possibly of mesquite (*Prosopis*) has been reported by Sobolik and Gerick (1992) in a study of pollen in coprolites from an Archaic age cave in western Texas. In the historic period in the Galisteo Basin of New Mexico, two woven baskets dating to the mid-seventeenth century contained roots, bark/stems and herb bundles interpreted as assemblages intended for healing (Toll and McBride 1996b). The considerable diversity of materials present, coupled with the nonlocal origin of some of the specimens, and supported by well-documented Hispanic records of their use as medicinal plants, allowed researchers a window into the arena of past medicinal plants. This record also reinforced the links, often assumed, between the historic written record and plant usage by earlier groups.

Syntheses

A diverse set of syntheses are now available for the Southwestern archaeobotanical record (Table 5.1). Hohokam archaeobotanists have assessed a large and complicated record for general patterns of human behavior with plants in the southern Ari-

TABLE 5.1. Some Southwestern archaeobotanical syntheses.

Synthesis Topic	References
Hohokam, general	Gasser 1982b; Gasser and Kwaitkowski 1991a, 1991b
Hohokam, indigenous domesticates	Bohrer 1991
Hohokam, pollen	Gish 1991
Southwest, wild plants	Huckell and Toll, in press
Southwest, domesticated plants	Ford 1981, 1985; Fish, in press
Zea mays	Adams 1994
Gossypium	Huckell 1993
Phaseolus	Kaplan 1956, 1965; Kaplan and Lynch 1999; Nabhan and Felger 1978
Cucurbitaceae	Cutler and Whitaker 1961
Nicotiana	Adams and Toll 2001; Winter, 2001a, 2001b
Anthropogenic ecology	Adams, in press; Fish 2000
Seasonality	Adams and Bohrer 1998
Middle Little Colorado River	Adams 1996
Tucson Basin	Miksicek 1988
Archaic period plant use	Huckell 1996

zona desert area (Gasser 1982b; Gasser and Kwiatkowski 1991a, 1991b), as well as for specific insights into some indigenous Hohokam domesticates (Bohrer 1991) and resource use revealed by pollen (Gish 1991). The huge and complicated Ancestral Puebloan record of the Colorado Plateau region remains to be examined in a similar detailed way, as does the smaller Mogollon record of southern New Mexico and eastern Arizona. A recent general overview of the Southwestern wild plant record (Huckell and Toll, in press) and one for domesticates (Fish, in press) has started the process of updating this information.

For the Southwest, a number of targeted syntheses also exist. More recent efforts to pull together literature on specific domesticates such as *Gossypium* (Huckell 1993), *Zea mays* (Adams 1994), and *Phaseolus* (Kaplan and Lynch 1999) complement earlier efforts for beans (Kaplan 1956, 1965; Nabhan and Felger 1978), and squash/gourds (Cutler and Whitaker 1961). The record of tobacco (*Nicotiana*) use is also fairly current (Adams and Toll 2001; Winter 2001a, 2001b). A framework for evaluating the potential seasonality insights contained within ancient plant records, and possibly muted by human and animal behavior, is also available (Adams and Bohrer 1998), as is a look at anthropogenic ecology focusing on human impacts on ecosystems, populations and individual plants (Adams, in press; Fish 2000). Specific regions also have synthesized archaeobotanical records, for example the Tucson Basin (Miksicek 1988) and the middle Little Colorado River area (Adams 1996).

Some syntheses are difficult due to the timing of developing search images for particular plant taxa or parts. For example, *Agave* fibers were not recognized in Southwestern U.S. archaeobotanical records until research in the Tucson Basin first identified and described them (Fish et al. 1985). Likewise, recognition of little barley grass (*Hordeum pusillum*) and its role as a possible prehistoric domesticate was first brought to our attention by Bohrer (1984). Once a particular plant part gains widespread recognition, all analyses accomplished after that time can legitimately include it in discussions of significance. However, comparisons to sites excavated prior are particularly vulnerable to misinterpretation of missing data.

Theories, Models and Hypothesis-Testing

In the Midwest, Johannessen (1984, 1988) gave archaeobotanists a fine example of theory building when she looked at the American Bottom (Mississippi River) plant record in light of a current model of plant domestication (Rindos 1984). In the Southwestern U.S., archaeobotanists have primarily focused on retrieval and description of the plant record, including residues, contexts of recovery, and associated artifacts and features. With some notable exceptions, there has been little focus on building models and testing hypotheses (Bohrer 1986a:39), and it is not clear if our current methods and approaches are truly appropriate to this task (Adams 1989). Some Southwestern U.S. examples of models derived from ecological, ethnographic or other sources are listed below.

Models from Behavioral and Evolutionary Ecology

Behavioral ecology has offered us a series of models for assessing the viability of different strategies humans use to procure resources. One common theme is that of optimization, which suggests that when faced with numerous choices for acquiring resources, humans behave rationally and make choices that are to their benefit. Generally one expects the most efficient strategies to be utilized, often defined in terms of energy. Kelley (1995) provides a thorough overview of some of these models and their expectations. Although models such as these include a series of assumptions and various types of proxy records, nevertheless they provide independent ways of evaluating past agricultural efforts and reliance on wild plants.

A good example of using archaeobotanical data to test a behavioral ecology model is Diehl's examination of Late Archaic subsistence and land use in southern Arizona (1997). Going beyond the common approach of reporting and interpreting archaeobotanical ubiquity indices, he developed a diet breadth model for investigating the archaeobotanical record, complete with expectations related to choices of higher-ranked or lower-ranked resources. He then chose among three competing notions of Late Archaic period land use, arguing that these early farmers were seasonally sedentary, focused heavily on wild plants, and made use of multiple residential locations throughout the year.

Other researchers applied the principles of evolutionary ecology to a simulation of maize farming reliance by late pre-ceramic farmers/foragers in the variable environments of southeastern Arizona (Huckell et al. 2000). This simulation focused on understanding the forces that surrounded early agricultural decision-making. It utilized principles of risk and uncertainty as employed by human evolutionary ecologists to determine whether it is possible to identify a lower threshold of effort investment in agriculture. Researchers included historic climatic data to simulate maize productivity, and bell-shaped pit volume as a proxy for maize harvest volume, to simulate the optimal size agricultural fields. The resulting simulation suggested that fairly large field size (greater than 10 acres) reduced the probability of agricultural failure when compared to smaller field size (less than 2-3 acres) for a given target harvest determined through bell-shaped pit capacities with a holding potential of 6,205 ears. They concluded that early agriculturalists would have been better off making a serious commitment to agriculture (via large field size), rather than attempting a riskier strategy of casual agriculture in smaller fields.

Although not a prehistoric example, one recent diet optimization study using non-linear techniques is worth noting, as it provides perspective on approaches applicable to the archaeological record (LaFerriere 1991). The Mountain Pima of Chihuahua, Mexico, utilize both agricultural and wild plants, as well as domestic and wild animals. Diets that included adequate amounts of energy, protein, calcium and vitamins A and C were examined via two methods, one focusing on time minimization, and the other on nutrient-indexing. The nutrient-indexing model better approximated modern Mountain Pima diet, and predicted higher use of noncultivated plants and animal resources than did the time minimization model. This study took into account years of adequate and inadequate rainfall, as well as the seasonal nature of some resource availability.

Site Catchment Analysis

One example of a catchment analysis was performed at Pueblo Grande, a late Preclassic and Classic period pueblo in the Phoenix Basin of Arizona. There, Kwiatkowski focused on saguaro (*Carnegiea*), mesquite (*Prosopis*) and available arable land within a 5 km radius, which reflects the average spacing of large sites in the local settlement system (1994). The purpose of the catchment analysis was to estimate whether the inferred prehistoric population of the community existed below, at, or above the carrying capacity of these major plant resources and available irrigated land within the radius. Although many assumptions had to be made for this analysis, the number of people that could be supported by saguaro, mesquite and the available arable land approximated peak population estimates for the site by archaeologists. Implications were that the group occupying Pueblo Grande may not have been able to buffer natural disasters such as floods or droughts.

Models Based on Ethnographic Strategies

Southwestern archaeobotanists have developed ethnographically based models to examine the ancient plant record, recognizing the potential risk in trying to fit archaeological data to contemporary models of social organization. Bohrer was among the first to utilize extensive literature on the Akimel O'odham peoples (River Pima) to examine the Hohokam record of plant use at the pre-Classic (A.D. 700-1150) site of Snaketown in southern Arizona (1970, 1971). She then developed seed concentration indices to assess both successful riverine irrigation, and episodes of irrigation crop failure among ancient agriculturalists, and to point out similarities in food choice and possibly in agricultural scheduling between the modern and ancient groups.

Minnis formally recognized a series of common social adaptations to food stress that could be examined in the archaeological record (1985). He demonstrated that food shortage likely occurred during Classic Mimbres times, and suggested some possible social coping strategies. In subsequent research (1996) he broadened the range of potential responses that might be recognized in the ancient plant record, again based on ethnographic solutions to hunger. He also culled the literature for responses to severe food shortage in the borderlands area of the southern deserts, and utilized the archaeobotanical record to argue that patterns of food preference in the region have changed within the past 400 years (1991). In a similar vein, Adams and Bowyer selected a number of historic solutions to food shortages that could be reasonably examined in the archaeobotanical record of sites in southwestern Colorado, and concluded that some low level of food shortage was present as abandonment of the region approached (1998).

Another type of ethnographic model utilizes the historic record of plant use to build a "behavioral chain" to predict the nature of a prehistoric plant record. This approach, developed by Schiffer (1976), is best illustrated by papers published on cotton (*Gossypium*) and yucca (*Yucca*) from Antelope House in Arizona (Magers 1975; Stier 1975). In each case, extensive ethnographic records on cotton and yucca use were examined in light of the nature of the archaeobotanical record likely to be left from human actions in various places in and around a community. Such an exercise suggests that human behavior with plants often does not leave any recognizable evidence, and may help us understand the evidence that is recovered, especially when context and associated material culture remains are also considered.

Ethnoarchaeology and Experimental Archaeobotany

Ethnoarchaeology and experimental archaeology both help remove the temptation to speculate on what "might" happen to plants and plant parts as they become part of an ancient record. Such observations and experiments are, by default, performed on modern vegetation, and sometimes by researchers unskilled in the daily work strategies and skills of a forager or agriculturalist. Any experiment that asks the question "what happens over time" must be satisfied with a very short-term perspective, but there are insights available via this type of study.

A small number of ethnoarchaeological studies have focused on modern Native American activities with plants. A trio of scholars (Greenhouse et al. 1981) studied a Pima cholla bud roasting event in southern Arizona, taking both flotation and pollen samples at the end of the process and again a year later, and finding that little evidence of cholla remained, but pollen from fleshy vegetation utilized in the roasting process was conspicuous. Researchers examined the charred seeds and pollen remaining from a saguaro (*Carnegiea*) processing camp, learning the best locations for each type of plant remains, and how underrepresented the actual levels of saguaro fruit processing were (Miksicek 1987b:221-22). At a Hopi village in northern Arizona, researchers examined trash deposited over time into abandoned structures for a perspective on long-term plant degradation and rodent, insect and fungal effects on plant remain in midden deposits (Gasser and Adams1981). They also studied the moving of trash for construction purposes, which rearranges and combines deposits of different ages and sources.

Numerous other perspectives have added additional insights pertinent to archaeobotanical interpretation. For example, Minnis related some sources and interpretive problems of seeds recovered from archaeological sites, based on modern observations of how seeds might become accidentally incorporated into a record (1981). Miksicek (1987b) then offered a thorough look at formation processes of the archaeobotanical record. Even a simple experiment that consisted of burying modern non-black seeds in the nearly black soil of an archaeological site for three months revealed that the site soil itself could darken seeds in a relatively short period of time (Adams 1987b). Because of this, darkened (but not clearly burned) seeds from archaeological contexts were conservatively considered to be darkened by the soil, rather than by some limited amount of ancient parching.

In the realm of pollen analysis Bohrer (1972) was one of the first to wash harvested plant parts for the pollen types they might carry with them, to help palynologists interpret whether pollen presence of specific plants in archaeological sites has cultural meaning. She then published a broad framework for thinking about pollen transport in terms of plant anatomy, pollination strategy, experimentation, ethnographic, environmental, and archaeological evidence (1981a). Adams (1988) pointed out the variety of wind-pollinated pollen types that can become attached to other reproductive plant parts in natural settings, to such an extent that a resulting pollen record might actually reflect that of the hitchhiker and not the plant that carried it. In yet another effort, Hasbargen (1997) harvested flowers of several crop plants and native plants to document pollen per flower, extrapolated to pollen per plant. More recently, Smith and Geib (1999) performed quantified experimental studies to determine the nature of pollen retention on grinding tools after winnowing, parching and grinding a variety of seeds, including maize. They are exploring the dynamic between plant structure, pollen ecology and human behavior to understand more fully how archaeological pollen records can form.

Despite these fine examples given above, the level of experimentation in South-western U.S. archaeobotany is presently low. Simple experiments conceived to look at one variable, holding others constant, are needed. The effect of burning on plant part morphology (Brugge 1965; Stewart and Robertson 1971; Toll and McBride 1996a) should be further documented, as burned plant parts are our primary source of information, and morphological changes are cited as one source of evidence for domestication. Available determinations of the caloric and mineral content of common native foods (Ross 1941; Greenhouse 1979; Greenhouse et al. 1981; Calloway et al. 1974; Cummings 1991, 1995) could be expanded upon with targeted research questions. Experiments that determine an energetic return rate for different seeds and fruit per unit of time spent gathering and processing would add to the limited literature already available, and increase success in assessing behavioral archaeology models (Diehl 2000).

Methodological Contributions

Field Guides

Over the past three decades, Southwestern archaeobotanists have written guides for archaeologists in the field. The unique conditions of preservation previously described calls for methods and techniques appropriate for the region. Bohrer and Adams (1977) wrote a dual field/lab guide to retrieving and studying plant remains from Salmon Ruin in New Mexico, and Adams and Gasser (1980) tried to distill critical issues related to field sampling decisions in a journal article. However, we also realize that such documents are not to be transferred wholesale to each new research project, and that there is no one size of field procedures that fits all archaeological sites. For example, if flotation samples are to be of a standard size, the volume chosen for a given research project or area can be determined at the outset of excavation during a series of trial runs on strata considered optimal to answer the questions asked. Nearly every large archaeological project has had an associated archaeobotanical specialist or two that have written sets of field procedures tailored to the specific archaeological research questions of the project.

Laboratory Guides: Macrofossils

There are currently no basic standardized laboratory methods followed by South-western archaeobotanists in their analysis of flotation samples and macrofossils (larger plant remains). This is in part because of different investigator solutions to the problem of balancing the resources available for a project against the methods of analysis that most efficiently provide interpretable information about past human behavior. However, as the group routinely gathers to discuss their speciality, an underlying

theme over recent years has been to adopt a standardized set of laboratory procedures. We do not yet know the level of inter-investigator differences amongst us, nor
can we easily grasp the level of intra-investigator differences as each of us becomes
better at our craft over time. Differences in analysis are not an issue if two investiga-
tors can come to relatively similar conclusions about past human/plant relationships,
despite alternative approaches to sample analysis. This, however, remains to be evaluated.

Among the guides available for laboratory procedures is Bohrer's (1962) prime
example of thorough reporting on macrobotanical materials recovered from Tonto
National Monument. Later, Bohrer and Adams (1977) delineated the laboratory
methods and procedures followed during multiyear excavation of the large Ancestral Puebloan site of Salmon Ruin in northwestern New Mexico. More recently, Toll
and Huckell (1996) compiled a set of directions for describing and measuring maize
(*Zea mays*) remains, although it is unknown to what extent this list of detailed observations are obscured or altered by both charring and the environmental conditions
under which the maize grew, or which ones are best suited to distinguishing Southwestern U.S. maize varieties. Sauer and Kaplan (1969) and Huckell (1986) pulled
together helpful information on describing cultivated jackbeans (*Canavalia
ensiformis*). Much additional guidance to understanding and describing prehistoric
plant remains is contained within the publications of many individuals.

Flotation analysis has received much attention over the years. Emil Haury was
one of the first to acquire flotation samples systematically from the site of Snaketown
during excavations in the 1960s (Bohrer 1970; 1986a). Bohrer and Adams (1977)
delineated details related to flotation processing and analysis for a large excavation
project in New Mexico. Toll (1988) advocated a dual system of scanning and full
sort procedures for flotation samples as a cost-efficient way of accumulating thorough datasets. Adams (1993) suggested use of a "species area curve" approach to
sorting flotation samples, to allow the complexity or simplicity of a sample help
determine how much effort should be devoted to analysis.

Southwestern archaeobotanists should routinely report anatomical and morphological details of identification of ancient remains, as exemplified consistently in
publications by Bohrer (e.g. 1962, 1987). Published identification criteria accom-
plish three functions: (1) enabling others to corroborate any identifications we make,
(2) enabling others to identify unknowns from these written descriptions, and (3)
making metric details available for use in new domestication models based on anatomical and morphological changes. To this end, some identification guides are already available. For aid in identifying prehistoric charcoal, Minnis (1987) gave us a
key to the identification of gymnosperms. Perhaps a group effort is needed to develop keys to the identification of angiosperms, which comprise a large diversity of
trees and shrubs in regions such as the Colorado Plateau, the New Mexican Highlands, and the Lower Sonoran Desert. On occasion, unknown items recovered in
archaeobotanical samples become known, such as the finding that common hexago-

nal specimens in flotation samples were termite fecal pellets (Adams 1984). Another specific set of anatomical and morphological traits were outlined for reedgrass (*Phragmites*) "cigarettes" with tobacco (*Nicotiana*) stem contents in archaeological deposits (Adams 1990).

In terms of charcoal analysis, most analysts still make identifications based on freshly snapped cross-section (transverse) views, although Bohrer (1986a:34) has recommended a more thorough and labor-intensive approach that includes scrutiny of radial and tangential sections under high-power magnification. For some upland regions which host relatively limited numbers of trees and shrubs, the cross-section anatomies of many genera are often unique, or share overlapping similarities with a rather small number of other taxa. In these situations, relying on cross-section anatomy to broadly identify the major categories of wood charcoal at an archaeological site seems reasonable, acknowledging a lower level of reliability. In lowland areas, such as valley bottoms that potentially receive driftwood from uplands, the range of wood choices for prehistoric groups can be much higher, and successful identification of charcoal from prehistoric sites can require a much broader comparative collection of both lowland and upland taxa. Modern comparative collections of wood charcoal should include a range of sizes from twig to branch to trunk wood, including root material, and should be backed by herbarium voucher specimens. A master compilation of wood anatomy descriptions and photos of charred tree and shrub woods from major Southwestern regions (e.g. Colorado Plateau, Sonoran Desert, Mogollon Highlands) would be a welcome aid for analysts.

Many archaeobotanists rely on "ubiquity" indices, or the presence/absence of plant taxa within a suite of analyzed flotation samples, to make arguments about past human behavior. Bohrer points out that ubiquity calculations based on samples with a constant volume are more reliable than those where samples differ in volume (1981b). Having large numbers of flotation samples from a site or a region increases confidence in the plant patterns revealed. It is recommended that the relationship between plant taxonomic diversity and sample size (e.g. number or total volume) be evaluated statistically, to eliminate sampling bias as a possible source of plant patterning. These issues have been examined by archaeologists with other datasets (Leonard 1989; Leonard and Jones 1989; Plog and Hegmon 1993). It is also advised to use a very broad framework when interpreting macrofossils from archaeological sites (Table 5.2).

Some methodological advances made in the past have not been explored to their full potential. For example, nearly seventy years ago researchers discovered that sun-dried adobe bricks often contained examples of both charred and uncharred plant remains, providing insights into the presence of cultivars, and the introduction, distribution and spread of weedy European plant taxa (Hendry 1931; Hendry and Bellue 1936; Hendry and Kelly 1925). Although this form of construction material is primarily found in the historic period, a few examples of prehistoric adobe bricks also exist (Huckell 1992). With few exceptions (O'Rourke 1983; Huckell 1992), archaeo-

TABLE 5.2. Evaluating macrofossils and pollen for ethnobotanical significance.

Each plant part type recovered can be assessed from viewpoints listed below.

MACROFOSSILS

1. Archaeological context. Where does the plant part occur? What other plant materials (e.g. pollen, other economic taxa) is it associated with? What other material culture items?

2. Ethnographic analogy. What modern groups have used the plant, and in what ways? This could include the perspective of a behavioral chain, to point out possible distributions of plant parts according to processing and use within a household or community.

3. Archaeological analogy. Where else does this plant part occur within archaeological sites in the region? What are the interpretations offered for it there?

4. Signs of preparation. Charred? Systematically damaged (could indicate rodent or human use)?

5. Habitat of the plant. What is its ecology? How likely could its parts get into a household or community accidentally? Is it part of the modern seed rain, present in non-cultural overburden or fill?

6. Inherent characteristics. What is the general preservation potential of the part?

POLLEN

1. Archaeological context. How is the pollen type patterned at the site? Does it accompany other reproductive (seeds, fruit) or vegetative parts (leaves, charcoal) of its own taxon? What other potential economic resources does it occur with?

2. Ethnographic analogy. (See comments for macrofossils).

3. Archaeological analogy. (See comments for macrofossils).

4. Comparisons to other cultural settings. How does this pollen type compare between various feature types, or site types? Are there any prehistoric samples that would possibly represent natural vegetation pollen rain?

5. Comparisons to other natural settings. Does it occur in percentages higher than normally found in modern natural settings, or in settings with various levels of human modification? Does it occur as pollen grain "aggregates"?

6. Modern experiments. How and in what amounts does pollen travel on plant parts of interest to humans?

botanists have not taken advantage of the potential information on past plant/human relationships that are contained within adobe bricks.

There are still many significant methodological contributions to be made, as illustrated by the following example of grass (Poaceae) grains. With the exception of ricegrass (*Stipa hymenoides*) and dropseed (*Sporobolus*) type grains, Southwestern archaeobotanists often report grass caryopses (grains) in archaeological sites at the family level only. Yet, specimens identified to the genus or species level could provide information on seasonality (cool or warm); photosynthetic pathway (C_3 or C_4) with implications for reconstructing human diets via analysis of carbon isotopes; the possibilities of long-distance gathering; and potential evidence of human interactions with them that could range from simple to complex, up to and including cultivation or domestication. The large number of grass types in the American Southwest (Gould 1951) has made it a difficult task to attach names to ancient specimens, based on anatomical and morphological descriptions. Although there are some published documents that include detailed drawings of grasses (e.g. Musil 1963), the attached chaffy parts cover the grains, obscuring the grain shape and other features important to the archaeobotanist.

The following framework is suggested as a strategy for systematically accumulating data on grass grains that might ultimately allow their identification in archaeological deposits (see also Bohrer 1987). For all grass types known ethnographically or archaeologically from the American Southwest (Doebley 1984; Bohrer 1975), including native grasses known to have been of human interest in other parts of the world (Harlan 1975:17-18), basic descriptive information should be accumulated on those traits that can be easily observed in ancient burned specimens (Table 5.3). Even before the range of variability of modern grass grains is fully known, ancient grass grain types can be described for archaeological sites or projects, facilitating comparisons and eventual identification.

Pollen Analysis

Many methodological or procedural advances have been made in the realm of pollen analysis. Early on, researchers recognized the value of acquiring modern surface samples for interpreting prehistoric pollen. In a masterful work, Jannifer Gish (1993) conducted an extensive modern pollen analog study for comparison with archaeological pollen spectra. Her study included quantifying perennial vegetation in Sonoran Desert settings, and extended over more than one season and year. Complementing earlier studies (Schoenwetter and Doerschlag 1971; Hevly et al. 1965; Gish 1975), she documented responses in modern pollen rain to annual weather fluctuations. At Arroyo Hondo, Bohrer was one of the first to use subsurface sediments to provide prehistoric analog samples for comparison to possible cultural pollen signatures (1986b). In this document she brings to our attention anomalous out-of-range populations of plants, and has a thoughtful discussion of the scale and intensity of

TABLE 5.3. Systematic framework for describing modern and ancient grass (Poaceae) caryopses (grains).

Shape: defined by the ratio of length to width, complete grains can be long and slender (length 2.0 or more times longer than width), or short and sturdy (length less than 2.0 times longer than width).

Actual measurements: of length, width and thickness.

Nature of grain compression: this can vary from (a) laterally compressed, with the dorsal (embryo) and ventral surfaces forming two rather narrow ridges, while the wide flattened lateral surfaces are expansive and form the facets upon which the grains easily rest, to (b) dorsal-ventrally compressed, that is the dorsal and ventral surfaces are broad and expansive and the grain rests comfortably on either one, the embryo is clearly visible on the dorsal side, and the two lateral surfaces form the narrowest dimensions, to (c) rounded, when by nature or by burning the grain has plumped up into a fairly rounded profile, to (d) indented, in which the grain has either a "U" or a "V" shape.

Relative length of the embryo to entire grain: a calculated ratio, the relative proportion an embryo occupies of the entire grain length can vary from quite small (< 25%) to very large (>66%), a relationship helpful in placing grains into very general grass categories (Reeder 1957).

Facet profile: when the grain is lying on a stable facet (dorsal, ventral or lateral surface), noting whether the widest dimension is at the base, just above the embryo, or whether the grain is equally wide for most of its length.

Condition: burned or broken or both.

Other features: presence of grooves, central nerves, ridges, striations, or evidence of attached chaffy parts (paleas, lemmas).

post-European vegetation changes that might affect pollen records. She and others realized that humanly modified environments provide a strong pollen signal, and that prehistoric pollen signals of disturbed floras in southern Arizona are unlike those of modern humanly modified environments, arguing against incautious use of modern analogs for prehistoric disturbance floras (Bohrer 1986a:35; Fish 1985; Gish 1991). Suzanne Fish supplements the use of modern analogs by comparing and contrasting ancient pollen records, for example by examining pollen from different structure and site types for insight into the organization of subsistence activities (1998a), and points out how pollen in archaeological sites represents a dynamic mixture of windblown types, anthropogenic plant communities, and plants carried in by occupants (1984b). She also advocates use of floor samples as particularly efficient and meaningful units of comparison that both encapsulate and average the record of resource use by a specific household or social group over time (1998a).

In other advances in pollen analysis, Gish pointed out the potential of pollen grain aggregates as an indicator of ethnobotanical significance (1979, 1991). Bohrer (1981a) then summarized methods for recognizing the cultural significance of pollen types in archaeological deposits. Scott (1986) applied an intensive pollen sampling scheme to the floor of an Ancestral Puebloan pit structure, and when the results were combined with those of intensive flotation sampling, was able to suggest the location of food processing areas. In the laboratory, Glenna Dean (1998) shared with us a new way to search for larger, rare pollen grains, such as cotton (*Gossypium*), to provide a more complete record of pollen types preserved in archaeological contexts. By experimenting, Susan Smith (1998) showed that even a minor change in procedure during pollen sample processing can lead to a major change in variety and concentration of pollen types recovered, and that synthetic studies of archaeological pollen should not assume that pollen data derived from different processing methods are comparable. Fish (1987) offered a taphonomic perspective on pollen recovered from canal sediments by reviewing a range of variables known to affect pollen distribution in these features. She also provided a thorough framework for thinking about pollen studies of both gardens and fields (Fish 1998b). As with macrofossil specimens, a broad approach to evaluating the significance of pollen in archaeological sites is suggested (Table 5.2).

The use of absolute pollen concentration calculations has been advocated for recording pollen (e.g. Gish 1991). This approach complements the determination of pollen percentages based on routine counts of 200 pollen grains. Significance of pollen concentrations may be closely tied to the amount of time represented by the pollen deposit, which often is not known, and can be assumed to vary between short (e.g. on a briefly used house floor) to long (e.g. a trash midden spanning the lifetime of a community). Variability in pollen concentrations at a site could represent (a) different activities in different loci, (b) varying amounts of time for pollen accumulation, or (c) both. Establishing the mean and range of pollen abundance per volume of soil for different types of archaeological contexts should be part of any effort to utilize pollen concentration calculations.

Phytoliths and Other Microremains

Archaeobotanical analysis in the Southwest has also included examination of molluscs, ostracodes, phytoliths, starch granules, plant protein residues, and calcium oxide (CaO) crystals on tools. Unlike macrofossil and pollen analyses, these methods are in their infancy, and their basic contributions to interpretation of past human behavior with plants are currently limited in the American Southwest. One of the issues for most of these approaches is to be able to argue on reasonable grounds not only the anatomical, morphological, or chemical signatures of a correct identification, but also why closely related or even nonrelated specimens or materials have been reasonably eliminated from consideration. While it is true that material or part X may indeed seem to match specimen Y, readers must be appraised of the level of effort that has been made to eliminate other reasonable alternatives. Such information provides a balanced level of confidence in early efforts applied to relatively new research approaches.

Molluscs and ostrocodes within archaeobotanical samples have been recognized as useful organisms to characterize the hydrological history (water temperature, speed, salinity, permanence) of ancient earthern Hohokam canals in Arizona (Vokes and Miksicek 1987; Miksicek 1989, 1995; Palacios-Fest 1989, 1994, 1997a, 1997b). What remains is to establish baseline data by gathering environmental data (e.g. water temperature, pH, salinity, sediment particle size) in association with assemblages of living microcrustaceans in modern earthen canals still in use in the region. Sediment analysis from a prehistoric reservoir in the same area suggested long-term, perennial water storage, based on recovery of minute duckweed (*Lemna*) seeds (Bayman et al.1997).

Phytoliths and plant protein residues have been examined in various locations (Scott-Cummings and Puseman 1994; Puseman 1995; Scott-Cummings et al. 1998; Bozarth 1994, 1997), as have starch granules (Scott-Cummings 1998), all with limited results. For example, some have argued that cross-shaped phytoliths may not indicate prehistoric maize cultivation, as previously assumed (Doolittle and Frederick 1991). The same can be said of CaO crystals, known to occur commonly in monocots including agave and yucca, but also known from other common Southwestern plant taxa (Bohrer 1987:72; McNair 1932). More background work must be accomplished to establish the presence, variability, population characteristics, and diagnostic potential of these minute remains in Southwestern plant taxa, as well as to document any postdepositional complications or contamination affecting them.

Molecular and Chemical Approaches

Molecular and chemical approaches to Southwestern plant materials are limited, and efforts are in their infancy to understand the pitfalls and possibilities of some of these approaches (Adams 1997). To date, there have been few attempts to document prehistoric crops via molecular studies of both modern and prehistoric crops, including cotton (McDaniel 1993) and agave (Nabhan et al. n.d.). In one case, molecular efforts to tackle an archaeological question has had far-reaching implications for understanding plant evolution generally. For example, studies of maize (*Zea mays* L.) under human selection pressures has focused on delineating molecular events and processes responsible for morphological changes in plants (Doebley et al. 1983; Doebley 1990; Doebley and Stec 1991; Doebley 1992; Dorweiler et al. 1993; Doebley et al. 1995; Doebley et al. 1997; Gaut and Doebley 1997; Doebley and Wang 1997; Doebley and Lukens 1998; Want et al. 1999). In this case, data generated by archaeologists and archaeobotanists have elicited questions whose answers are contributing fundamental knowledge about the plant kingdom. Initial attempts to examine unburned maize cobs from dry Southwestern cave deposits (Helentjaris 1989; Golubinoff et al. 1994) suggested the presence of intact genetic material, but followup studies have not been conducted, nor were the cobs confirmed via AMS dating to be prehistoric in age.

Chemical approaches in the American Southwest are also relatively rare. Efforts to extract nicotine and nicotinic acid in the dottle of ancient pipes have met with only mild success, perhaps largely due to the instability of these chemical substances (Johnson et al. 1959; Dixon and Stetson 1922; Jones and Morris 1960). Researchers have successfully demonstrated the presence of lipids, likely from maize, in Ancestral Puebloan sites (Priestly et al. 1981; Wetterstrom 1986). On the basis of both microscopic and unnamed chemical tests, the lid sealant from a prehistoric jar in Arizona has been identified as lac from the creosote bush lac insect, *Tachardiella larrae* (Euler and Jones 1956). Efforts to recognize burned trees and shrubs in firepits by examining the chemical signatures of the resulting hearth ash have pointed the way to additional necessary analysis (Pierce et al. 1998). The same is true for chemical attempts to try and pinpoint general source locations for major conifer trees carried some distances to Chaco Canyon in New Mexico for use as building timbers (Durand et al. 1999). With instrumentation, it is possible to correctly characterize organic (carbon) based vs. mineral (iron) paint types on Ancestral Puebloan black on white pottery (Stewart and Adams 1999). Recent restoration efforts at historic missions have included addition of prickly pear (*Opuntia ficus-indica*) pad juice as a binder in exterior wall plaster applied over low-fired adobe bricks, and an archaeobotanist helped unravel the chemical explanation for adoption of this practice (Adams et al., in press).

How We Become Archaeobotanists

Archaeobotany requires background in both anthropology and botany. The current group of Southwestern archaeobotanists have all entered through one discipline or the other, or at times via such related specialties as packrat midden studies. There are few Southwestern archaeobotanists currently on the rosters of university faculty or museums, so the opportunities for formalized academic training in the Southwest are currently limited to the Arizona State Museum, Northern Arizona University (Quaternary Studies Program), and Texas A & M University. Much of the training today occurs "on the job," at times without a mentor to smooth the way. Contracting agencies are hard pressed to pay for the development of comparative collections, or to fund long hours in the herbarium working out the identity of unknown specimens.

A significant commitment is required to become familiar with the taxonomic, ecological, ethnographic, and archaeobotanical literature of the region, and to hone laboratory skills. Presently, Crow Canyon Archaeological Center in southwestern Colorado has supervised summer internships in archaeobotany, but other similar opportunities are rare. Such mentoring relationships must be expanded to insure the development of future Southwestern archaeobotanical scholars.

A number of Southwestern archaeobotanists have presently crafted nontraditional careers to be able to practice their profession. Some are independent contractors, having part-time affiliations with teaching or research institutions. Others are employed full- or part-time by contracting agencies. This group publishes, reviews articles and grant proposals, holds office in professional societies, mentors younger scholars, and struggles to make a decent living wage, plan for retirement, and maintain viable professional affiliations as visiting scholars or adjunct faculty. In the Southwest, the list of active archaeobotanists has waxed and waned over the years, and currently their numbers seem low. The first generation of archaeobotanists has nearly all retired, and over half of the second generation of individuals is no longer active, having focused their interests elsewhere (Table 5.4).

Where Do We Publish?

While we continue to publish in refereed journals and books, most of what we write enters the grey literature of reports and syntheses published by museums, governmental agencies, and private contracting companies (Table 5.5). Because it is often difficult to locate this primary literature, listed in Table 5.5 are many of the locations where one will find archaeobotanical reports on Southwestern sites or projects accomplished by the individuals in Table 5.4. What is needed to facilitate access to this information is for some Southwestern institution to provide a regularly updated database of references to all archaeobotanical reports, especially including those in the grey literature, organized by key words, and made available via the Internet or computer disk. A future application of the Internet would also be to host a clearinghouse where photos and descriptions of unknown specimens could be displayed and reviewed by practicing archaeobotanists.

Collaborative Colleagues

Southwestern archaeobotanists have archaeological colleagues that apply diverse approaches to understanding past human/plant relationships. For example, due primarily to vagaries of preservation, archaeobotanical records are generally not relied upon for productivity estimates. However, using a GIS approach, Van West has utilized dendrochronological reconstructions of paleoclimate to model environmental variability and agricultural productivity in various locations (Van West 1996, 1994a, 1994b; Van West and Altschul 1997). Others have also focused on agricultural pro-

TABLE 5.4. Southwestern archaeobotanists, listed in alphabetical order.

First Generation

Leonard W. Blake	Lawrence Kaplan
Vaughn Bryant, Jr.	Paul S. Martin
Hugh Cutler	Jonathan Sauer
Vorsila Bohrer	James Schoenwetter
Richard Ford	C. Earl Smith
Richard Hevly	Thomas Whitaker
Volney Jones	

Second Generation

Karen R. Adams	Scott Kwiatkowski
Steven Bozarth	Meredith Matthews
Carol Brandt	Pamela McBride
Owen Davis	Janet McVickar
Glenna Williams-Dean	Charles Miksicek
Phil Dering	Jo Anne Miller
Michael Diehl	Paul Minnis
John Doebley	Bruce Phillips
Suzanne K. Fish	Guy Prouty
Robert Gasser	Kathy Puseman
Jannifer W. Gish	Alan C. Reed
Julia Hammett	Linda Scott Cummings
Richard Holloway	Kristin D. Sobolik
Lisa W. Huckell	Susan Smith
Andrea Hunter	Mollie S. Toll
Johna Hutira	

ductivity, using archaeological data and paleoenvironmental records to take a very broad view of regional abandonments (Jones et al. 1999). An entire volume has been devoted to prehistoric agricultural strategies in the Southwest (Fish and Fish 1984). Doolittle has made extensive observations on both prehistoric and modern irrigation systems in Mexico, with implications for understanding prehistoric irrigation systems in the American Southwest (1990). An extensive study of the agricultural systems of the Marana Area Community in the Tucson Basin was accomplished in part by a palynologist, and relied heavily on archaeobotanical evidence from roasting pits and other contexts (Fish et al. 1992b). A maize agronomist experimentally studying drought tolerance of a modern Southwestern variety (Muenchrath 1995) made available her data and field specimens for archaeobotanists to evaluate specific effects of natural and applied moisture on maize morphological traits routinely examined by archaeobotanists (Adams et al. 1999).

TABLE 5.5. Journals and cultural resources management literature likely to contain Southwestern US archaeobotanical reports by individuals listed in Table 5.4.[a]

Title or Series	Publisher	City
American Antiquity	Soc. for American Archaeology	Washington, DC
Annals of the Missouri Botanical Garden	Missouri Botanical Garden	St. Louis, MO
Anthropological Field Studies	Arizona State University	Tempe, AZ
Anthropological Papers	Center for Desert Archaeology	Tucson, AZ
Anthropological Papers	Institute for American Research	Tucson, AZ
Anthropological Papers	Northland Research	Tempe, AZ
Anthropological Papers	Pueblo Grande Museum	Phoenix, AZ
Anthropological Papers	University of Arizona	Tucson, AZ
Anthropological Papers	University of Utah	SLCity, UT
Anthropological Papers	University of Michigan	Ann Arbor, MI
Anthropological Research Papers	Arizona State University	Tempe, AZ
Anthropological Research Papers	S.W.C.A.	Tucson, AZ
Archaeological Reports	S.W.C.A.	Tucson, AZ
Archaeological Series	Arizona State Museum	Tucson, AZ
Botanical Museum Leaflets	Harvard University	Boston, MA
Contributions in Anthropology	Eastern New Mexico University	Portales, NM
Cultural Resources Reports	Arch. Consulting Services, Ltd.	Tempe, AZ
Cultural Resource Reports	S.W.C.A.	Tucson, AZ
Desert Plants	University of Arizona	Tucson, AZ
Dolores Archaeological Reports	Bureau of Reclamation	Denver, CO
Economic Botany	NY Botanical Garden Press	Bronx, NY
Ethnobiological Technical Series	Zuni Archaeology Program	Zuni, NM
Ethnobotanical Lab Reports	University of Oklahoma	Norman, OK
Ethnobotanical Reports	Museum of Anthropology, University of Michigan,	Ann Arbor, MI
Fieldiana, Anthropology	Chicago Natural History Museum	Chicago, IL
Internet Site Studies (crowcanyon.org)	Crow Canyon Arch. Center	Cortez, CO

[a]Other sources for archaeobotanical literature are contained within the bibliography that accompanies this article.

cont.

Title or Series	Publisher	City
Journal of Archaeological Science	Society of Archaeological Science	
Journal of Ethnobiology	Society of Ethnobiology	
Kiva (fomerly The Kiva)	Archaeological & Historical Society	Tucson, AZ
Navajo Nation Papers in Anthropology	Navajo Nation Archaeology Division	Window Rock, AZ
New World Studies Seminar Series	Amerind Foundation/Other Publishers	Dragoon, AZ
Occasional Papers	Arizona Archaeological Society	Phoenix, AZ
Occasional Papers	Center for Archaeological Investigations	Carbondale, IL
Occasional Papers	Crow Canyon Archaeological Center	Cortez, CO
Office of Archaeological Studies	Museum of New Mexico	Santa Fe, NM
Publications in Archaeology	Soil Systems, Inc	Phoenix, AZ
Research Publications in Archaeology	Amerind Foundation	Dragoon, AZ
Reports of the Chaco Center	National Park Service	Denver, CO
Reports	Human Systems Research	Las Cruces, NM
Reports	Zuni Archaeology Program	Zuni, NM
Research Reports	Center for Archaeological Investigations	Carbondale, IL
Research Series	Zuni Cultural Resource Enterprise	Zuni, NM
Reports	Southwest Ethnobotanical Enterprises	Portales, NM
Technical Reports	Center for Desert Archaeology	Tucson, AZ
Technical Reports	Dames and Moore	Phoenix, AZ
Technical Reports	Desert Archaeology, Inc.	Tucson, AZ
Technical Reports	Paleo Research Laboratories	Golden, CO
Technical Series	Castetter Laboratory for Ethnobotanical Studies	Albuquerque, NM
Technical Series	SW Parks & Monuments Assoc.	Tucson, AZ
Technical Series	Statistical Research Inc.	Tucson, AZ

[a]Other sources for archaeobotanical literature are contained within the bibliography that accompanies this article.

cont.

Title or Series	Publisher	City
The Artifact	El Paso Archaeological Society	El Paso, TX
Western Arch. & Conservation Center	National Park Service	Tucson, AZ
(Individually named volumes)	Archaeological Research Services	Tempe, AZ
(Individually named volumes)	Museum of Northern Arizona	Flagstaff, AZ
(Individually named volumes)	Northland Research, Inc.	Flagstaff, AZ; Tempe, AZ
(Individually named volumes)	Office of Contract Archaeology	Albuquerque, NM
(Individually named volumes)	Statistical Research Press	Tucson, AZ
(Individually named volumes)	US Forest Service, SW Region	Albuquerque, NM

[a]Other sources for archaeobotanical literature are contained within the bibliography that accompanies this article.

Looking Toward the Future

Cultural Resource Management

Currently Cultural Resource Management (CRM) provides the bulk of research projects and funds available for archaeobotany in the American Southwest. Archaeological managers of these contracts can be encouraged to support reasonable amounts of basic background research, and to collaborate with archaeobotanists on developing new methods and approaches to the record of prehistoric plant remains. It is within this contract arena that overviews and syntheses of archaeobotanical research within regions are often completed.

Integrated Interpretations

Although the present conventions related to reporting pollen, macrofloral, and animal data do not easily lend themselves to direct comparison, some excellent examples of integrated interpretations have been published that have Southwestern archaeobotanical remains as a focus. In one case, a single scholar (Wetterstrom 1986) used the following datasets to assess diet and health at the site of Arroyo Hondo in New Mexico: archaeobotanical data, archaeofaunal data, human population estimates, local available resource (plants, animals, arable land) estimates, paleoclimatic data, and human skeletal information. This landmark study provides a blueprint for all-inclusive research. Elsewhere, a trio of scholars (Fish 1983, 1984a; Miksicek 1983, 1984; Szuter 1984) working on archaeobotanical and archaeofaunal records in central Arizona produced complementary interpretations about past resource use and environmental alteration; these results were further integrated by Bohrer within an ecological framework (1992). Others examining land use in the Mimbres area of New Mexico integrated plant, animal, artifact, architectural, and settlement data, to assess the role of mobility within a dispersed land-use system (Nelson and Diehl 1999). These three examples show that efforts to integrate interpretations of multiple lines of evidence are valuable, provide a more thorough assessment than could be made on single datasets alone, and should be accomplished by the specialists working with the archaeologists.

It is clear that Southwestern archaeobotanists have learned a great deal about past humans and their relationships with both plants and landscapes. In addition to serving as a time machine, the archaeobotanical record has revealed two key guiding principles of ethnobiology: biodiversity and sustainability. We now know that ancient groups consistently relied upon a diversity of plants, both domesticated and wild. We also know they occupied some Southwestern landscapes for centuries, gathering many of the same resources through time. These landscapes are currently at risk from modern human occupation of barely more than a century.

There are lessons for the future in this well-preserved plant record of the past. The first generation of Southwestern archaeobotanists gave us many reasonable ways to coax sound interpretations out of those "black burned bits" that are our daily reality. The second generation has been able to greatly strengthen and expand our perspective on ancient human/plant interactions, by analyzing thousands of samples over the past twenty years, and by moving into new technological arenas. This synthesis is both targeted and dedicated to that third generation of bright young scholars eager to take us into the new millennium and the next level of excellence.

Acknowledgments

When I accepted Dick Ford's challenge to write this paper, I contacted many of my archaeobotanical colleagues for their perspective on the current accomplishments, status, and future tasks of Southwestern archaeobotany. Many of them, listed here in alphabetical order, responded, and provided citations to their own works to ease my task of pursuing the grey and not-so-grey literature: Steven Bozarth, Carol Brandt, Glenna Dean, Michael Diehl, Suzanne Fish, Gayle Fritz, Richard Holloway, Lisa Huckell, Johna Hutira, Scott Kwiatkowski, Pam McBride, Janet McVickar, Bruce Phillips, Kathy Puseman, Linda Scott-Cummings, Susan Smith, and Mollie Toll. I appreciate the time and effort each one took to send me their thoughts and manuscripts.

References Cited

Adams, Karen R.

1984 Evidence of wood-dwelling termites in archaeological sites in the southwestern United States. Journal of Ethnobiology 4(1):29-43.

1987a Little barley (*Hordeum pusillum* Nutt.) as a possible New World domesticate. In: La Ciudad, Specialized Studies in the Economy, Environment and Culture of La Ciudad, Part III, edited by JoAnn E. Kisselburg, Glen E. Rice, and Brenda L. Shears, pp. 203-37. Anthropological Field Studies No. 20, Arizona State University. Tempe.

1987b Domesticated and native plants recovered from Robinson Pueblo and other regional sites in the Capitan, New Mexico area. Ms. on file with the author.

1988 The Ethnobotany and Phenology of Plants in and Adjacent to Two Riparian Habitats in Southeastern Arizona. Doctoral dissertation, University of Arizona. University Microfilms.

1989 Review of *A Current Paleoethnobotany, Analytical Methods and Cultural Interpretations of Archaeological Plant Remains*, edited by Christine A. Hastorf and Virginia S. Popper. Journal of Ethnobiology 9(2):200-205.

1990 Prehistoric reedgrass (*Phragmites*) "cigarettes" with tobacco (*Nicotiana*) contents: a case study from Red Bow Cliff Dwelling, Arizona. Journal of Ethnobiology 10(2):123-39.

1993 Carbonized plant remains. In: The Duckfoot Site, Vol. 1, Descriptive Archaeology, edited by Ricky R. Lightfoot and Mary C. Etzkorn, pp. 195-220. Crow Canyon Archaeological Center Occasional Papers No. 3. Cortez, CO.

1994 A regional synthesis of *Zea mays* in the prehistoric American Southwest. In: Corn and Culture in the Prehistoric New World, edited by Sissel Johannessen and Christine A. Hastorf, pp. 273-302. Boulder, CO: Westview Press.

1996 Archaeobotany of the middle Little Colorado River valley. In: River of Change: Prehistory of the Middle Little Colorado River Valley, Arizona, edited by E. Charles Adams, pp. 163-86. Archaeological Series, No. 185, Arizona State Museum, University of Arizona. Tucson.

1997 Molecular and Chemical Approaches to Southwestern Archaeobotany. Paper presented at the 62nd Annual Meeting, Society for American Archaeology. Nashville, TN.

1998 Plant Remains from State Route 87 Sites. Manuscript on file, Statistical Research, Inc. Tucson, AZ.

In press Southwest anthropogenic ecology. In: People and Plants in Ancient North America, edited by Paul Minnis. Washington, DC: Smithsonian Institution Press.

Adams, Karen R., and Rex K. Adams

1998 How does our *Agave* grow? Reproductive biology of a suspected ancient Arizona cultivar, *Agave murpheyi* Gibson. Desert Plants 14(2):11-20.

Adams, Karen R., and Vorsila L. Bohrer

1998 Archaeobotanical indicators of seasonality: examples from arid southwestern United States. In: Seasonality and Sedentism: Archaeological Perspectives from Old and New World Sites, edited by Thomas R. Rocek and Ofer Bar-Yosef, pp. 129-41. Peabody Museum Bulletin 6, Peabody Museum of Archaeology and Ethnology, Harvard University. Cambridge, MA.

Adams, Karen R., and Vandy E. Bowyer
1998 Plant Use in the Sand Canyon Locality, A.D. 1180-1280. Manuscript on file, Crow Canyon Archaeological Center. Cortez, CO.

Adams, Karen R., and Robert E. Gasser
1980 Plant microfossils from archaeological sites: research considerations and sampling techniques and approached. The Kiva 45(4):293-300.

Adams, Karen R., Christine Gottardo and Robert W. Vint
In press The role of prickly pear cactus (*Opuntia ficus-indica* [L.] Mill.) pad mucilage as a binder in mission wall plaster. Journal of the Southwest.

Adams, Karen R., Deborah A. Muenchrath and Dylan M. Schwindt
1999 Moisture effects on the morphology of ears, cobs and kernels of a southwestern U.S. Maize (*Zea mays* L.) cultivar, and implications for the interpretation of archaeological maize. Journal of Archaeological Science 26:483-96.

Adams, Karen R., and Mollie S. Toll
2001 Tobacco (*Nicotiana*) use and manipulation in the prehistoric and historic southwestern United States. In: Tobacco Use by Native North Americans: Sacred Smoke and Silent Killer, edited by Joseph C. Winter. Norman: University of Oklahoma Press.

Adams, Karen R., and John R. Welch
1994 Tonto Basin plant geography and ecology. In: The Roosevelt Rural Sites Study: Changing Land Use in the Tonto Basin, Vol. 3, edited by Richard Ciolek-Torrello and John R. Welch, pp. 121-33. Statistical Research Technical Series No. 28. Tucson, AZ.
1997 Landform associations, seasonal availability, and ethnobotany of plants in the Lower Verde. In: Vanishing River: Landscapes and Lives of the Lower Verde Valley: The Lower Verde Archaeological Project, Vol. 2, Agricultural, Subsistence and Environmental Studies, edited by Jeffrey A. Homburg and Richard Ciolek-Torrello, pp. 33-54. CD-ROM. Tucson, AZ: Statistical Research Inc. Press.

Anschuetz, Kurt F.
1995 Saving a rainy day: the integration of diverse agricultural technologies to harvest and conserve water in the Lower Rio Chama valley New Mexico. In: Soil, Water, Biology, and Belief in Prehistoric and Traditional Southwestern Agriculture, edited by H. Wolcott Toll, pp. 25-39. New Mexico Archaeological Council. Albuquerque, NM.

Bayman, James M., Manuel R. Palacios-Fest and Lisa W. Huckell
1997 Botanical signatures of water storage duration in a Hohokam reservoir. American Antiquity 62(1):103-11.

Betancourt, Julio L., and Thomas R. Van Devender
1981 Holocene vegetation in Chaco Canyon, New Mexico. Science 214:656-58.

Betancourt, Julio L., A. Long, D. J. Donahue, A.J. T. Jull and T. H. Zabel
1984 Pre-Columbian age for North American *Corispermum* L. (Chenopodiaceae) confirmed by accelerator radiocarbon dating. Nature 311(5986):653-55.

Betancourt, Julio L., Elizabeth A. Pierson, Kate Aasen Rylander, James A. Fairchild-Parks and Jeffrey S. Dean
1993 Influence of history and climate on New Mexican pinyon-juniper woodlands. In: Managing Pinyon-Juniper Ecosystems for Sustainability and Social Needs, by Earl F. Aldon and Douglas W. Shaw (Technical Coordinators), pp. 42-62. USDA Forest Service General Technical Report RM-236.

Bohrer, Vorsila L.
1962 Nature and interpretation of ethnobotanical materials from Tonto National Monument. In: Archeological Studies at Tonto National Monument, Arizona, by Charlie R. Steen, Lloyd M. Pierson, Vorsila L. Bohrer, and Kate Peck Kent, pp. 75-114. Southwestern Monuments Association Technical Series Vol. 2. Globe, AZ.
1970 Ethnobotanical aspects of Snaketown, a Hohokam village in southern Arizona. American Antiquity 35(4):413-30.
1971 Paleoecology of Snaketown. The Kiva 36(3):11-19.
1972 Paleoecology of the Hay Hollow site, Arizona. Fieldiana: Anthropology 63(1):1-30.
1975 The prehistoric and historic role of the cool-season grasses in the Southwest. Economic Botany 29(3):199-207.
1978 Plants that have become locally extinct in the Southwest. New Mexico Journal of Science 18(2):10-19.
1981a Methods of recognizing cultural activity from pollen in archaeological sites. The Kiva 46(3):135-42.
1981b The research potential of plant remains from Fresnal shelter, an Archaic site in south-central New Mexico. Annals of the New York Academy of Sciences, Vol. 376:387-92.
1983 And before crops came: the Fresnal shelter. El Palacio 89(1):13-14.
1984 Domesticated and wild crops in the CAEP study area. In: Prehistoric Cultural Development in Central Arizona: Archaeology of the Upper New River Region, edited by Patricia M. Spoerl and G. J. Gumerman, pp. 183-259. Southern Illinois University at Carbondale Center for Archaeological Investigations Occasional Paper No. 5. Carbondale.
1986a Guideposts in ethnobotany. Journal of Ethnobiology. 6(10):27-43.
1986b The ethnobotanical pollen record at Arroyo Hondo Pueblo. In: Food, Diet, and Population at Prehistoric Arroyo Hondo Pueblo, New Mexico, edited by Wilma Wetterstrom, pp. 187-293. Arroyo Hondo Archaeological Series, Vol. 6. Santa Fe, NM.
1987 The plant remains from La Ciudad, a Hohokam site in Phoenix. In: La Ciudad: Specialized Studies in the Economy, Environment and Culture of La Ciudad, Part III, edited by JoAnn E. Kisselburg, Glen E. Rice, and Brenda L. Shears, pp. 67-202. Anthropological Field Studies No. 20, Arizona State University. Tempe.
1991 Recently recognized cultivated and encouraged plants among the Hohokam. Kiva 56(3):227-35.
1992 New life from ashes II: the tale of burnt brush. Desert Plants 19(3):122-25.
1997 Pieces of the landscape: flotation analysis of plant remains from sites in the vicinity of Kitty Jo canyon. In: Rocks, Roaster, and Ridgetops: Data Recovery Across the Pioneer Road Landscape, State Route 87 Segment F, Maricopa and Gila Counties, Arizona, edited by G. R. Woodall, D. D. Barz, and M. P. Neeley, pp. 295-314. Archaeological Research Services, Project Report 94:77B. Tempe, AZ.

Bohrer, Vorsila L., and Karen R. Adams
1977 Ethnobotanical techniques and approaches at Salmon Ruin, New Mexico. Eastern New Mexico University Contributions in Anthropology 8(1):1-215.

Bozarth, Steven
1994 Pollen and phytolith analysis. In: The Roosevelt Rural Sites Study, Changing Land Use in the Tonto Basin, Vol. 3, edited by Richard Ciolek-Torrello and John R. Welch, pp. 189-222. Statistical Research Technical Series No. 28. Tucson.
1997 Pollen and phytolith analysis. In: Vanishing River: Landscapes and Lives of the Lower Verde Valley: The Lower Verde Archaeological Project. Vol. 2. of Agricultural, Subsistence and Environmental Studies, CD-ROM, edited by Jeffrey A. Homburg and Richard Ciolek-Torrello, pp. 179-204. Tucson, AZ: Statistical Research Inc. Press.

Brand, M. J.
1994 Prehistoric Anasazi Diet: A Synthesis of Archaeological Evidence. Master's thesis, University of British Columbia. Burnaby.

Brown, David E.
1982 Biotic communities of the American Southwest—United States and Mexico. Desert Plants 4(1-4), Special Issue.

Brugge, David M.
1965 Charred maize and "nubbins." Plateau 38(2):49-51.

Calloway, Doris H., R. D. Giauque and F. M. Costa
1974 The superior mineral content of some Indian foods in comparison to federally donated counterpart commodities. Ecology of Food and Nutrition 3:203-11.

Carpenter, John P., Guadalupe Sanchez de Carpenter and Elisa Villalpando
1999 Preliminary investigations at La Playa, Sonora, Mexico. Archaeology Southwest 13(1):6.

Chisholm, B., and R. G. Matson
1994 Carbon and nitrogen isotopic evidence on Basketmaker II diet at Cedar Mesa, Utah. Kiva 60(2):239-55.

Cutler, Hugh C., and Thomas W. Whitaker
1961 History and distribution of the cultivated cucurbits in the Americas. American Antiquity 26(4):469-85.

Dean, Glenna
1998 Finding a needle in a palynological haystack: a comparison of methods. In: New Developments in Palynomorph Sampling, Extraction, and Analysis, edited by Vaughn M. Bryant, Jr. and John H. Wrenn, pp. 53-59. American Association of Stratigraphic Palynologists Contribution Series No. 33. Dallas, TX.

Dean, Jeffrey S.
1969 Chronological Analysis of Tsegi Phase Sites in Northeastern Arizona. Papers of the Laboratory of Tree-Ring Research, No. 3. Tucson: University of Arizona Press.

Diehl, Michael
1997 Rational behavior, the adoption of agriculture, and the organization of subsistence
during the Late Archaic period in the Greater Tucson Basin. In: Rediscovering Darwin,
edited by C. Michael Barton and Geoffrey A. Clark, pp. 251-65. Archaeological Papers of
the American Anthropological Association No. 7, American Anthropological Association.
Arlington.
1999 *Zea mays*: the bountiful crop. Archaeology Southwest 13(1):2.
2000 Macrobotanical remains and land use: subsistence and strategies for food acquisition.
In: Excavations in the Santa Cruz River Floodplain: The Early Agricultural Period Component at Los Pozos, edited by David Gregory, pp. 95-106. Anthropological Papers No.
21. Center For Desert Archaeology. Tucson, AZ.

Dixon, Roland B., and John B. Stetson, Jr.
1922 Analysis of Pre-Columbian pipe dottles. American Anthropologist 24(N.S.):245-46.

Doebley, John F.
1976 A Preliminary Study of Wild Plant Remains Recovered by Flotation at Salmon Ruin,
New Mexico. Master's thesis, Eastern New Mexico University. Portales, NM.
1981 Plant remains recovered by flotation from trash at Salmon Ruin, New Mexico. The
Kiva 46(3):169-88.
1984 "Seeds" of wild grasses: a major food of Southwestern Indians. Economic Botany
38(1):52-64.
1990 Molecular evidence and the evolution of maize. Economic Botany 44(Supp. 3):6-27.
1992 Mapping the genes that made maize. Trends Genet 8:302-7.

Doebley, John F., Major Goodman and Charles W. Stuber
1983 Isozyme variation in maize from the southwestern United States: taxonomic and anthropological implications. Maydica 28:97-120.

Doebley, John F., and L. Lukens
1998 Transcriptional regulators and the evolution of plant form. Plant Cell 10:1075-82.

Doebley, John F., and A. Stec
1991 Genetic analysis of the morphological differences between maize and teosinte. Genetics 129:285-95.

Doebley, John F., A. Stec and C. Gustus
1995 Teosinte branced1 and the origin of maize: evidence for epistasis and the evolution of
dominance. Genetics 141:333-46.

Doebley, John F., A. Stec and L. Hubbard
1997 The evolution of apical dominance in maize. Nature 386:485-88.

Doebley, John F., and R. L. Wang
1997 Genetics and the evolution of plant form: an example from maize. Cold Spring Harbor
Symposia on Quantitative Biology 62:361-67.

Doerweiler, J., A. Stec., J. Kermicle and J. Doebley
1993 Teoginte glume architecture 1: a genetic locus controlling a key step in maize evolution. Science 262:233-35.

Doolittle, William E.
1990 Canal Irrigation in Prehistoric Mexico: The Sequence of Technological Change. Austin: University of Texas Press.

Doolittle, William E., and Charles D. Frederick
1991 Phytoliths as indicators of prehistoric maize (*Zea mays* sp. Mays, Poaceae) cultivation. Plant Systematics and Evolution 177:175-84.

Durand, S. R., P. H. Shelley, R. C. Antweiler, and H. E. Taylor
1999 Trees, chemistry and prehistory in the American Southwest. Journal of Archaeological Science 26(2):185-203.

Elson, Mark D., Suzanne Fish, Steven James and Charles Miksicek
1995 Prehistoric subsistence in the Roosevelt Community Development study area. In: The Roosevelt Community Development Study, Vol. 3: Paleobotanical and Osteological Analyses, edited by Mark Elson and Jeffrey Clark, 217-60. Anthropological Papers 14, Center for Desert Archaeology. Tucson, AZ.

Euler, Robert C., and Volney H. Jones
1956 Hermetic sealing as a technique of food preservation among the Indians of the American Southwest. Proceedings of the American Philosophical Society 199(1):87-99.

Ezzo, J. A.
1993 Human Adaptation at Grasshopper Pueblo, Arizona: Social and Ecological Perspectives. Archaeological Series 4. International Monographs in Prehistory. Ann Arbor, MI.

Fish, Suzanne K.
1983 Appendix A: pollen from agricultural features. In: Hohokam Archaeology along the Salt-Gila Aqueduct Central Arizona Project, Vol. 3: Specialized Activity Sites, edited by Lynn S. Teague and P. L. Crown, pp. 575-603. Arizona State Museum Archaeological Series No. 150, University of Arizona. Tucson.
1984a Agriculture and subsistence implications of the Salt-Gila Aqueduct pollen analysis. In: Environment and Subsistence: Hohokam Archaeology Along the Salt-Gila Aqueduct Central Arizona Project, Vol. 7, edited by Lynn S. Teague and Patricia L. Crown, pp. 111-38. Arizona State Museum Archaeological Series No. 150, University of Arizona. Tucson.
1984b The modified environment of the Salt-Gila Aqueduct project sites: a palynological perspective. In: Environment and Subsistence: Hohokam Archaeology Along the Salt-Gila Aqueduct Central Arizona Project, Vol. 7, edited by Lynn S. Teague and Patricia L. Crown, pp. 39-51. Arizona State Museum Archaeological Series No. 150, University of Arizona. Tucson.
1985 Prehistoric disturbance floras of the lower Sonoran Desert and their implications. American Association of Stratigraphic Palynologists, Contribution Series No. 16:77-88.

1987 Pollen results from the Las Acequias-Los Muertos irrigation system and related features. In: Archaeological Investigations of Portions of the Las Acequias-Los Muertos Irrigation System, edited by W. Bruce Masse, pp. 159-67. Archaeological Series 176, Arizona State Museum. Tucson.

1989 Hohokam plant use at Las Colinas: the pollen evidence. In: The 1982-1984 Excavations at Las Colinas, Environment and Subsistence, edited by Donald A. Graybill et al., pp. 79-93. Arizona State Museum Archaeological Series 162, Vol. 5. Tucson.

1998a A pollen perspective on variability and stability in Tonto Basin subsistence. In: Environment and Subsistence in the Classic Period Tonto Basin, edited by Katherine A. Spielmann, pp. 49-69. The Roosevelt Archaeology Studies, 1989 to 1998. Anthropological Field Studies 39, Arizona State University, Tempe, AZ.

1998b Archaeological palynology of gardens and fields. In: The Archaeology of Garden and Field, edited by Naomi F. Miller and Kathryn L. Gleason. Philsdelphia: University of Pennsylvania Press.

2000 Hohokam impacts on Sonoran Desert environment. In: Imperfect Balance: Landscape Transformations in the Precolumbian Americas, edited by David Lentz, pp. 251-80. New York: Columbia University Press.

In press Corn, crops and cultivation in the ancient Southwest. In: People and Plants in Ancient North America, edited by Paul Minnis. Washington, DC: Smithsonian Institution Press.

Fish, Suzanne K., and Marcia Donaldson
1991 Production and consumption in the archaeological record: a Hohokam example. Kiva 56(3):255-75.

Fish, Suzanne K., and Paul R. Fish, editors
1984 Prehistoric Agricultural Strategies in the Southwest. Arizona State University Anthropological Research Papers 33. Tempe.

Fish, Suzanne K., Paul R. Fish, and John H. Madsen
1992a Evidence for large-scale agave cultivation in the Marana community. In: The Marana Community in the Hohokam World, edited by Suzanne K. Fish, Paul R. Fish and John H. Madsen, pp. 73-87. Tucson: University of Arizona Press.

Fish, Suzanne K., Paul R. Fish, and John H. Madsen (editors)
1992b The Marana community in the Hohokam world. Anthropological Papers of the University of Arizona, No. 56. Tucson: University of Arizona Press.

Fish, Suzanne K., Paul R. Fish, Charles Miksicek, and J. Madsen
1985 Prehistoric *Agave* cultivation in southern Arizona. Desert Plants 7:107-12.

Fish, Suzanne K., and Gary P. Nabhan
1991 Desert as context: the Hohokam environment. In: Exploring the Hohokam: Prehistoric Desert Peoples of the American Southwest, edited by George J. Gumerman, pp. 29-60. Amerind Foundation, New World Study Series 1. Albuquerque: University of New Mexico Press.

Ford, Richard I.
1981 Gardening and farming before A.D. 1000: patterns of prehistoric cultivation north of Mexico. Journal of Ethnobiology 1(1):6-27.
1985 Patterns of prehistoric food production in North America. In: Prehistoric Food Production in North America, edited by Richard I. Ford, pp. 341-64. Anthropological Papers No. 75, Museum of Anthropology, University of Michigan. Ann Arbor.

Fritz, Gayle, Karen R. Adams, Robert Hard, and John Roney
1999 Evidence for cultivation of *Amaranthus* sp. (Amaranthaceae) 3,000 years ago at Cerro Juanaquena, Chihuahua. Paper given at the 22nd Annual Conference, Society of Ethnobiology. Oaxaca, Mexico.

Fry, G., and H. J. Hall
1975 Human coprolites from Antelope House: preliminary analyses. The Kiva 41(1):87-96.

Gaut, B., and J. Doebley
1997 DNA sequence evidence for the segmental allotetraploid origin of maize. Proceedings of the National Academy of Science 94:6809-14.

Gasser, R. E.
1982a Anasazi diet. In: The Coronado Project Archaeological Investigations, the Specialists' Volume: Biocultural Analyses, edited by R. E. Gasser, pp. 8-95. Museum of Northern Arizona Research Paper No. 23, Coronado Series No. 3. Flagstaff.
1982b Hohokam use of desert plant foods. Desert Plants 3(4):216-34.

Gasser, R. E., and E. C. Adams
1981 Aspects of deterioration of plant remains in archaeological sites: the Walpi archaeological project. Journal of Ethnobiology 1(1):182-92.

Gasser, R. E., and Scott M. Kwiatkowski
1991a Food for thought: recognizing patterns in Hohokam subsistence. In: Exploring the Hohokam, edited by George Gumerman, pp. 417-59. Jointly published by American Foundation, Dragoon, AZ, and University of New Mexico Press, Albuquerque.
1991b Regional signatures of Hohokam plant use. The Kiva 56:207-26.

Gasser, R. E., and Charles Miksicek
1985 The specialists: a reappraisal of Hohokam exchange and the archaeobotanical record. In: Proceedings of the 1983 Hohokam Symposium, Part II, edited by Alfred E. Dittert, Jr. and Donald E. Dove, pp. 483-98. Phoenix chapter of the Arizona Archaeological Society, Occasional Paper 2.

Gish, Jannifer W.
1975 Appendix A: preliminary report on pollen analysis from Hecla I, II, and III. In: Hecla II and III: An Interpretive Study of Archeological Remains from the Lakeshore Project, Papago Reservation, South-Central Arizona, by Albert C. Goodyear III, pp. 254-70. . Arizona State University Anthropological Research Paper No. 9. Tempe.
1979 Palynological research at Pueblo Grande ruin. The Kiva 44:159-72.

1987 Structured diversity in the resource base of a Hohokam village: the pollen evidence from La Ciudad. In: La Ciudad: Specialized Studies in the Economy, Environment and Culture of La Ciudad, Part III, edited by JoAnn E. Kisselburg, Glen E. Rice, and Brenda L. Shears, pp. 1-66. Anthropological Field Studies No. 20, Arizona State University. Tempe.
1991 Current perceptions, recent discoveries, and future directions in Hohokam palynology. The Kiva 56(3):237-54.
1993 Palynology of Shelltown and the Hind site. In: Shelltown and the Hind Site: A Study of Two Hohokam Craftsman Communities Southwestern Arizona, Vol. 1, edited by William S. Marmaduke and Richard J. Martynec, pp. 449-562. Northland Research, Inc. Flagstaff, AZ.

Golubinoff, Pierre, Svante Paabo, and Allan C. Wilson
1994 Molecular characterization of ancient maize: potentials and pitfalls. In: Corn and Culture in the Prehistoric New World, edited by Sissel Johannessen and Christine A. Hastorf, pp. 113-25. Boulder, CO: Westview Press.

Gould, Frank W.
1951 Grasses of Southwestern United States. Tucson: University of Arizona Press.

Greenhouse, Ruth
1979 The Iron and Calcium Content of Some Traditional Pima Foods and the Effects of Preparation Methods. Master's thesis, Department of Home Economics, Arizona State University. Tempe.

Greenhouse, Ruth, Robert E. Gasser, and Jannier W. Gish
1981 Cholla bud roasting pits: an ethnoarchaeological example. Kiva 46(4):227-42.

Hammett, Julia
1993 Paleoethnobotanical evidence of tobacco use along the transwestern pipeline. In: Across the Colorado Plateau: Anthropological Studies for the Transwestern Pipeline Expansion Project. Vol. XV, Subsistence and Environment, edited by Jannifer W. Gish et al., pp. 509-18. Office of Contract Archaeology and Maxwell Museum of Anthropology, University of New Mexico. Albuquerque.

Hard, Robert J., and John R. Roney
1998 A massive terraced village complex in Chihuahua, Mexico, 3000 years before present. Science 279:1661-64.

Harlan, Jack R.
1975 Crops and Man. American Society of Agronomy, Crop Science Society of America. Madison, WI.

Hasbargen, J.
1997 Identification of Prehistoric Fields through Palynological Evidence. Master's thesis, Northern Arizona University. Flagstaff.

Hastorf, C.A.
1999 Recent research in paleoethnobotany. Journal of Anthropological Research 7(1):55-103.

Helentjaris, Tim
1989 Does RFLP analysis of ancient Anasazi samples suggest that they utilized hybrid maize? Maize Genetic Cooperation Newsletter 62:104-5.

Hendry, George W.
1931 The adobe brick as a historical source. Agricultural History 5:110-27.

Hendry, George W., and M. K. Bellue
1936 An approach to Southwestern agricultural history through adobe brick analysis. The University of New Mexico Bulletin, Symposium on Prehistoric Agriculture, 296:65-72.

Hendry, George W. and Margaret Kelly
1925 The plant content of adobe bricks. California Historical Society Quarterly 4:361-73.

Hevly, R. H., P. J. Mehringer, Jr., and H. Yokum
1965 Modern pollen rain in the Sonoran desert. Journal of the Arizona Academy of Science 3:123-35.

Hillman, G. C.
1984 Interpretation of archaeological plant remains: the applications of ethnographic models from Turkey. In: Plants and Ancient Man: Studies in Paleoethnobotany, edited by W. van Zeist and W. A. Casparie. Rotterdam: A. A. Balkema.

Housley, Lucille K.
1974 *Opuntia imbricata* Distribution on Old Jemez Indian Habitation Sites. Master's thesis, Department of Botany, Pomona College. Claremont, CA.

Huckell, Bruce B.
1995 Of Marshes and Maize: Preceramic Agricultural Settlements in the Cienega Valley, Southeastern Arizona. Anthropological Papers of the University of Arizona No. 59. Tucson.

Huckell, Bruce B., Lisa W. Huckell, and M. Steven Shackley
1999 McEuen cave. Archaeology Southwest 13(1):12.

Huckell, Bruce B., Lisa W. Huckell, and Karl K. Benedict
2000 Maize Agriculture and the Rise of Mixed Farming-Foraging Economies in Southeastern Arizona during the Second Millennium B.C. Paper presented at the Southwest Symposium 2000. Santa Fe, NM.

Huckell, Lisa W.
1986 Botanical remains. In: The 1985 excavations at the Hodges Site, Pima County, Arizona, edited by Robert W. Layhe, pp. 241-69. Arizona State Museum Archaeological Series No. 170. Tucson, AZ.
1992 Plant macroremains in adobe bricks. In: San Miguel de Guevavi: The Archaeology of an Eighteenth Century Jesuit Mission on the Rim of Christendom, edited by Jeffrey F. Burton, pp. 113-24. Western Archeological and Conservation Center Publications in Anthropology 57. Tucson, AZ.

1993 Plant remains from the Pinaleno cotton cache. The Kiva 59:147-204.

1996 Southwestern Archaic Period Paleoethnobotany: An Overview. Paper presented at the Conference on the Archaic Prehistory of the North American Southwest. University of New Mexico. Albuquerque.

1998 Macrobotanical remains. In: Archaeological Investigations of Early Village Sites in the Middle Santa Cruz Valley, edited by Jonathan Mabry, pp. 113-24. Anthropological Papers 19, Center for Desert Archaeology. Tucson, AZ.

1999 Silver Creek Archaeological Research Project paleoethnobotany. In: Living on the Edge of the Rim: The Silver Creek Archaeological Research Project, 1993-1997, edited by Barbara J. Mills, Sara A. Herr and Scott Van Kueren, pp. 459-504. Arizona State Museum Archaeological Series No. 192. Tucson.

Huckell, Lisa W., and Mollie S. Toll
In press People and plants in ancient North America: wild plant use in the Southwest. In: People and Plants in Ancient North America, edited by Paul Minnis. Washington, DC: Smithsonian Institution Press.

Johannessen, S.
1984 Paleoethnobotany. In: American Bottom archaeology, edited by C. J. Bareis and J. W. Porter, pp. 197-214. Urbana: University of Illinois Press.

1988 Plant remains and culture change: are paleoethnobotanical data better than we think? In: Current Paleoethnobotany, edited by C. A. Hastorf and V. S. Popper, pp. 145-66. Chicago: University of Chicago Press.

1993 Food, dishes, and society in the Mississippi. In: Foraging and Farming in the Eastern Woodlands, edited by C. M. Scarry, pp. 182-205. Gainesville: University Press of Florida.

Johnson, V. C., F. L. Gager and J. C. Holmes
1959 A Study of the History of the Use of Tobacco. Special Report No. 8, El Paso Archaeological Society, Inc. (Cited in Pipes and Cigarettes of the Prehistoric Southwest, by Ronald R. Switzer, 1969.)

Jones, T., G. M. Brown, L. M. Raab, J. L. McVickar, W. G. Spaulding, D. J. Kennett, A. York, and P.L. Walker
1999 Environmental imperatives reconsidered: demographic crisis in western North America during the medieval climatic anomaly. Current Anthropology 40(2):137-70.

Jones, G. E. M.
1984 Interpretation of archaeological plant remains: ethnographic models for Greece. In: Plants and Ancient Man: Studies in Paleoethnobotany, edited by W. Van Zeist and W. A. Casparie, pp. 43-61. Rotterdam: A. A. Balkema.

Jones, Volney H.
1942 Report No. 96, Lab Nos. 1319-1343. Manuscript on file, University of Michigan, Museum of Anthropology, Ethnobotanical Laboratory. (Letter to E. B. Sayles, Gila Pueblo, Globe, Arizona.)

Jones, Volney H., and Elizabeth Ann Morris
1960 A seventh-century record of tobacco utilization in Arizona. El Palacio 67(4):115-17.

Kaplan, Lawrence
1956 The cultivated beans of the prehistoric Southwest. Annals of the Missouri Botanical Garden 43:189-251.
1965 Archaeology and domestication in American *Phaseolus* (beans). Economic Botany 19(4):358-68.

Kaplan, Lawrence, and Thomas F. Lynch
1999 *Phaseolus* (Fabaceae) in archaeology: AMS radiocarbon dates and their significance for pre-Columbian agriculture. Economic Botany 53(3):261-72.

Kelley, Robert L.
1995 The Foraging Spectrum: Diversity in Hunter-Gatherer Lifeways. Washington, DC: Smithsonian Institution Press.

Kohler, Timothy A.
1992 Prehistoric human impact on the environment in the upland North American Southwest. Population and Environment: A Journal of Interdisciplinary Studies 13(4):255-68.

Kohler, Timothy A., and Meredith H. Matthews
1988 Long-term Anasazi land use and forest reduction: a case study from southwestern Colorado. American Antiquity 53(3):537-64.

Kwiatkowski, Scott
1994 Prehistoric biotic communities and ecosystem dynamics near Pueblo Grande. In: The Pueblo Grande Project, Volume 5: Environment and Subsistence, edited by Scott Kwiatkowski, pp. 5-34. Soil Systems Publications in Archaeology No. 20. Phoenix, AZ.

LaFerriere, Joseph E.
1991 Optimal use of Ethnobotanical Resources by the Mountain Pima of Chihuahua, Mexico. Doctoral dissertation, University of Arizona. Tucson.

Leonard, Robert D.
1989 Anasazi Faunal Exploitation: Prehistoric Subsistence on Northern Black Mesa, Arizona. Occasional Paper No. 13. Center for Archaeological Investigations, Southern Illinois University. Carbondale.

Leonard, Robert D., and George T. Jones
1989 Quantifying Diversity in Archaeology. New York: Cambridge University Press.

Mabry, Johnathan B.
1999 Changing concepts of the first period of agriculture in the southern Southwest. Archaeology Southwest 13(1):3.

Mabry, Jonathan B., editor
1998 Archaeological Investigations of Early Village Sites in the Middle Santa Cruz Valley: Analyses and Synthesis. Anthropological Papers No. 19(1-2). Center for Desert Archaeology. Tucson, AZ.

Mabry, Jonathan B., Deborah L. Swartz, Helga Wocherl, Jeffrey J. Clark, Gavin H. Archer, and Michael W. Lindeman
1997 Archaeological Investigations of Early Village Sites in the Middle Santa Cruz Valley: Descriptions of the Santa Cruz Bend, Square Hearth, Stone Pipe, and Canal Sites. Anthropological Papers No. 18, Center for Desert Archaeology. Tucson, AZ.

Magers, Pamela C.
1975 The cotton industry at Antelope House. Kiva 41(1):39-47.

Martin, S. L.
1999 Virgin Anasazi diet as demonstrated through the analysis of stable carbon and nitrogen isotopes. Kiva 64(4):495-514.

Matson, R. G.
1991 The Origins of Southwestern Agriculture. Tucson: University of Arizona Press.

Matson, R. G., and B. Chisholm
1991 Basketmaker II subsistence: carbon isotopes and other dietary indicators from Cedar Mesa, Utah. American Antiquity 56(3):444-59.

McDaniel, Robert
1993 Microscopic evaluation of the cotton. In: A Prehistoric Cotton Cache from the Pinaleno Mountains, edited by Emil W. Haury and Lisa W. Huckell. Kiva 59(2):128-34.

McNair, James B.
1932 The interrelation between substances in plants: essential oils and resins, cyanogens and oxalates. American Journal of Botany 19:255-71.

Miksicek, C. H.
1983 Appendix B: plant remains from agricultural features. In: Hohokam Archaeology along the Salt-Gila Aqueduct Central Arizona Project, Vol. III: Specialized Activity Sites, edited by Lynn S. Teague and P. L. Crown, pp. 604-20. Arizona State Museum Archaeological Series No. 150, University of Arizona. Tucson.
1984 Historic desertification, prehistoric vegetation change, and Hohokam subsistence in the Salt-Gila Basin. In: Hohokam Archaeology along the Salt-Gila Aqueduct, Central Arizona Project, Vol. VII: Environment and Subsistence, edited by Lynn S. Teague and Patricia L. Crown, pp. 53-80. Arizona State Museum Archaeological Series No. 150. Tucson.
1987a Formation processes of the archaeobotanical record. In: Advances in Archaeological Method and Theory, Vol. 10, edited by Michael Schiffer, pp. 211-47. New York: Academic Press.
1987b Late Sedentary-Early Classic period Hohokam agriculture: plant remains from the Marana Community complex. In: Studies in the Hohokam Community of Marana, edited by Glen E. Rice, pp. 197-216. Arizona State University Anthropological Field Studies. Tempe.

1988 Rethinking Hohokam paleoethnobotanical assemblages: a progress report for the Tucson Basin. In: Recent Research on Tucson Basin Prehistory: Proceedings of the Second Tucson Basin Conference, edited by William Doelle and Paul Fish, pp. 9-30. Institute for American Research, Anthropological Paper No. 10, Institute for American Research. Tucson.

1989 Snails, seeds and charcoal: macrofossils from the Las Acequias canal system. In: Prehistoric Agricultural Activities on the Lehi-Mesa Terrace: Perspectives on Hohokam Irrigation Cycles, edited by N. W. Ackerly and T. K. Henderson, pp. 235-62. Northland Research. Flagstaff, AZ.

1995 Canal mollusks and plant remains. In: Archaeology at the Head of the Scottsdale Canal System, Vol. 3, edited by M. R. Hackbarth and T. K. Henderson, pp. 121-31. Anthropological Papers No. 95-1, Northland Research, Inc. Tempe, AZ.

Miksicek, Charles H., and Robert E. Gasser
1989 Hohokam plant use at Las Colinas: the flotation evidence. In: The 1982-1984 Excavations at Las Colinas: Environment and Subsistence, edited by D. A. Graybill, D. A. Gregory, F. L. Nials, S. Fish, R. Gasser, C. Miksicek, and C. Szuter, pp. 115-45. Archaeological Series 162, Arizona State Museum. Tucson.

Minnis, Paul E.
1978 Paleoethnobotanical indicators of prehistoric environmental disturbance: a case study. In: The Nature and Status of Ethnobotany, edited by Richard I. Ford, pp. 347-66. Anthropological Papers 67, Museum of Anthropology, University of Michigan. Ann Arbor.

1981 Seeds in archaeological sites: sources and some interpretive problems. American Antiquity 46:143-52.

1985 Social Adaptation to Food Stress. Chicago: University of Chicago Press.

1987 Identification of wood from archaeological sites in the American Southwest, I: keys for gymnosperms. Journal of Archaeological Science 14:121-31.

1989 Prehistoric diet in the northern Southwest: macroplant remains from Four Corners feces. American Antiquity 54(3):543-63.

1991 Famine foods of the northern American desert borderlands in historical context. Journal of Ethnobiology 11:231-57.

1996 Notes on economic uncertainty and human behavior in the prehistoric North American Southwest. In: Evolving Complexity and Environmental Risk in the Prehistoric Southwest, edited by J. Tainter and B. B. Tainter, pp. 57-78. Santa Fe Institute Studies in the Sciences of Complexity, Proceedings Vol. XXIV. Reading, MA: Addison-Wesley.

Muenchrath, Deborah A.
1995 Productivity, Morphology, Phenology and Physiology of a Desert-Adapted Native American Maize (*Zea mays* L.) Cultivar. Doctoral dissertation, Iowa State University. Dissertation Abstracts 95-40927.

Musil, Albina F.
1963 Identification of crop and weed seeds. USDA Agricultural Handbook 219:1-171.

Nabhan, Gary Paul, and Richard S. Felger
1978 Teparies in southwestern North America: a biogeographical and ethnohistorical study of *Phaseolus acutifolius*. Economic Botany 32(1):2-19.

Nabhan, Gary Paul, and Jan M. J. de Wet
1984 Panicum sonorum in Sonoran desert agriculture. Economic Botany 38(1):65-82.

Nabhan, Gary Paul, Wendy Hodgson and James Hickey
n.d. Domestication, Cultural Diffusion and In Situ Conservation of *Agave murpheyi* Gibson: An Ethnobiological Perspective. Manuscript on file, Arizona-Sonora Desert Museum. Tucson.

Nabhan, Gary Paul, Alfred Whiting, Henry Dobyns, Richard Hevly and Robert Euler
1981 Devil's claw domestication: evidence from southwestern Indian fields. Journal of Ethnobiology 1(1):135-64.

Nelson, Margaret C., and Michael W. Diehl
1999 Foraging and farming. In: Mimbres During the Twelfth Century: Abandonment, Continuity, and Reorganization, edited by Margaret C. Nelson, pp. 142-66. Tucson: University of Arizona Press.

O'Rourke, Mary Kay
1983 Pollen from adobe brick. Journal of Ethnobiology 3(1):39-48.

Palacios-Fest, Manuel R.
1989 Late Holocene ostracodes as hydrochemical indicators in the Phoenix Basin. In: Prehistoric Agricultural Activities on the Lehi-Mesa Terrace: Perspectives on Hohokam Irrigation Cycles, edited by N. W. Ackerly and T. K. Henderson, pp. 263-78. Northland Research. Flagstaff, AZ.
1994 Nonmarine ostracode shell chemistry from ancient Hohokam irrigation canals in central Arizona: a Paleohydrochemical tool for the interpretation of prehistoric human occupation in the North American Southwest. Geoarchaeology: An International Journal 9:1-29.
1997a Paleoenvironmental reconstruction of human activity in central Arizona using shell chemistry of Hohokam canal ostracodes. Geoarchaeology: An International Journal 12:211-26.
1997b Continental ostracode paleoecology from the Hohokam Pueblo Blanco area, central Arizona. Journal of Archaeological Science 24:965-83.

Pierce, Christopher, Karen R. Adams and Joe D. Stewart
1998 Determining the fuel constituents of ancient hearth ash via ICP-AES analysis. Journal of Archaeological Science 25:493-503.

Plog, Stephen, and Michelle Hegmon
1993 The sample size-richness relation: the relevance of research questions, sampling strategies, and behavioral variation. American Antiquity 58(3):489-96.

Priestly, D. A., W. C. Galinat, and A. C. Leopold
1981 Preservation of polyunsaturated fatty acid in ancient Anasazi maize seed. Nature 292:146-48.

Puseman, Kathryn
1995 Protein Residue Analysis of Ten Lithic Artifacts from Site LA110143, Southeast New Mexico. Paleo Research Labs Technical Report 95-68. Denver, CO.

Reeder, John R.
1957 The embryo in grass systematics. American Journal of Botany 44:756-68.

Rindos, David
1984 The Origins of Agriculture: An Evolutionary Perspective. New York: Academic Press.

Ross, Winifred
1941 The Present Day Dietary Habits of the Papago Indians. Master's thesis, Department of Home Economics, University of Arizona. Tucson.

Samuels, Michael L., and Julio L. Betancourt
1982 Modeling the long-term effects of fuelwood harvests on pinyon-juniper woodlands. Environmental Management 6(6):505-15.

Sauer, Jonathan D.
1950 The Grain Amaranths: A Survey of Their History and Classification. Annals of the Missouri Botanical Garden, Vol. 37.

Sauer, Jonathan, and Lawrence Kaplan
1969 Canavalia beans in American prehistory. American Antiquity 34(4):417-24.

Schiffer, Michael B.
1976 Behavioral Archeology. New York: Academic Press.

Schoenwetter, James
1979 Initial assessments of the palynological record: Gila Butte-Santan region. In: An Archaeological Test of Sites in the Gila Butte-Santan Region, South-Central Arizona, edited by Glen Rice, David Wilcox, Kevin Rafferty, and James Schoenwetter, pp. 164-77. Arizona State University Anthropological Research Papers 18. Tempe.

Schoenwetter, J., and L. A. Doerschlag
1971 Surficial pollen records from central Arizona, I: Sonoran desert scrub. Journal of the Arizona Academy of Science 6:216-21.

Scott, Linda
1986 The pollen record at Windy Wheat hamlet: Appendix 9C. In: Dolores Archaeological Program: Anasazi Communities at Dolores: Early Anasazi Sites in the Sagehen Flats Area, compiled by Allen E. Kane and G. Timothy Gross, pp. 773-804. Bureau of Reclamation, Engineering and Research Center. Denver, CO.

Scott-Cummings, Linda
1991 Anasazi diet: variety and nutritional analysis. In: Proceedings of the Anasazi Symposium 1991, compiled by Art Hutchinson and Jack E. Smith, pp. 303-18. Mesa Verde Musuem Association. Mancos, CO.

1995 Agriculture and the Mesa Verde area Anasazi diet: description and nutritional analysis. In: Soil, Water, Biology and Belief in Prehistoric and Traditional Southwestern Agriculture, edited by H. Wolcott Toll, pp. 335-52. New Mexico Archaeological Council, Special Publication No. 2. Albuquerque, NM.
1998 Starch Granules and Fremont Subsistence. Paper presented at the 26th Great Basin Anthropological Conference. Bend, Oregon.

Scott-Cummings, Linda, and Kathryn Puseman
1994 Phytolith and Protein Residue Analysis of Forty Tabular Stone Knives from the Lower Verde Project in Central Arizona. Paleo Research Labs Technical Report 94-54. Denver, CO.

Scott-Cummings, Linda, Kathryn Puseman, and Thomas E. Moutoux
1998 Pollen, Phytolith, and Macrofloral Analysis of Samples from the Rimrock Hamlet (5RB2792) and Sky Aerie (5RB104) Sites, Western Colorado. Paleo Research Labs Technical Report 95-57. Denver, CO.

Simmons, Alan H.
1986 New evidence for the early use of cultigens in the American Southwest. American Antiquity 51(1):73-89.

Smith, Bruce D.
1992 Rivers of Change: Essays on Early Agriculture in Eastern North America. Washington, DC: Smithsonian Institution Press.

Smith, Susan J.
1997 El Rito Pollen Analysis. Manuscript on file, Rio Grande Foundation. Santa Fe, NM.
1998 Processing pollen samples from archaeological sites in the southwest United States: an example of differential recovery from two heavy liquid gravity separation procedures. In: New Developments in Palynomorph Sampling, Extraction, and Analysis, edited by V. M. Bryand and J. H. Wrenn, pp. 29-34. American Association of Stratigraphic Palynologists Foundation, Contributions Series Number 33. Dallas, TX.

Smith, Susan J., and Phil R. Geib
1999 An Experimental Study of Grinding Tool Pollen Washes: Bridging the Inferential Gap between Pollen Counts and Past Behavior. Poster presented 64th Annual Meeting, Society for American Archaeology. Chicago, IL.

Sobolik, Kristin D., and Deborah J. Gerick
1992 Prehistoric medicinal plant usage: a case study from coprolites. Journal of Ethnobiology 12(2):203-11.

Stewart, Joe D., and Karen R. Adams
1999 Evaluating visual criteria for identifying carbon- and iron-based pottery paints from the Four Corners region using SEM-EDS. American Antiquity 64(4):675-96.

Stewart, Robert B., and William Robertson, III
1971 Moisture and seed carbonization. Economic Botany 25(4):381.

Stier, Frances
1975 Behavioral chain analysis of yucca remains at Antelope House. The Kiva 41(1):57-64.

Stiger, Mark A.
1977 Anasazi Diet: The Coprolite Evidence. Master's thesis, University of Colorado. Boulder.
1979 Mesa Verde subsistence patterns from Basketmaker to Pueblo III. The Kiva 44(2-3):133-44.

Sutton, M. Q., and K. J. Reinhard
1995 Cluster analysis of the coprolites from Antelope House: implications for Anasazi diet and cuisine. Journal of Archaeological Science 22:741-50.

Szuter, Christine R.
1984 Paleoenvironmental and species richness along the Salt-Gila aqueduct. In: Environment and Subsistence: Hohokam Archaeology along the Salt-Gila Aqueduct Central Arizona Project, Vol. VII, edited by Lynn S. Teague and Patricia L. Crown, pp. 81-93. Arizona State Museum Archaeological Series No. 150, University of Arizona. Tucson.

Tagg, Martyn D.
1996 Early cultigens from Fresnal shelter, southeastern New Mexico. American Antiquity 61(2):311-24.

Toll, Mollie S.
1985 An overview of Chaco Canyon macrobotanical materials and analyses to date. In: Environment and Subsistence at Chaco Canyon, edited by Frances J. Mathien and Thomas C. Windes, pp. 247-77. Chaco Canyon Studies, Publications in Archeology 18E. National Park Service, US Department of the Interior.
1988 Flotation sampling: problems and some solutions, with examples from the American Southwest. In: Current Paleoethnobotany: Analytical Methods and Cultural Interpretations of Archaeological Plant Remains, edited by Christine A. Hastorf and Virginia S. Popper, pp. 36-52. Prehistoric Archeology and Ecology Series. Chicago: The University of Chicago Press.

Toll, Mollie S., and Lisa W. Huckell, compilers
1996 Guidelines for Standardizing Collection of Zea mays Morphometric Data. Manuscript on file, Museum of New Mexico, Office of Archaeological Studies. Santa Fe.

Toll, Mollie S., and Pamela J. McBride
1996a Flotation and Macrobotanical Materials from Early Pithouse and Early Pueblo Period Sites of the Quemado Area, NM: The Gallo Mountain Project, MNM#41.411. Museum of New Mexico, Office of Archaeological Studies, Ethnobotany Lab Technical Series No. 37. Santa Fe, NM.
1996b Botanical Contents of Two 17th Century Baskets from a Dry Shelter in the Galisteo Basin, NM. MNM Project #41.573. Museum of New Mexico, Office of Archeological Studies. Santa Fe, NM.

Van West, Carla R.
1996 Modeling prehistoric agricultural strategies and human settlement in the middle Little Colorado River Valley. In: River of Change: Archaeology of the Middle Little Colorado River Valley, Arizona, edited by E. C. Adams, pp. 15-35. Arizona State Museum Archaeological Series, No. 185. University of Arizona. Tucson.
1994a Agricultural productivity and carrying capacity in the Tonto Basin. In: The Roosevelt Rural Sites Study: Changing Land Use in the Tonto Basin, Vol. 3, edited by R.S. Ciolek-Torrello and J. R. Welch, pp. 361-435. Statistical Research Technical Series No. 28. Tucson, AZ.
1994b Modeling Prehistoric Agricultural Productivity in Southwestern Colorado: A GIS Approach. Washington State University Reports of Investigations 67. Department of Anthropology, Washington State University. Pullman.

Van West, Carla R., and Jeffrey H. Altschul
1997 Environmental variability and agricultural economics along the Lower Verde River, A.D. 750-1450. In: Vanishing River, Landscapes and Lives of the Lower Verde Valley: The Lower Verde Archaeological Project, Overview, Synthesis and Conclusions, edited by S. M. Whittlesey, R. Ciolek-Torrello, and J. H. Altschul, pp. 337-92. Statistical Research, Inc. Press. Tucson, AZ.

Vokes, A. S., and C. H. Miksicek
1987 Snails, clams and canals: an analysis of nonmarine molluscan remains. In: Archaeological Investigations of Portions of the Las Acequias-Los Muertos Irrigation System: Testing and Partial Data Recovery within the Tempe Section of the Outer Loop Freeway System, Maricopa County, Arizona, edited by W. B. Masse, pp. 177-78. Arizona State Museum Archaeological Series 176. Tucson.

Wang, R. L., A. Stec. J. Hey, L. Lukens and J. Doebley
1999 The limits of selection during maize domestication. Nature 398:236-39.

Welch, P. D., and C. M. Scarry
1995 Status-related variation in foodways in the Moundville chiefdom. American Antiquity 60:397-419.

Wetterstrom, Wilma
1986 Food, Diet, and Population at Prehistoric Arroyo Hondo Pueblo, New Mexico. Arroyo Hondo Archaeological Series 6, School of American Research Press. Santa Fe.

Whiting, Alfred F.
1966 Ethnobotany of the Hopi. Flagstaff, AZ: Northland Press.

Williams-Dean, Glenna
1978 Ethnobotany and Cultural Ecology of Prehistoric Man in Southwest Texas. Doctoral dissertation, Texas A & M University. College Station.

Wills, Wirt H.
1988 Early Prehistoric Agriculture in the American Southwest. Santa Fe, NM: School of American Research Press.

1996 Archaic foraging and the beginning of food production in the American Southwest. In: Last Hunters, First Farmers, edited by T. Douglas Price and Anne B. Gebauer, pp. 215-42. Santa Fe, NM: School of American Research Press.

Winter, Joseph C.
2001a The North American tobacco species and their uses by Native Americans. In: Tobacco Use by Native North Americans: Sacred Smoke and Silent Killer, edited by Joseph C. Winter. Norman: University of Oklahoma Press.
2001b Botanical description and archaeological record of the North American tobacco species. In: Tobacco Use by Native North Americans: Sacred Smoke and Silent Killer, edited by Joseph C. Winter. Norman: University of Oklahoma Press.

6

An Ethnozoological Perspective on the Ethnobiological Enterprise

Eugene S. Hunn, University of Washington

Ethnobiology as a deliberate intellectual project is scarcely a century old. The term "ethnobiology" is even younger, apparently first used in print by Castetter in 1935 (Clément 1998:162), though its components, "ethnobotany" (Harshberger 1895) and "ethnozoology" (Mason 1899; Henderson and Harrington 1914), were introduced before the turn of the twentieth century (Clément 1998:175, 184). Of course, "folk biology," which in contrast to "ethnobiology" we might define as the activity of "humanizing nature" (Marx), is as old as our species. I won't trace this history here, but will focus instead on the place of ethnozoology within the larger ethnobiological project.

There is a paradoxical asymmetry in the relationship of ethnozoology to ethnobotany. That is, ethnozoology is now, and apparently always has been, a bit of an afterthought with respect to ethnobotany, despite the fact that we might expect the contrary on both biosystematic and psychological grounds. I will explore this apparent paradox below.

Counts of publications, whether popular or scholarly, indicate a ratio greater than 2:1 in favor of ethnobotany. For example, during my recent tenure as editor of the *Journal of Ethnobiology* we published 27 ethnobotanical articles but just 6 focused on ethnozoology, despite the predilections of the editor (Hunn 1998b). Summaries of recent dissertations of interest to ethnobiologists compiled for the *Journal of Ethnobiology* list 116 of primarily ethnobotanical interest compared to 58 of primarily ethnozoological interest (with 96 of general or indeterminate emphasis) (Laferrière and Hays 1995; Hays 1997, 1998). However, the number of animal species known to

TABLE 6.1. Numbers of species by major taxonomic group and number of scientific papers published per species per year by taxonomic group (May 1988; Toledo and Ordóñez 1993).

Taxonomic group	Number of species[a]	Publications/ species/year
All living things	1,500,000++	
Monerans and protists	5%	
Fungi and plants	22%	
Vascular plants	/266,000	
Fungi	/46,983	
Animals	~73%/1,400,000	
Protozoa	260,000	0.15
Porifera, Coelenterata, Echinodermata	26,000	
Nematoda	1,000,000?/12,000	0.002
Annelida	15,000/12,000	
Mollusca	100,000/200,000	0.04
Anthropoda		
Crustacea	39,000/38,723	0.09
Chelicerata	63,000	0.03
Insecta	1,000,000?/750,000	0.02
Coleoptera	300,000	
Diptera	85,000	
Lepidoptera	100,000/220,000	
Hymenoptera	100,000	
Hemiptera	40,000	
Chordata/Vertebrata	41,300+/45,202	
Pisces	19,000/21,763[b]	0.37
Amphibia	2,800/4014	0.47
Reptilia	6,000/5965	0.41
Aves	9,000	1.00
Mammalia	4,500	1.80
Chiroptera	951	
Rodentia	1,702	

[a]The first number is from May, the number after the slash from Toledo and Ordóñez.
[b]Marine fish only.

modern science exceeds the number of presently known plant species by approximately the ratio of 3.5:1 (see Table 6.1). This ratio would likely be much greater—perhaps by an order of magnitude—if the true number of arthropod and nematode species were known (May 1988). Thus, in terms of intellectual effort per species, plants have a better than 10:1 advantage! My analysis of the reasons for this disproportionate effort on behalf of the plant kingdom will provide some useful insights into the nature of the larger ethnobiological enterprise.

How might we account for this bias? In particular, we may ask if the bias is perceptually based or motivated by "utilitarian" concerns. This contrast reflects a related debate with regard to the basis of folk biological classification (Berlin 1992).

TABLE 6.2. Relative emphasis on the ethnobotanical and ethnozoological domains.

Cultural group	Plant generics	rank order[a]	Animal generics	% plant	Total generics	#a/p[b]
Hanunóo[c]	956	1:3	461	67%	1417	0.47
Aguaruna[c]	566	3:1	606	48%	1172	1.07
Tobelo[c]	689	2:4	420	62%	1109	0.61
Wayampí[c]	516	4:2	589	47%	1105	1.14
Tzeltal[c]	471	5:6	335	58%	806	0.71
Zapotec[d]	435	6:8	320	65%	665	0.53
Anindilyakwa[c]	199	9:5	417	32%	616	2.10
Ndumba[c]	385	7:9	186	67%	571	0.48
Sahaptin[c]	213	8:7	236	47%	449	1.11
Koyukon[e]	33	10:10	158	17%	191	4.79

[a]Relative rank order with respect to the number of generic plant versus animal taxa recognized
[b]Ratio of animal to plant folk generic taxa recognized.
[c]Berlin 1992: 98, 100; [d]Hunn 1998a; [e]Nelson 1983:265-271

One con⸍   ᵘal factor is the simple matter of size. As I have shown
elsev⸍   ctor affecting the cultural attention devoted to a given
s⸍   1999). It is a fact that the vast majority of animal
                    ⸍asitic nematodes such that the modal size of all
                    ⸍y 1988:1447). By contrast, a typical vascular
p.   ᵃes larger than the average animal. I have demon-
stra⸍   ⸍ifications of both plants and animals are highly sen-
sitive⸍   ⸍isms classified, the larger the organism the more refined
the clas⸍   . 1999). The size bias clearly affected the degree of scholarly
effort, as in⸍   ⸍ı Table 6.1, column 3, which summarizes scholarly papers/spe-
cies/year for vᵃ⸍ ⸍us groups. If we correct for size, the disproportionate ethnobiological
and folk biological attention to plants in proportion to the ratio of plant to animal
species in the local environment is far less striking.

Next we may inquire if the residual disproportion reflects a biased "scholarly
focus" on the various subject matters of ethnobiology. To evaluate this issue I compare the ethnobiological effort with the corresponding "folk biological" effort. In
other words, are ethnobiologists accurately reflecting the interests of the "folk biologists" whose Traditional Environmental Knowledge we seek to document? How might
this be determined?

We may compare the numbers of named animal taxa with comparable numbers of
plant taxa when such figures are available for a single community. Table 6.2 summarizes such figures for ten well-documented cases. I admit I was surprised by the
results. I expected a greater folk botanical bias, based on my own experience with

three of the ten cases. I expected that animals would be preponderant only at very high latitudes. However, the central tendency is quite well balanced.

In three quite disparate cases, the number of generic plant taxa (Berlin 1992) named is nearly equal to that for animals (plants are 47-48% of total taxa for the horticultural Aguaruna and Wayampí of lowland South American forests and the Sahaptin gatherer-fisher-hunters of the semi-arid Columbia River plateau); five cases showed a strong folk botanical bias, with the number of named plant generics between 58% and 67% of total taxa. These cases include cultivators of wet tropical forests (Hanunóo, Ndumba, Tobelo) but also agriculturalists of less humid Mesoamerican highland regions (Tzeltal, Zapotec). The last two cases exhibit the most extreme asymmetry of all ten cases, curiously, in favor of recognizing folk zoological taxa. Both until recently practiced subsistence foraging economies; the Anindilyakwa in coastal tropical Australia (plants 32% of total named generics) and the Koyukon in the subarctic Alaskan interior (plants only 17% of total named generics).

I believe we may take these numbers as roughly accurate. In most cases the researchers were not obviously biased in their investigations towards plants or animals. The wide range of disparities is clearly due to a variety of factors, sometimes working at cross purposes. Prominent factors include the relative diversity of flora and fauna in a given region. In particular, note the limited floral diversity in the Koyukon and Anindilyakwa habitats. Note also the importance of marine fauna for the Anindilyakwa of Groote Eylandt of Australia's tropical northern coast. By contrast, highland Papua New Guinea, home to the Ndumba, has rather limited faunal diversity. The extraordinary biodiversity of the humid tropical environments of the Hanunóo, Tobelo, Wayampí, and Aguaruna help justify the high total biotaxa counts in these cases, but this does not explain why plants are more often named in the first two cases, while the opposite is true for the last two.

In these and the remaining cases, the relative emphasis on agriculture versus foraging activities may be key, with more intensive agricultural emphases leading to a folk botanical bias. This may account as well for the contrast between the Mixtepec Zapotec and Tzeltal Mayan cases. In the first case the traditional settlement pattern is concentrated with a subsequent depletion of game near town, limiting hunting to a very occasional pasttime of a few individuals (Hunn 1998a). By contrast, the Tzeltal settlement pattern is dispersed, which may foster a more balanced encounter-rate with respect to flora and fauna. In conclusion, it would seem that the strong bias evident in the scholarly literature towards ethnobotany is more "ethnobotanical" than "folk-botanical" in origin.

At this point, utilitarian biases loom large. However, utilitarian biases are grounded in perceptible differences among the organisms subjected to human scrutiny. To anticipate, the biochemical relevance of plants for human survival is much greater than that of animals. This reflects the ecological roles of plants and animals as prey and predator respectively in most global food chains (Johns 1990). This ecological contrast is reflected also in the fact that though "animals are good to think" (Tambiah 1969), plants are more relevant with respect to the practical, material necessities of daily life.

I next consider the situation from a rather different perspective. After assessing the impact of the taxonomic, perceptual, and utilitarian factors discussed above, we might still expect to find that animals hold a greater fascination for the human imagination than plants. This is suggested by the general *anthropocentric principle* that humans are more sympathetic to other living creatures roughly in proportion to the human perception of similarity, and hence, of kinship with them. This is true not only with respect to modern urbanites' obsessive concern for their pets, and other "charismatic megafauna." It is rather more difficult to love a fish, clam, mosquito, or shrub (tree-huggers may be an exception to this anthropocentric rule, but I doubt it) than a cat, dog, chimp, or dolphin.

This anthropocentric principle has clouded our understanding of our own evolutionary history. The persistence of variants of the Hunting Hypothesis testifies to this. This is the notion that humans are "killer apes" and that our most distinctively human characteristics—our large brains, our linguistic capacities, our tool-making prowess, our cooperative social forms, even our penchant for murder, mayhem and male chauvinism—are due to our obsession with animals as prey (Lorenz 1966; Laughlin 1968; Ardrey 1976). The ethnobiological bias towards plants has served as a much-needed antidote to the misconception that humans are carnivores rather than omnivores (Johns 1990).

The anthropocentric principle is exposed as well by linguistic and cognitive psychological studies that demonstrate a universal cognitive basis for the recognition of *animacy*. For example, a clear hierarchy of animacy is applied by Navajo speakers in judging the capacity of one entity to affect another (Witherspoon 1977:78). Thus, in Navajo it is considered absurd to assert, in effect, that "the horse kicked the man," since the man, with the full capacity for speech, is more intelligent than the horse, thus in control of any such intentional interaction between man and horse. The following hierarchy of control is implicit in Navajo syntax: (1) adult persons, (2) larger animals and especially intelligent medium-sized animals, predators, and human infants, (3) medium-sized animals, (4) small animals, (5) insects, (6) natural forces, (7) plants and inanimate objects, and (8) abstract concepts.

It is also the case that the mythic charters of tribal peoples attribute a far more central role to animal personages than to plants. For example, within the "Coyote Cycle" of sacred stories among Sahaptin-speaking Indians of the Columbia Plateau of the Pacific Northwest the role of mythic person (as indicated by the honorific suffix *-yáy*) is a role played by dozens of animal species (cf. Jacobs 1931:219-20). Prominent among Sahaptin personages of the Myth Age are the Bear and Grizzly sisters (or co-wives), *anahuiyáy* and *tuwit'áya* (> *anahuí* 'black bear' and *tuwit'ásh* 'grizzly bear'); Rattlesnake Person, *waxpúuya* (< *wáxpush* 'rattlesnake'); Cougar and Wild Cat, *kʷ'ayawiyái* and *ptch'íimya* (< *kʷ'ayawí* 'cougar' and *pích'im* 'bobcat'); Coyote and Eagle, *spilyáy* and *xʷayamayái* (<*spílya* 'coyote' and *xʷáyama* 'golden eagle'). Even the cannibals Flea and Tick are so recognized: *ashnamyái* and *pshxyái* from *áshnam* 'flea' and *apshíx* 'tick' (Jacobs 1934, 1937). Entities other than animals may be so honored, but such instances are rare: Sun and his younger brother Moon are *anyái* and *alxayxyái*, from *an* 'sun' and *alxáyx* 'moon'. The Soft Basket Person is *t'at'atíya*, from *t'át'ash* 'twined basket'. In one story Little Vulva (*taníktaníkyáy*) outraces Little Penis (*iwashiwashyái*)! The only plants treated in this way that I have been able to locate are Hemlock Tree and Cedar, *waqutqutyáy* and *nankyáy* (< *waqutqút* 'hemlock' and *nánk* 'Western red cedar'). Hemlock Tree retrieves Coyote's head from the bottom of the river by catching it with its hooked lead shoot (James Selam, pers. comm.), while Cedar teaches young girls how to weave (Nettie Kuneki Jackson, pers. comm.). It is clear that the anthropocentric principle exerts a powerful influence in defining the significant actors of the Myth Age as predominantly animal.

Recently, a number of cognitive psychologists have developed research programs to investigate what sorts of innate "theoretical" understandings infants and children might employ to draw inferences about the internal dynamics of entities of various "ontological types" (Atran 1998). In particular, theoretical lines are drawn with respect to whether young children (those too young to have learned these principles either from experience or instruction) employ an innate "biological theory" distinct from innate "psychological" and "mechanical" theories. Or, do they interpret what is going on inside an animal or plant by extrapolating from their intuitive understanding of human motivations? Do they attribute any special qualities to living beings as opposed to inanimate or constructed objects? The evidence is not entirely clear, but it appears that even preschool children appreciate the fact that living things grow, eat, feel, resemble their parents, get sick, and die (Kit-fong Au and Romo 1999). The "accuracy" of their inferences with respect to prototypical human, animal, plant, and inanimate exemplars increases dramatically between three and seven years of age (Hatano and Inagaki 1999). (One odd demonstration of this improvement was the abandonment of the view, more commonly expressed by younger children, that plants "feel." This was judged incorrect. I wonder.) As in the case of the Navajo, the "anthropocentric" principle seems at work—interpreted by some cognitive psychologists as evidence that a distinct "folk biological" theoretical understanding is not innate, but an extension of "folk psychology" according to perceived resemblance. "Generally, the closer the target object is biologically to a human being, the more often children recognize its similarity and thus apply the person analogy" (Hatano and Inagaki 1999:336).

This line of cognitive research supplies largely untapped questions for ethnobiology. Have we too readily assumed the essential unity of our subject matter? Have we attributed to our "folk biological" colleagues (our consultants and teachers in the communities we study) our understanding of the unity of all life, and the essential difference between animals and plants within that larger domain? The salience of the category "living thing" is taken for granted in most studies of ethnobiological classification, which then proceed to focus on how within the two domains of living things, the ethnobotanical and the ethnozoological, our knowledge of the living world is organized. As a consequence, have we failed to ask some very interesting (and perhaps important) questions about how we might understand our place in nature?

My recent Zapotec research has raised some doubt in my mind in this regard. I have presented a series of questions to a sample of San Juaneros, in a crude attempt to address the "theoretical understandings" that might lie beneath their impressive empirical knowledge of local biodiversity. I asked if a range of entities, from people to rocks, had "heart" (*zdòo*), "life" (*guièl-mbán*), and/or "intelligence" (*guièl-bìinî*). Responses, if taken as literal translations of the English dictionary glosses, would in many cases be judged by our cognitive psychological colleagues as inaccurate—childish perhaps. In particular, corn, avocados, and columnar cacti have "heart," while many were uncertain about snakes and worms. They explained that the corn plant and the avocado tree grows from the kernel or seed, which is its "heart"; by a somewhat different logic, the columnar cactus has "heart" because it has strong "heart wood" inside. "Life" was freely granted to plants and animals, but with little reservation also to the moon, rain, and wind, as is evident in the power of their spontaneous movement. "Intelligence" proved a challenging concept for my respondents. They argued about it and in justifying their answers developed some quite astute analyses. In particular, two of my friends—both knowledgeable and intelligent young men—took opposing views with respect to goats and sheep. Pedro was confident that sheep were smarter than goats while Santiago was just as adamant that goats were smarter. Pedro reasoned that sheep learn quickly to follow their master while goats are slow to learn. Santiago judged from the same evidence that goats, being by nature "*travieso*" 'mischievous', were smarter. I think they were telling me more about themselves than about sheep and goats, but it is clear that they were close observers of animal behavior and needed no special schooling to wonder what was going on inside their animals' heads.

One final anomaly has caused me to reflect on the complexity of folk biological classification at the largely unexamined domain and super-domain rank. That is the fact that in Mixtepec Zapotec macro-fungi are classed together under the heading *měy*, which incorporates the "animate" prefix *m-*, presumed to represent a contraction of *mâ* 'animal'. This is given additional support by the fact that if you ask in Zapotec if there are any mushrooms available when there aren't, the answer will be *guiènd mâ* 'there is no [animal]'. There are at least 20 consistently named macro-fungi folk genera, all named binomially on the pattern of *měy-guièdz* 'hives mushroom' (*Amanita muscaria*, the name descriptive of the warty growth on the cap). This nicely parallels the naming pattern for plant "life-forms" such as *dòb* '*Agave* spp. +' and *yàg* 'tree/shrub'. So, I feel comfortable treating *měy* as a life-form. But a life-form of what? It is from the local perspective in some sense "animal," but they reject that as literally true, just as they reject the assertion that *měy* are "plants." However, there is a simple solution:

měy is an "unaffiliated life-form," just as there are "unaffiliated generics" (Berlin 1992:171ff) that fit no life-form (and, as I have argued elsewhere [Hunn 1998a], unaffiliated folk species and varieties that fit within no folk genus).

And why not? My sense of the general drift of thinking about ethnobiological classification since Berlin et al.'s first statement of their general principles of classification and nomenclature (1973) is that the grip of taxonomic structure is progressively being loosened, the better to appreciate the subtlety of peoples' understandings of the complex relationships among living things (and not so obviously living things). I hope that we return in our future ethnobiological investigations to these fundamental questions: What is life? What is a plant, an animal, a person? What can our consultants teach us about these questions that we may have forgotten or learned to ignore?

References

Anonymous [Harshberger, John W.]
1895 Some new ideas. Philadelphia Evening Telegraph, 5 December, p. 2.

Ardrey, Robert
1976 The Hunting Hypothesis: A Personal Conclusion Concerning the Evolutionary Nature of Man. New York: Atheneum.

Atran, Scott
1998 Folk biology and the anthropology of science. Behavioral and Brain Sciences 21: 597-611.

Berlin, Brent
1992 Ethnobiological Classification: Principles of Categorization of Plants and Animals in Traditional Societies. Princeton, NJ: Princeton University Press.

Castetter, Edward F.
1935 Uncultivated native plants used as sources of food. Ethnobiological Studies in the American Southwest I. Biological Series 4(1). University of New Mexico Bulletin 266, Albuquerque.

Clément, Daniel
1998 The historical foundations of ethnobiology (1860-1899). Journal of Ethnobiology 18:161-87.

Hatano, Giyoo and Kayoko Inagaki
1999 A developmental perspective on informal biology. In: Folkbiology, edited by Douglas L. Medin and Scott Atran, pp. 321-54. Cambridge, Mass.: Harvard University Press.

Hays, Terence E.
1997 Recent doctoral dissertations of interest to ethnobiologists XIV. Journal of Ethnobiology 17:109-17.

Hays, Terence E.
1998 Recent doctoral dissertations of interest to ethnobiologists XV. Journal of Ethnobiology 18:129-36.

Henderson, Junius, and John Peabody Harrington
1914 Ethnozoology of the Tewa Indians. Bureau of American Ethnology Bulletin 56. Washington, D.C.

Hunn, Eugene S.
1998a Mixtepec Zapotec ethnobiological classification: A preliminary sketch and theoretical commentary. Anthropologica 40:35-48.
1998b Ethnobiotica. Journal of Ethnobiology 18(2).
1999 Size as limiting the recognition of biodiversity in folk biological classifications; one of four factors governing the cultural recognition of biological taxa. In: Folkbiology, edited by Douglas L. Medin and Scott Atran, pp. 47-69. Cambridge, Mass.: Harvard University Press.

Jacobs, Melville
1931 A sketch of Northern Sahaptin grammar. University of Washington Publications in Anthropology 4:85-292.
1934 Northwest Sahaptin texts. Columbia University Contributions to Anthropology No. 19, Part 1. New York: Columbia University Press.
1937 Northwest Sahaptin texts. Columbia University Contributions to Anthropology No. 19, Part 2. New York: Columbia University Press.

Johns, Timothy
1990 With Bitter Herbs They Shall Eat It: Chemical Ecology and the Origins of Human Diet and Medicine. Tucson: University of Arizona Press.

Kit-fong Au, Terry, and Laura F. Romo
1999 Mechanical causality in childrens' folkbiology. In: Folkbiology, edited by Douglas L. Medin and Scott Atran, pp. 355-402. Cambridge, Mass.: Harvard University Press.

Laferrière, Joseph E., and Terence E. Hays
1995 Recent doctoral dissertations of interest to ethnobiologists XIII. Journal of Ethnobiology 15:281-86.

Laughlin, William S.
1968 Hunting: an integrating biobehavior system and its evolutionary importance. In: Man the Hunter, edited by Richard B. Lee and Irven De Vore, pp. 304-20. Chicago: Aldine.

Lorenz, Konrad
1966 On Agression. New York: Harcourt, Brace and World.

Mason, Otis Tufton
1899 Aboriginal American zoötechny. American Anthropologist 1:45-81.

May, Robert M.
1988 How many species are there on earth? Science 241: 1441-49.

National Research Council (NRC)
1999 Perspectives on Biodiversity: Valuing Its Role in an Everchanging World. Washington, D.C.: National Academy Press.

Nelson, Richard K.
1983 Make Prayers to the Raven: A Koyukon View of the Northern Forest. Chicago: University of Chicago Press.

Tambiah, S. J.
1969 Animals are good to think, and good to prohibit. Ethnology 7:423-59.

Toledo, Victor Manuel, and Ma. de Jesús Ordóñez
1993 The biodiversity scenario of Mexico: a review of terrestrial habitats. In: Biological Diversity of Mexico: Origins and Distribution, edited by T. P. Ramamoorthy, R. Bye, A. Lot, and John Fa, pp. 757-77. New York: Oxford University Press.

Witherspoon, Gary
1977 Language and Art in the Navajo Universe. Ann Arbor: University of Michigan Press.

7

Linguistic Ethnobiology
Amerindian Oak Nomenclature

Cecil H. Brown, Northern Illinois University

Introduction

Linguistic ethnobiology treats the relationship of people to plants and animals as mediated by language. This can encompass any aspect of linguistic behavior involved in the interaction of humans with other living things, but linguistic ethnobiologists mostly have focused on how ordinary people, the "folk," name organisms. Classification and nomenclature constitute primary emphases in the study of folk biological naming. Classification refers to the grouping of organisms implied in the application of names to them. Nomenclature refers to the nature of names used in classification. Biological classification has been of interest to scholars from as early as the time of Aristotle (Atran 1990). Biological nomenclature has only relatively recently emerged as a focus of linguistic ethnobiology (e.g., Bartlett 1940; Conklin 1954; Berlin 1972). This essay deals primarily with nomenclature, especially with names employed by speakers of Native American languages to designate oak trees (*Quercus* spp., Fagaceae).

There are two basic types of labels used in folk biological naming: (1) binomial terms, and (2) non-binomial terms. A binomial label, as its name suggests, shows two constituent elements: for example, a word for a class of organisms to which a living thing belongs, e.g., *oak*, and a modifier, e.g., *white*, as in *white oak*. In English, *white oak* designates *Quercus alba* which is a kind of oak. Not all labels that appear to be binomial terms are in fact binomials. For example, English *poison oak*, which designates *Rhus radicans*, consists of a word for a class of botanical things, *oak*, plus a modifier, *poison*. *Poison oak*, however, is not formally a binomial since the organism it designates is not an oak.

Poison oak fits into the second nomenclatural category, non-binomial terms. Non-binomial labels typically are monomial terms such as *tree, oak, fish,* and *trout*. But some non-binomials, like *poison oak*, are polylexemic, having two or more constituent elements each of which has a distinct meaning. Other English examples of non-binomial polylexemic terms include labels such as *Queen Anne's lace, cow-parsnip, false Solomon's-seal*, and *Jack-in-the-pulpit*.

Some Personal History

My interest in linguistic ethnobiology developed as a result of engagement in the study of cognitive anthropology. Pioneered in the 1950s and 1960s, cognitive anthropology assumes that the vocabularies or lexicons of languages reflect ways in which knowledge is organized in people's heads (Tyler 1969). In 1969, I undertook dissertation field research among Huastec (Mayan) speakers, a swidden agricultural group of Northern Veracruz, Mexico, with the goal of investigating several different lexical domains using the methods of cognitive anthropology. These domains included kinship terminology, body part terms, color terms, disease vocabulary, and social status terms. I also intended to research words for plants and animals, but only as a minor focus.

I began with kinship terminology, eliciting from Huastec consultants detailed personal genealogies and lists of kinship terms, a task that was tedious, both for me and for my consultants. The pace of research picked up a bit when we began to investigate body part terms and disease vocabulary, but consultants could hardly be described as enthusiastically involved in the enterprise. However, when we took up plants, the situation improved considerably. I began by asking consultants to supply me with as many Huastec names for plants they could think of. I was overwhelmed with the results. Consultants were able to produce lists of botanical names in excess of 200 lexical items in less than an hour. In addition, they were eager to identify plants in their local environment and frequently voluntarily brought me cardboard boxes stuffed with collections of specimens.

This line of research, then, proved extremely productive. Unfortunately, I did not have the tools to take full intellectual advantage of the robust amount of information the Huastec were so eager to share. I was trained as an anthropologist, not as a botanist. I had no problem in compiling an extensive inventory of Huastec plant names. I had no problem in assessing, as was appropriate to cognitive anthropology, semantic relationships holding among these names. For example, I easily determined that the Huastec consider a tree called *hoθ* to be a kind of *teʔ, teʔ* being the Huastec word closest to English *tree* in meaning, and also that *hoθ* has two subtypes, *yaš hoθ* and *t'unuʔ hoθ*. (The labels, *yaš hoθ* and *t'unuʔ hoθ,* are binomial terms; *yaš* means "green" and *t'unu?*, "black.") I was, then, able to flesh out details of a Huastec system of botanical classification, i.e., of a Huastec plant taxonomy. However, I was unable to connect standard scientific nomenclature to plants named in Huastec and, hence, could not inform the scientific community to which botanical species Huastec names, such as *hoθ*, *yaš hoθ*, and *t'unu? hoθ*, were applied.

In addition to Huastec names, consultants, all of whom were fully bilingual in Huastec and Spanish, supplied local Mexican-Spanish words for plants. Using the latter, I made a rough attempt to determine scientific identifications by consulting literature in which Mexican-Spanish plant names were glossed by scientific terms. For example, *hoθ* was identified in Spanish as *palo de negrito,* and the literature I consulted identified *palo de negrito* as *Karwinskia humboldtiana* Zucc. In my Ph.D. dissertation I (1971) presented the Huastec plant taxonomy, glossing all Huastec plant terms with both Mexican-Spanish names and with the roughly determined scientific names, characterizing the latter as "only a first approximation to be corrected and refined through future research."

Some years later, a trained botanist, Janis Alcorn (Alcorn and Hernández V. 1983), as part of a larger project, undertook to "refine" my rough identifications through field research with Huastec speakers, including one of my earlier major consultants. For example, she determined that Huastec *hoθ* actually designates *Bumelia celastrina* HBK rather than *Karwinskia humboldtiana* Zucc. In fact, she found that only 19% of the items I roughly identified were in fact accurate, concluding that "common names are very unreliable guides to scientific identifications" (1983:15), a conclusion with which I fully agree.

Alcorn (Alcorn and Hernández V. 1983:15) also made the further observation that "Brown's list is of limited value for comparative purposes," a conclusion with which I am in strong disagreement. What she failed to realize is that systems of folk biological classification and nomenclature can be productively compared without detailed reference to the actual plants and animals being classified and named.

After finishing my dissertation research among the Huastec, I became acquainted with a now well-known article by Berlin, Breedlove, and Raven entitled "General Principles of Classification and Nomenclature in Folk Biology" (1973). By comparing the folk botanical taxonomies of several globally distributed human groups, including, for example, that of the Tzeltal of southern Mexico collected by Berlin and his colleagues, and that of the Hanunóo of the Philippines collected by Conklin (1954), these scholars proposed, among other things, that there was a nearly perfect match between ethnobiological rank and the type of name assigned to biological classes. For example, classes of the "specific" rank in folk taxonomies of all human groups are always labeled by binomial terms, such as *white oak* and *yaš hoθ*, while classes of the "generic" rank are always labeled by non-binomial terms such as *oak* and *hoθ*. On reading this work, I was struck by how very closely my Huastec data agreed with this and other cross-language generalizations outlined in the paper. The resemblance was remarkable and, significantly, had nothing whatsoever to do with the scientific identification of the actual plants involved. Whether one knew or did not know the exact plants to which terms referred, cross-language regularities entailing classification and nomenclature were nonetheless very apparent.

It was awareness of the detailed similarity of folk biological taxonomies across human groups that launched me (often in collaboration with my recently deceased colleague, Stanley R. Witkowski) on a relentless pursuit of lexical universals by comparing the vocabularies of large numbers of languages. This involved domains such as color (Witkowski and Brown 1977, 1981), body parts (Brown 1976; Witkowski and Brown 1985), cardinal direction concepts (Brown 1983), time concepts (Brown 1987, 1989), figurative language (Brown and Witkowski 1981), items of acculturation (Brown 1999), and others. However, the domain of folk biology has consistently been most productive in my comparative investigations (Brown 1977, 1979, 1984, 1985, 1986, 1992, 1995, 1996; Witkowski and Brown 1983; Witkowski, Brown, and Chase 1981), and, within that domain, the study of nomenclature has been particularly fertile.

Studies of Folk Biological Nomenclature

One finding of nomenclatural studies produced by the comparative approach is that the kind of label employed in folk biological classification correlates with the mode of subsistence of the group that uses it. Folk biological taxonomies surveyed in the original Berlin et al. (1973) study were limited to those of small-scale agrarian peoples like the Huastec, Tzeltal, and Hanunóo. These groups all manifest extensive use of binomial terms for biological classes. Comparative research undertaken independently by Hunn and French (1984) and me (Brown 1985) indicates quite a different situation for people practicing a mostly nonagricultural way of life. Folk biological taxonomies of foragers tend to employ very few, if any, binomial terms. Indeed, in such systems (and also in systems of some small-scale agriculturalists) it is possible to find classes of the specific ethnobiological rank that are not binomially designated. Such findings led Berlin to abandon his original proposal that specific classes are *always* labeled by binomial terms, motivating him to write, "I was in error to have originally framed the principle in a categorical rather than statistical fashion" (1992:118).

Comparative studies of nomenclature can contribute substantially to understanding how folk biological taxonomies develop and change over time. For example, a conclusion drawn from the finding mentioned above is that as societies have shifted from a hunter-gatherer way of life to an agrarian mode (the dominant historical trend), there has been an accompanying shift in the types of label used to name plants and animals, from non-binomial to binomial terms.

Berlin's contributions to a developmental perspective in linguistic ethnobiology have been especially important. In the early 1970s, in a brilliant speculative paper, he postulated stages in the growth of folk biological nomenclature involving ethnobiological ranks (1972). For example, he proposed that generic classes labeled by non-binomial terms, such as *oak*, emerge first in the development of folk taxonomies, followed later by inclusively related specific classes labeled by binomial terms such as *white oak*, *red oak*, and *live oak*.

Berlin's (1972) writing on this topic implied the following developmental details. (1) Initially, closely similar, but species-distinct organisms in a local environment, such as different species of oak, tend not to be lexically differentiated, but rather are classed together through use of a single non-binomial name, such as *oak* (designating a generic class). (2) Subsequently, these closely related species are distinguished nomenclaturally through use of binomial terms, such as *white oak*, *red oak*, and *live oak* (designating specific classes).

In response to Berlin, I proposed (Brown 1986) that data from hunter-gatherer groups suggest just the opposite, that specific classes labeled by non-binomial terms emerge first in folk taxonomies, followed later by the development of associated generic categories, and even later by a nomenclatural shift in which the non-binomial labels of original specific classes are replaced by binomial terms. This proposal is based on the observation that biological classes named in hunter-gatherer taxonomies tend strongly to encompass single species, meaning that the non-binomially labeled categories of hunter-gatherer folk biological taxonomies tend strongly to be monospecific.

In my (1986) model, a generic class typically emerges when a non-binomial label for a single species is expanded in use to denote other closely related species (which typically belong to the same genus). Thus, for example, a language may initially have monomial labels, X, Y, and Z, respectively for the species *Quercus alba*, *Q. stellata*, and *Q. prinus*, one of which, say X, subsequently expands in reference to all three species, creating a monomially labeled generic category which is roughly equivalent to English *oak*. Subsequently, respective monomial labels, X, Y, and Z, for the three species are replaced with respective binomial labels (based on the name of the generic category), for example, X, Y, and Z become aX, bX, and cX, where a, b, and c are modifying elements (such as English *white*) and X is the label for the generic class.[1] This development usually occurs with a shift from foraging to farming.

My proposal has been challenged by Berlin (1986, 1992). His response involves the observation that local environments mostly tend to support only one species of any scientific genus. Consequently, development of folk generics encompassing two or more closely related species in taxonomies of foragers is an unlikely occurrence. In the view of Berlin, hunter-gatherer monospecific categories labeled by non-binomials are in fact generic classes that, for environmental reasons, just happen to encompass only single species. That folk taxonomies of foragers show only monospecific classes labeled by non-binomials, then, does not necessarily imply that specific classes develop before generic ones in folk biological taxonomies.

Contrary to Berlin, there is evidence not only that two or more species of a single genus more than occasionally are found to occur natively in the local environments of foragers, but also that hunter-gatherers typically distinguish such species nomenclaturally through use of distinct non-binomial labels. For example, local environments of hunter-gatherer groups of California typically support several native species of oak. In addition, California foraging groups commonly have distinct names for each oak species in their habitats and these names are almost always non-binomial in structure, usually monomial terms (see detailed data below). Furthermore, it is often the case that a label for "oaks in general" is lacking (see below).

For example, the Diegueño of southern California nomenclaturally distinguish five species of oak, labeling each with a distinct monomial name. In addition, they do not have a word for "oaks in general," or, in other words, they lack a folk generic class encompassing several oak species (see detailed data below). Other California groups showing oak naming systems like that of the Diegueño include the Wintu, Yuki, Patwin, and Lake Miwok peoples (see below).

If the Diegueño were to develop a generic oak term, equivalent to English *oak,* this would result in a system in which a generic class immediately included folk categories labeled by monomial terms. Indeed, several California groups name and classify local oaks in just such a manner, including the Wappo, Nisenan, Tübatulabal, and Kawaiisu (see below).

Amerindian Oak Nomenclature

The remainder of this essay is a comparative investigation of how Native American groups name oak trees. This approach is especially instructive with respect to understanding aspects of nomenclatural development and change. For example, data on Amerindian oak-naming suggest that a shift from a hunter-gatherer way of life to farming does not always result in an accompanying shift from non-binomial to binomial naming. When such a shift involves a change from foraging to a mode of subsistence only marginally involving farming, people may not employ binomial naming. Binomial names may emerge as a significant aspect of biological nomenclature only when an agricultural way of life is fully embraced.

The present comparative study entails a survey of oak-naming systems in 80 Native American languages and dialects. The latter are distributed from the northern borders of the United States to Costa Rica, a spread closely matching the natural dispersal of oak species through the New World.

In the Americas, oaks occur only in the Northern Hemisphere. Eighty-seven species are found in North America, exclusive of Mexico (Nixon 1993:447). Six or so of these occur north of the United States, none of which extend northward much beyond the U.S./Canada border (Elias 1987:310-85). Mexico shows as many as 150 species (Nixon 1993:447), but there are no oaks on the Yucatan Peninsula. There are about 30 species in Central America, and a single species in South America restricted to Colombia (Nixon 1993:447, 451).

Sample Systems

Oak naming systems of Amerindian groups vary in two major ways: (1) whether they have a generic oak term (GOT) or, in other words, a label for oaks in general which is extended in reference to all local oak species, for example, English *oak* (*Quercus* spp.); and (2) whether subgeneric oak terms (SOTs), or, in other words, labels for subgeneric oak classes, e.g., English *white oak* (*Quercus alba*), are labeled binomially. In this treatment, a compound label that combines a modifier with an oak term, either a GOT or a SOT, is formally considered a binomial construction.

Tenejapa Tzeltal (Mayan, Mexico) and Diegueño (Yuman, California) constitute two sample systems differing from one another with respect to both of these variables. (Language case sources, locations, and genetic affiliations are given in Appendix A.) The first of these shows both a GOT and binomial SOTs.

TENEJAPA TZELTAL SYSTEM

GOT:	hih te?	
SOT:	bac'il hih te?	*Q. peduncularis, Q. rugosa, Q. crassifolia, Q. segoviensis, Q. dysophylla*
	k'ewš hih te?	*Q. polymorpha, Q. rugosa*
	sakyok hih te?	*Q. candicans, Q. crassifolia*
	čikinib hih te?	*Q. acatenangensis, Q. mexicana, Q. sapotifolia, Q. conspersa*
	č'iš hih te?	*Q. corrugata*

Tenejapa Tzeltal SOTs are all binomials since each entails the compounding of an oak term, in every instance the language's GOT (*hih te?*), with a modifying element (*bac'il* 'genuine', *k'eweš* 'custard apple', *sakyok* 'white-trunked', *čikinib* 'armadillo-eared', and *č'iš* 'spine'). In the terminology of Hunn and French (1984:86), binomial labels such as these entail "hierarchic subordination" between classes at higher and lower levels of a taxonomy (the higher level class being the GOT, and lower level classes, binomially labeled SOTs nomenclaturally based on the GOT).

The second sample system lacks both a GOT and binomial SOTs:

DIEGUEÑO SYSTEM

GOT:	(not present)	
SOT:	semtaay	*Q. chrysolepis*
	neshaaw	*Q. douglasi*
	'esnyaaw	*Q. agrifolia*
	'ehwap	*Q. dumosa*
	kuphaall	*Q. kelloggii*

SOTs in Diegueño are not binomial since none are constructions combining an oak term (either a GOT or SOT) with a modifier.

Some Amerindian systems are intermediate with respect to the contrastive systems of Tenejapa Tzeltal and Diegueño. For example, that of Mixtepec Zapotec (Otomanguean, Mexico) lacks a GOT, but uses some binomials as labels for subgeneric oak classes:

MIXTEPEC ZAPOTEC SYSTEM

GOT: (not present)
SOT:

yàg-lbís	*Q. laurina, Q. acutifolia*
yàg-rèdz	*Q. magnoliifolia*
yàg-pxù	*Q. glaucoides*
yàg-pxù-diè	*Q. obtusata?*
yàg-pxù-làs	*Quercus* sp.
yàg-xíid	*Q. castanea*
yàg-xíid-diè	*Q. obtusata*
yàg-xíid-zêd	*Q. cerifera*
yàg-zhòg	*Q. conzattii*
yàg-zhòg-yëts	*Q. crassifolia*

Note: *yàg* designates "tree."

Binomial labels in Mixtepec Zapotec differ from those of Tenejapa Tzeltal since they are formed by compounding a modifier (e.g., *diè* 'powdered' and *zêd* 'salt') with a SOT (e.g., *yàg-pxù* and *yàg-xíid*) rather than with a GOT (not present in Mixtepec Zapotec). In the terminology of Hunn and French (1984:86), binomial labels such as these entail "conceptual coordination" between classes at the same taxonomic level, one focal (the original SOT), and the other peripheral (the binomially labeled SOT nomenclaturally based on the original SOT).

Lake Miwok (Utian, California) constitutes another intermediate system of a different sort showing a GOT, but lacking binomial SOTs:

LAKE MIWOK SYSTEM

GOT: wajáaʔala
SOT:

jutéeʔala	*Q. kelloggii*
penéel	*Q. chrysolepis*
múuleʔala	*Q. douglasi*
sáata	*Q. wislizeni*
hákjaʔala	*Q. lobata*
wátalʔala	*Q. dumosa* [original transcription from Merriam (1979): wah-tahl al-wah]

Note: -ʔala designates "tree."

Acorn Terms

The nuts of all species of oak are closely perceptually similar, entailing a seed enclosed in a shell and seated in a cup. Oak nuts are highly distinctive as a group compared to nuts of all other trees (with the notable exception of the acornlike fruit of tanoaks of which only one species, *Lithocarpus densiflorus*, found in California and Oregon, is native to the New World). Reflecting these perceptual conditions, languages often show generic acorn terms (GATs), such as English with *acorn*, designating oak nuts in general, but which are referentially exclusive with respect to nuts of all other trees. While Native American languages frequently show GATs, some do not. In addition, Amerindian groups often have subgeneric acorn terms (SATs) which are individual names for acorns of distinct oak species. The naming of oak species and the naming of their acorns are often closely interrelated. For this and other reasons, it is informative to include acorn nomenclature in our inventory of Amerindian systems of oak naming.

Nomenclatural interrelationship is observed in Lake Miwok, which shows both a GAT and SATs. The GAT, *wája*, is used as a constituent of the language's GOT, *wajáaʔala*, a compound label translating literally "acorn tree." With regard to SATs, the language shows terms for acorns of at least three different subgeneric oak classes: *wátal* (probably acorns of *Q. dumosa*), *júte* or *jutéewaja* (acorns of *Q. kelloggii*), and *múulewaja* (acorns of *Q. douglasi*). The first two of these both combine with Lake Miwok's word for tree in general (-*ʔala*) yielding the SOTs *wátalʔala* and *jutéeʔala* which designate oak trees that produce acorns denoted respectively by *wátal* and *júte*. The word *jutéewaja* is an alternative to *júte* which compounds the latter with the GAT, *wája*. Similarly, *múulewaja* is a compound of which *wája* is a constituent. The other constituent of the latter compound is also a constituent of a SOT, *múuleʔala*, whose referent is the source of acorns known as *múulewaja*.

The other sample case from California, Diegueño, lacks a GAT, but shows SATs. SATs and SOTs are nomenclaturally related in the language since each term for a subgeneric oak class is also used to designate the particular acorns produced by oak trees pertaining to the class. The other sample cases, Tenejapa Tzeltal and Mixtepec Zapotec, are similar to one another since neither system shows SATs, but different since Mixtepec Zapotec has a GAT, *mgàg*, while Tenejapa Tzeltal does not (Brent Berlin, pers. comm.).

Inventory of Systems

Table 7.1 is an inventory of oak classification systems in 80 Native American language cases organized by culture area. Noted for each case is: (1) whether or not a GOT is present; (2) number of SOTs; (3) number of binomial oak terms (BOTs) in evidence among SOTs; (4) whether or not a GAT is present; (5) number of SATs; (6) whether or not speakers of the language are traditional agriculturalists (AGR); (7)

whether or not speakers of the language traditionally consume acorns (ACN). In (1), (4), (6), and (7), "+" = present and "-" = absent.

Sources for language cases include bilingual dictionaries and studies focusing on ethnobotany. These are identified in Appendix A. For a number of cases, e.g., Mixtepec Zapotec, consulted sources include ethnobotanical studies combined with dictionaries. Data for many cases were extracted solely from dictionaries, for all of which prior experience suggests their accurate (if not complete) reporting of classification and naming strategies. My general approach to data collection was exhaustive, involving consulting all sources (of both types) among materials readily available to me.

A strict convention was used in deciding whether or not to include data from a particular language in Table 7.1. Data were used only if terms for at least two subgeneric oak classes were listed for a language case or, in other words, only if a language case showed at least two nonsynonymous SOTs (see below discussion of synonymy). This convention was adopted for a couple of reasons. First, an Amerindian group may not show more than one subgeneric oak class because no more than one species of oak occurs in a locale. This, for example, is true of a number of native groups of the Pacific Northwest Coast where *Q. garryana* is the only oak in evidence.[2] Such cases are of little relevance to the current study, which focuses on how *different* kinds of oak, implying two or more, are classified and named. Second, in instances where two or more species of oak are known to be present in a group's environment, sources reporting fewer than two nonsynonymous SOTs for the group are suspicious with respect to thoroughness of documentation. By this I do not mean to imply that empirically *no* groups fail to distinguish lexically between two or more different species of oak in their environments, but only that such a circumstance seems very unlikely given the many known systems.

Languages commonly show synonymous SOTs or, in other words, two or more terms that designate the same subgeneric oak class. For example, the referential range associated with Tenejapa Tzeltal's *sakyok hih te?* (one of four SOTs, see above) includes *Q. crassifolia* and *Q. candicans*. The same subgeneric oak class is denoted by both *sakil hih te?* and *k'an tulan* as well. For purposes of determining number of SOTs reported for cases in Table 7.1, each subgeneric oak class is counted only once regardless of the number of synonyms used to designate it. In addition, if any one of two or more labels for the same subgeneric oak class is binomial (even if one or more labels may not be binomial, e.g., *k'an tulan*), then that class is judged to be designated by a BOT in calculating the number of BOTs pertaining to each language case in Table 7.1.

Many sources for data of Table 7.1, especially dictionaries, identify oaks through use of vernacular or popular oak names (from English, French, or Spanish), such as English *live oak* and Spanish *encino prieto*, rather than through use of scientific-Latin nomenclature. Since some popular names are not especially consistent from region to region with respect to species identification (see above discussion), it is

TABLE 7.1. Inventory of oak naming systems in Native American languages organized by culture area with information on mode of subsistence and acorn consumption.

	GOT	SOT	BOT	GAT	SAT	AGR	ACN
NORTHWEST COAST							
1. Clallam[2]	-	2	0	?	?	-	-
PLATEAU:							
2. Klamath	-	2	0	-	2	-	-
CALIFORNIA:							
3. Karok	-	3	0	+	3	-	+
4. Chimariko	-	3	0	+	1	-	+
5. Achumawi	-	7	0	+	7	-	+
6. Yana	-	8	0	+	6	-	+
7. Wintu	+	5	0	+	5	-	+
8. Yuki	+	5	0	+	5	-	+
9. Patwin	+	6	0	+	6	-	+
10. Lake Miwok	+	6	0	+	3	-	+
11. Wappo	-	7	0	+	5	-	+
12. Nisenan	-	6	0	+	?	-	+
13. Maidu	-	3	2	+	0	-	+
14. Plains Miwok	-	5	0	+	4	-	+
15. Northern Sierra Miwok	-	6	0	+	2	-	+
16. Central Sierra Miwok	-	5	0	+	0	-	+
17. Southern Sierra Miwok	-	4	0	+	0	-	+
18. Chumash (Santa Inez)	-	4	0	+	1	-	+
19. Tübatulabal	-	6	0	+	6	-	+
20. Kawaiisu	-	7	0	+	1	-	+
21. Cahuilla	-	4	0	+	3	-	+
22. Cupeño	-	4	0	-	1	-	+
23. Luiseño	-	5	0	-	1	-	+
24. Diegueño	-	5	0	-	5	-	+
BAJA CALIFORNIA							
25. Kiliwa	-	3	0	+	?	-	+
SOUTHWEST							
26. Tewa	+	2	1	+	0	+	+
27. Western Apache	+	3	0	+	0	+	+
28. Papago-Pima	+	2	0	+	0	+	+
29. Mountain Pima	-	5	0	+	0	+	+
30. Nevome	-	5	0	+	2	+	+
31. Tarahumara	+	7	0	+	0	+	+
PLAINS							
32. Dakota	+	2	0	+	2	+	+
33. Pawnee	-	2	0	+	0	+	+
34. Osage	+	6	0	-	2	+	+
35. Comanche	+	2	0	+	0	-	-
36. Kiowa-Apache	+	3	3	?	?	-	-
37. Kiowa	+	3	0	+	0	-	+

Table 7.1 (cont.)

	GOT	SOT	BOT	GAT	SAT	AGR	ACN
NORTHEAST							
38. Ojibwa	+	3	0	+	0	+	+
39. Ottawa	-	4	1	-	2	+	+
40. Mississaga	-	2	0	-	1	+	+
41. Algonquin	-	2	0	-	2	+	+
42. Menominee	+	4	0	+	1	+	+
43. Fox	+	3	0	?	2	+	+
44. Maliseet	-	2	0	-	2	+	?
45. Western Abenaki	-	2	0	-	2	+	-
46. Natick	+	2	0	+	0	+	+
47. Delaware	-	4	0	+	0	+	+
48. Mohawk	-	2	0	+	0	+	+
49. Onondaga	+	4	0	+	0	+	+
50. Seneca	-	2	0	+	0	+	+
SOUTHEAST							
51. Tuscarora	-	5	0	+	0	+	+
52. Cherokee	-	6	0	+	0	+	+
53. Creek	+	10	5	+	1	+	+
54. Alabama	+	4	0	+	0	+	+
55. Koasati	-	9	1	+	0	+	+
56. Choctaw	+	10	2	+	3	+	+
57. Chickasaw	-	4	0	+	1	+	+
58. Biloxi	+	7	5	+	1	+	+
59. Ofo	+	3	3	+	0	+	+
60. Tunica	+	8	8	+	0	+	+
61. Atakapa	+	3	0	+	0	+	+
MESOAMERICA							
62. Huichol	-	4	1	?	?	+	-
63. Tarascan	+	4	3	+	?	+	-
64. Ixcatec	+	6	4	?	0	+	-
65. Cuicatec	+	7	5	+	0	+	-
66. Amuzgo	+	2	2	+	?	+	-
67. Zapotec (Mixtepec)	-	9	4	+	0	+	?
68. Zapotec (Mitla)	-	6	4	+	?	+	-
69. Zapotec (Juárez)	+	4	2	+	0	+	-
70. Tequistlatec	-	3	0	+	0	+	-
71. Huave	?	3	1	?	?	+	-
72. Mixe (Coatlán)	+	7	7	?	?	+	-
73. Mixe (Totontepec)	+	8	8	+	0	+	-
74. Tzeltal (Tenejapa)	+	5	5	-	?	+	-
75. Tzotzil (Zinacantán)	-	10	7	+	0	+	-
76. Tzotzil (San Andrés)	+	3	0	+	0	+	-
77. Kekchi	+	2	2	?	0	+	-
78. Cakchiquel	+	3	0	+	0	+	-
79. Tzutujil	-	3	0	+	0	+	-
LOWER CENTRAL AMERICA							
80. Cabecar	-	3	0	?	?	+	-

GOT = generic oak term, SOT = subgeneric oak term, BOT = binomial oak term,
GAT = generic acorn term, SAT = subgeneric acorn term, AGR = traditional agricultural group,
ACN = traditional acorn consumers

sometimes difficult to determine from their use the exact oak species designated by an Amerindian term. Fortunately, use of popular names in sources does not usually interfere significantly with determination of the *number* of subgeneric oak classes pertinent to a language case. The number of popular oak names used in a source is typically no more or no less reliable in this regard than is the number of scientific-Latin names given in a source.

In addition to data concerning oak classification and naming, Table 7.1 provides information regarding the traditional mode of subsistence of language speakers (agricultural or nonagricultural) and whether or not acorn consumption is a constituent of traditional cultural behaviors. This information is pertinent to findings discussed below. Three major reference sources were especially useful in codifying language cases with respect to these variables, *The Handbook of North American Indians* (Sturtevant 1978), *Handbook of Middle American Indians* (Wauchope 1964), especially volumes 7 and 8, and Swanton's (1946) *The Indians of the Southeastern United States*. A useful source on Native American acorn consumption was Driver (1953). Various other ethnographic and ethnobotanical sources were consulted when pertinent information was not forthcoming from major reference works.

Table 7.1 organizes language cases by culture area. Within culture areas, languages are grouped according to geographic proximity, involving a more-or-less north-to-south order. Culture areas are similarly listed, as much as possible, in a north-to-south manner.

Statistical Findings

Table 7.2 presents descriptive statistics based on data of Table 7.1. Each value of Table 7.1 is interpreted in Table 7.2 as either present (+) or absent (-) for language cases. Thus, for example, there are 36 language cases (N) showing a generic oak term (+GOT) and 43 cases lacking a generic oak term (-GOT), where the former number represents 45.6% of the total number of cases involved (79) and the latter, 54.4%. Similarly, the N associated with +SAT (33) is the number of cases showing at least one subgeneric acorn term, while that associated with -SAT (35) is the number of cases totally lacking subgeneric acorn terms, with respective pertinent percentages of 48.5 and 51.5.

While language cases tend to be evenly split in number with respect to the presence or absence of a GOT, the vast majority of cases (84.5%) show GATs. A total of 29 cases show both a GOT and a GAT (see Table 7.1). Nine cases lack both of these. Interestingly, the latter tend to cluster geographically (see Table 7.1): Cupeño, Luiseño, and Diegueño in southern California (see discussion below); Ottawa, Mississauga, and Algonquin in the Great Lakes region of the Northeast; and Maliseet and Western Abenaki in the eastern region of the Northeast.

Twenty-eight groups of those treated (35.0%) are nonagricultural (-AGR) and all of these except six are located in California. Most groups (65.0%) are agricultural (+AGR),

TABLE 7.2. Basic descriptive statistics organizing data of Table 7.1.

	N	%
+GOT	36	45.6
–GOT	43	54.4
+SOT	80	100.0
–SOT	0	0.0
+BOT	24	30.0
–BOT	56	70.0
+GAT	60	84.5
–GAT	11	15.5
+SAT	33	48.5
–SAT	35	51.5
+AGR	52	65.0
–AGR	28	35.0
+ACN	55	70.5
–ACN	23	29.5

cultivating the traditional Amerindian staple triad of maize, beans, and squash. These are found mainly in the Southwest, Northeast, Southeast, and Mesoamerica culture areas.

Agrarian peoples differ with respect to intensity of agricultural practices. Many groups of the Northeast manifest marginal food-producing economies wherein farming has traditionally been at best only auxiliary to hunting and gathering. Peoples of Mesoamerica show the most thorough dedication to agriculture with very little supplementary food acquired through other activities. Southeast and Southwest groups are typically somewhere between the extremes represented by the Northeast and Mesoamerica. In addition, it should be noted that some of the California groups, all of which are codified as non-agrarian (Table 7.1), traditionally cultivate tobacco.

Seventy-one percent of listed cases are traditional acorn consumers (+ACN). Close to all groups associated with culture areas north of Mesoamerica collect and eat acorns, while there are no Mesoamerican groups for which this practice is reported in the ethnographic literature I have surveyed (see Table 7.1). Of the traditional acorn consumers, acorns constitute a staple food only for the hunter-gatherer peoples of California. (As far as I can determine, acorns are a primary dietary source for all 22 listed California groups [cf., Driver 1953; Todt and Hannon 1999].) In other parts of the Americas where acorns are gathered and eaten, they are typically a minor, if not insignificant component of the Native American diet (Driver 1953).

Table 7.3 presents averages for culture areas of values presented in Table 7.1. For example, the SAT average for California is 3.10, meaning that the average number of subgeneric acorn terms in language cases from the culture area slightly exceeds three. For four values, GOT, GAT, AGR, and ACN, culture area averages do not exceed one since variables of these values are dichotomous and discontinuous (a case does or does not show a GOT; a case is or is not agricultural; and so on). Averages for these values range from 0.00 to 1.00. Thus, the average GOT for California of 0.18 indicates very few cases of the culture area show GOTs compared to, say, Mesoamerica, which has an average GOT of 0.65. Similarly, the average AGR for California of 0.00 indicates that no groups of the area are agricultural, while an average AGR of 1.00 for Mesoamerica indicates that all groups of the area are agrarian. Four areas, the Northwest Coast, the Plateau, Baja California, and Lower Central America, are not included in Table 7.3 since each is represented by only one language case.

Two of the six culture areas of Table 7.3, California and the Northeast, show some averages which appear to be significant deviations from corresponding averages associated with the other four culture areas. GOT averages for these culture areas, respectively 0.18 and 0.39, are substantially smaller than those for others, as are BOT averages at 0.09 and 0.08 respectively for both areas (also note the Southwest at 0.17). In addition, the SAT average for California, 3.10, is noticeably greater than those for other culture areas. These differences indicate that languages of California and the Northeast (1) have a greater tendency to lack generic oak terms than Amerindian languages of other regions, and (2) tend to show fewer binomial terms for subgeneric oak classes than languages of other areas. Also, (3) California languages tend to manifest greater numbers of subgeneric acorn terms.

The deviation of averages for California and the Northeast from corresponding averages for other culture areas may relate to areal differences in mode of subsistence, consumption of acorns, or both. They probably differ from peoples of other areas because California groups lack agriculture and Northeastern groups have only marginal agriculture, while other Amerindian groups are variously more intensely agricultural. In addition, California groups are distinctive since for them alone acorns constitute a primary food source.

Statistics assembled in Table 7.4 attest to possible correlations between variables of oak classification and naming and of agriculture (AGR) and acorn consumption

TABLE 7.3. Culture area averages.

	GOT	SOT	BOT	GAT	SAT	AGR	ACN
California	0.18	5.18	0.09	0.86	3.10	0.00	1.00
Southwest	0.67	4.00	0.17	1.00	0.33	1.00	1.00
Plains	0.83	3.00	0.50	0.80	0.80	0.50	0.80
Northeast	0.39	2.77	0.08	0.58	0.92	1.00	0.92
Southeast	0.64	6.27	2.18	1.00	0.55	1.00	1.00
Mesoamerica	0.65	4.94	3.06	0.92	0.00	1.00	0.00

TABLE 7.4. Averages relating to variables of AGR and ACN.

	GOT	SOT	BOT	GAT	SAT
+AGR	0.56	4.44	1.56	0.84	0.55
–AGR	0.25	4.61	0.18	0.85	2.79
+ACN	0.42	4.64	0.51	0.87	1.60
–ACN	0.59	4.04	2.30	0.80	0.31

(ACN). The average GOT for agriculturalists (+AGR), 0.56, is substantially larger than the average GOT for foragers (-AGR), 0.25, suggesting a stronger tendency among agrarian peoples to develop generic oak classes compared to hunter-gatherers. The BOT average for farmers, 1.56, is considerably greater than for nonagriculturalists, 0.18, indicating farmers tend to designate subgeneric oak classes through use of binomials more than do foragers. BOT averages also differ noticeably with respect to acorn consumption, with an average BOT of 0.51 associated with +ACN, and one of 2.30 with -ACN. Thus, nonconsumers of acorns tend more strongly than consumers to use binomials. Nonconsumers also appear to distinguish lexically fewer subgeneric acorn types than do consumers (with respective SAT averages of 0.31 and 1.60), and fewer subgeneric acorn types are lexically distinguished by farmers than by nonagriculturalists (SAT averages of 0.55 and 2.79).

The chi square statistic and a correlation coefficient, gamma, are employed to measure respectively the statistical significance and strength of these apparent associations (see Tables 7.5-7.9). Table 7.5 shows a reasonably strong and statistically significant relationship between AGR and GOT: farmers tend to develop generic oak terms more commonly than do nonfarmers. Table 7.6 attests to a very strong and statistically significant association between AGR and BOT: agrarian groups, substantially more so than hunter-gatherers, tend to use binomials as labels for subgeneric oak classes. Table 7.7 shows a strongly negative and statistically significant correlation between ACN and BOT: acorn consumers tend more strongly to lack binomial labels for subgeneric oak classes than do nonconsumers. There is also a strongly negative and statistically significant relationship between AGR and SAT (Table 7.8): agriculturalists show a substantially stronger tendency to lack subgeneric acorn terms compared to foragers. (Note that in Tables 7.8 and 7.9, "+" for SAT indicates at least one subgeneric acorn term in a language and "-" for SAT indicates no subgeneric acorn terms). There is also a very strong and statistically significant association between ACN and SAT (Table 7.9): acorn consumers tend to have more subgeneric acorn terms than nonconsumers.

Strong associations hold between BOT and both AGR and ACN (see Tables 7.6 and 7.7) and between SAT and both AGR and ACN (see Tables 7.8 and 7.9). For the most

TABLE 7.5. Association between AGR and GOT.

GOT	+ AGR	–
+	29	7
–	22	21

gamma = 0.60, *p* < .01, N = 79

TABLE 7.6. Association between AGR and BOT.

BOT	+ AGR	–
+	22	2
–	30	26

gamma = 0.81, *p* < .01, N = 80

TABLE 7.7. Association between ACN and BOT.

BOT	+ ACN	–
+	9	14
–	46	9

gamma = –0.78, *p* < .001, N = 78

TABLE 7.8. Association between AGR and SAT.

SAT	+ AGR	–
+	14	19
–	30	5

gamma = –0.78, *p* < .001, N = 68

TABLE 7.9. Association between ACN and SAT.

SAT	+ ACN	–
+	30	2
–	23	11

gamma = 0.76, *p* < .01, N = 66

TABLE 7.10. Association between AGR and ACN.

ACN	+ AGR	–
+	31	24
–	19	4

gamma = 0.57, *p* < .05, N = 78

part, these parallel connections involving AGR and ACN probably exist as a result of a reasonably strong and statistically significant (negative) correlation holding between AGR and ACN (Table 7.10): nonconsumers of acorns are more often farmers than they are foragers. In any case—ignoring coefficient valence—AGR is more strongly associated with both BOT and SAT (with respective correlation coefficients of 0.81 and 0.78) than is ACN (with respective correlation coefficients of 0.78 and 0.76), suggesting, if only weakly, AGR to be the explanatorily significant factor (see below discussion). In this regard it is informative to note that a reasonably strong and statistically significant relationship is apparent for AGR and GOT (see Table 7.5), but not for ACN and GOT (for which a 2 x 2 table analysis yields: gamma = -0.34, *p* < .20).

Nomenclatural Findings

A number of nomenclatural relationships occur repetitively and, probably, independently across language cases of the sample. For example, terms for generic oak classes (GOTs) are more than occasionally found to be derived through use of generic acorn terms (GATs), producing GOTs having literal translations comparable to "acorn tree" (shown by Yuki, Lake Miwok, Comanche, Creek, Choctaw, and Western Apache). The opposite naming situation is also found wherein GATs are derived through use of GOTs, translating literally "oak fruit," "oak seed," and the like (shown by Alabama, Ofo, Tunica, Tewa, Tzotzil, and Kiowa).

Oak/acorn terms are sometimes polysemous. For example, commonly a single label is used as both a GOT and a SOT, designating respectively both a generic oak class and a subgeneric oak class. This is the situation in Kiowa-Apache where the term *sóč'ił* (literally "star brush") denotes both oaks in general and a specific oak, *Q. marilandica*. (In Berlin's 1972 terminology, in such instances the category denoted by the SOT is dubbed a "type-specific" class.) Language cases of the sample manifesting GOT/SOT polysemy include—in addition to Kiowa-Apache—Patwin, Maidu, Kiowa, Ojibwa, Menominee, Creek, Choctaw, Tewa, and Tarahumara. In a parallel manner, a single label is sometimes used as both a GAT and a SAT, denoting respectively both acorns in general and a specific type of acorn. For example, Cahuilla *kʷíñil* is a term for the acorn of *Q. kelloggii,* which is also used to denote acorns in general. (The label is in fact three-way polysemous since it is as well a SOT designating *Q. kelloggii*.) Cases of the sample—in addition to Cahuilla—which show GAT/SAT polysemy include Achumawi, Plains Miwok, Dakota, and Alabama.

SOTs and SATs are frequently found to be nomenclaturally related. At least nine languages cases (Yuki, Northern Sierra Miwok, Plains Miwok, Diegueño, Luiseño, Cahuilla, Cupeño, Creek, and Nevome) show at least one term which denotes both a subgeneric oak class and the acorns produced (and only produced) by trees of that class. Sometimes SOT/SAT nomenclatural association involves double overt marking, wherein two different terms show a common base element, for example, Lake Miwok *múuleʔala* (a SOT denoting *Q. douglasi*) and *múulewaja* (a SAT denoting acorns of *Q. douglasi*), where *-ʔala* designates tree in general and *wája* denotes acorn in general. Other languages of the sample showing SOT/SAT double overt marking include Patwin, Western Abenaki, and, possibly, Kawaiisu.

More frequently, regular overt marking is in evidence. Fourteen cases (Klamath, Karok, Chimariko, Wappo, Achumawi, Yana, Wintu, Tübatulabal, Dakota, Osage, Algonquin, Maliseet, Western Abenaki, and Cherokee) show at least one SOT that is an overt marking construction based on a SAT, for example, Karok *xanpútip* (*Q. chrysolepis*) which consists of the language's word for the acorn of *Q. chrysolepis* (*xánput*) plus its label for "tree" (*-ʔip*). In all cases observed in which a SOT and a SAT are linked through regular overt marking, the SOT is always an overt marking construction based on the SAT. The reverse marking situation is not attested among cases of the current sample, suggesting that subgeneric acorn classes typically develop prior to subgeneric oak classes.

Diffusional Findings

That groups of the same area tend to share cultural practices which promote similar systems probably accounts for some regional commonalities found involving Amerindian oak classification and naming (see below discussion). However, some areal uniformities may be more appropriately explained by diffusion or, in other words, by borrowing.

I note above that language cases lacking both a GOT and a GAT tend to cluster geographically in distribution, for example, Cupeño, Luiseño, and Diegueño, neighboring languages of southern California. That these three all lack GOTs is not especially surprising since most languages of California also lack GOTs (see Table 7.1), an areal deficit that can probably be attributed to the lack of aboriginal agriculture in the region (see below discussion). On the other hand, that all three lack GATs is somewhat unexpected since these are the only languages of California (including Baja California) and of the broader western region including the Southwest in which GATs are missing (see Table 7.1). Possibly, the idea of a GAT diffused widely through the area, but for unknown reasons failed to reach the region in which Cupeño, Luiseño, and Diegueño are spoken.

Four neighboring languages of the central to northern area of California—Wintu, Yuki, Patwin, and Lake Miwok—all manifest a GOT. This is unusual since GOTs are found in no other California languages of the sample (see Table 7.1). While Wintu and Patwin belong to the same genetic grouping (Wintun), Yuki and Lake Miwok show other genetic affiliations (Yukian and Utian, respectively). Since possession of a GOT is both areally confined and extends across language genetic group frontiers, distribution of the feature through these four languages is probably due, at least in part, to diffusion.

The four languages show phonologically different terms for a generic oak class, indicating that the idea of a GOT, rather than an actual term, diffused (as a loan translation or semantic loan). There is evidence for the diffusion of actual oak/acorn labels across these languages. For example, a SOT in Lake Miwok and a SAT in Patwin (languages belonging to different genetic groupings) are phonologically closely similar, respectively, *penéel* and *pene·l*, the former denoting *Q. chrysolepis* and the latter acorns, probably of *Q. garryana*. This resemblance is almost certainly explained by borrowing. Patwin, Lake Miwok, and another Miwokan language, Northern Sierra Miwok, show closely similar terms for *Q. douglasi*, respectively, *mu·le*, *múule-*, and *mol·a-*, again, a likely result of borrowing.

Patwin shows several additional oak/acorn terms that are phonologically similar to labels in neighboring, but genetically unrelated, languages. The language's word for *Q. agrifolia* and/or *Q. wislizeni*, *sa·sa*, is also found with the same referents in Plains Miwok (*saʿsa*), Northern Sierra Miwok (*saʿsa-*), Central Sierra Miwok (*sáʿsa-*) and Southern Sierra Miwok (*saʿsa-*). Patwin and Maidu (Maiduan) show similar words for *Q. lobata*, respectively *to·* and *lôw*. Acorn terms in Patwin and Maidu are also closely phonologically similar: Patwin *hamsu*, designating acorns of *Q. garryana*, and Maidu *hámsi*, denoting acorns in general. Terms for acorns in general in Patwin and Atsugewi (Palaihnihan) are similar, *t'aka·* and *táʿqe*.

Oak nomenclature in some Amerindian languages of the sample has been influenced by European languages. For example, the GAT in Karok (isolate, California), *ʔékɔns*, is a loan from English (*acorns*). Bright (1957) suggests that the word may have been borrowed to fill the lack of a pre-contact generic term in the language. Haas (1953) proposes that several binomial SOTs in Tunica (isolate, Southeast) are loan translations (calques) based on oak terms of both English and French. For example, *čúhkimíli*, a term glossed by "red oak," is literally "oak red," which may be modeled on English *red oak*, and *čúhkirísa* 'oak sp.' is literally "oak grey," possibly based on French *chêne gris*.

Developmental Implications

Correlations between aspects of oak nomenclature and mode of subsistence are suggestive of patterns in the growth and development of oak naming systems. Systems lacking a generic oak term (GOT) and those lacking binomial terms for subgeneric oak classes (BOTs) are more typical of hunting and gathering groups than of farmers whose systems commonly manifest GOTs and BOTs (see Tables 7.5 and 7.6). Since a major thrust of human societal development over the last several millennia has been replacement of a foraging way of life with agriculture, the observed correlations suggest that over time systems have tended to shift from lacking a GOT and BOTs to having these features (cf., Anderson 1991).

In addition to mode of subsistence, acorn consumption is strongly correlated with SOT nomenclature (see Table 7.7). Acorn consumers tend to show fewer binomial SOTs (i.e., BOTs) than nonconsumers. This association may simply be a secondary expression of other relationships: (1) that hunter-gatherers tend more strongly to consume acorns than do farmers (Table 7.10), and (2) that foragers tend to show fewer oak binomials than agriculturalists (Table 7.6). The primacy of the latter association is indicated by its congruence with previously reported relationships involving ethnobiological nomenclature and mode of subsistence. As noted earlier, cross-language evidence (Brown 1985; Hunn and French 1984) shows that binomial names are very common in agrarian folk biological taxonomies, and very rare in taxonomies of non-agrarians. On the average, only 3.6% of plant classes and only 7.6% of animal classes in taxonomies of hunters and gatherers are labeled binomially. In striking contrast, small-scale agriculturalists on the average have binomial labels for 35.9% of all plant classes and for 31.6% of all animal classes (Brown 1985:43).

These statistics were the basis of the general proposal (Brown 1985, elaborated in

Brown 1986) that, as mode of subsistence shifts from foraging to agriculture, binomials are increasingly employed in folk biological taxonomies. The present findings suggest some possible fine-tuning of this hypothesis. For example, both the California and Northeast culture areas show very low BOT averages of 0.09 and 0.08 respectively compared to considerably greater averages for other culture areas (Table 7.3). In other words, languages of both California and the Northeast manifest very few binomial SOTs compared to Amerindian languages of other regions. With regard to California, this is expected since all groups of the region are nonagricultural. However, that the BOT average for the Northeast is actually less than that for California is surprising since all groups of the Northeast traditionally practice farming. On the other hand, among all agrarian groups of the current sample (Table 7.1), people of the Northeast show the most marginal agricultural practices, wherein food production is commonly only auxiliary to hunting and gathering. The mere acquisition of agriculture by a group, then, does not appear to be a sufficient condition for the development of binomial oak nomenclature. Binomial oak terms may only become numerically significant in a folk taxonomy when people develop something more than an ancillary interest in farming.

In a study mentioned above (Brown 1986), I speculated on processes leading to the development in folk biological taxonomies of polytypic generic categories, such as English *oak* and Tenejapa Tzeltal *hih te?* 'oaks in general'. For example, I proposed that with a shift from a foraging to an agricultural way of life, more and more such classes are added to taxonomies. This proposal entailed the assumption that polytypic generic categories (which I called "multispecies generics") tend to be more prominent in taxonomies of agriculturalists than in those of foragers. At the time, the validity of this assumption was only implied by assembled cross-language evidence. A contribution of the present study is presentation of some direct evidence, specifically, the finding that farmers tend to show terms for oaks in general, i.e. GOTs, considerably more than hunter-gatherers (Table 7.5).

As noted earlier, California and the Northeast culture areas resemble one another since languages of both regions commonly show substantially fewer GOTs than Amerindian languages of other culture areas (see Table 7.3). As noted above, groups of California and the Northeast have in common a minimal to nonexistent commitment to agriculture compared to the more substantial investment in farming shown by Amerindians of other areas. The development of a GOT in a language, then, like the development of BOTs (see above discussion), may not be so much influenced by the simple presence or absence of agriculture as it is by the extent to which a people are dependent on farming for a living. Groups may tend to develop generic oak terms only after replacing marginal agriculture with more intensive farming.

Table 7.8 shows a strong association (gamma = -0.78) between mode of subsistence and subgeneric acorn terms (SATs): foragers tend to show substantially more SATs than farmers. However, the essential factor here is almost certainly acorn consumption rather than mode of subsistence. The vast majority of foragers (85.7%) are also consumers of acorns (while slightly less than two-thirds of farmers are acorn consumers and the other third, nonconsumers). This is reflected by the association reported in Table 7.9 showing that acorn consumers strongly tend to have more SATs than nonconsumers (gamma = 0.76). In this regard, of considerable significance is a very strong association holding between SATs and culture area: languages of California show a substantially greater tendency to have SATs than languages of other culture areas combined (gamma = 0.86, $p < .001$). What sets California groups apart from all other groups of the sample is their universal use of acorns as a primary food source. Development of acorns as a dietary staple appears to result in greater lexical discrimination of different kinds of acorn.

Conclusion: Some Explanatory Possibilities

What are specific factors resulting in the development of generic oak terms (GOTs) and binomially labeled specific oak terms (BOTs) with a shift from a hunting-gathering/marginal-farming way of life to one involving full reliance on agriculture? Scholars have proposed explanations for the general increase in binomial terms of folk biological taxonomies as groups have replaced foraging with farming (Hunn and French 1984; Brown 1985, 1990; Berlin 1992; Ellen 1999). Hunn and French (1984:86-89) review several of these, justifiably rejecting some hypotheses which need not be discussed here. Two accounts, fitting into their category of "evolutionary" explanations, are highly plausible and deserve attention. Both of these, by implication, may contribute to understanding developments in the naming of oaks and, more broadly, to illuminating principles of linguistic ethnobiology.

Hunn and French (1984) and I (Brown 1985) have independently proposed one of these explanations. Our argument is as follows. Studies show that traditional agrarian groups name substantially more plants and animals in their environments than do hunter-gatherers or, in other words, that farmers show substantially larger folk biological taxonomies than do foragers. (For why this should be so, see Hunn and French 1984:89 and Brown 1985:48-50.) Use of binomial labels is positively correlated with size of biological taxonomies—the larger the taxonomy, the greater the percentage of binomial labels used. Thus, when taxonomies expand as economies shift from foraging to farming, so does the percentage of binomial terms employed.[3]

Binomial names may be especially useful in helping humans store and recall a larger quantity of folk biological knowledge. If so, this helps to explain increase in binomial percentage with augmentation in taxonomy size. For example, the binomial construction *white oak* may enhance the human ability to remember the tree it denotes (1) by calling attention to the general category of tree (i.e., oak) of which its referent is a member and (2) by signaling some special feature of the designated tree (e.g., the light tint of its bark) setting it apart from other members of the general category. Paralleling an example given in Hunn and French's (1984:88) discussion, it is probably easier to learn and remember a set of nomenclaturally related terms for oaks—one a GOT and the others, binomial SOTs based on the GOT, such as *oak, canyon live oak, blue oak, coast live oak, scrub oak,* and *black oak*—than to learn the unrelated names of several oak species—as in Diegueño with, respectively, *semtaay, neshaaw, 'esnyaaw, 'ehwap,* and *kuphaall.*

The second explanation involves reference to the process of domestication (Hunn and French 1984:88). Cultivars typically may have been the initial recipients of binomial names. A binomial naming strategy later may become generalized to wild relatives of cultivated plants and animals and, eventually, to other closely similar sets of organisms including both domesticated and wild examples. This view is championed by Berlin (1992:286). He points out that domestication involves the manipulation of new and distinctly different forms of life. As a result, groups acquire a cognitively qualitative difference in the perception of living things as they shift from foraging to farming. They begin to look more closely at nature in general and to become more systematic in their approach to biological things. A major component of this new systematicity is the development of binomial nomenclature and polytypic generic classes, first applied to cultivars and, subsequently, to plants and animals in general.

Both of these explanations are problematic. For example, folk biological taxonomies of some hunter-gatherer groups, especially those living in tropical forests, can be quite large, yet nonetheless show very few binomial terms (Ellen 1999). Berlin's explanation leaves open the crucial question of why a "new systematicity" typically involves the binomial naming of cultivars as opposed to any other nomenclatural strategy. Nevertheless, these are among the more compelling explanations forthcoming at present. In addition, there is no reason for supporting one of these arguments over the other since neither logically rules out the other. Both may constitute significant components of an explanation of observed differences between the ethnobiological nomenclature of hunter-gatherers and that of farmers, including differences relating to Amerindian naming of oaks.

Finally, comparative evidence assembled here indicates, among other things, that both generic oak terms and binomial oak labels typically emerge in a folk plant taxonomy only when groups develop something more than an ancillary interest in farming.[4] Does this conclusion generalize to the naming of all plants and animals? This possibility is worthy of further investigation through extension of the comparative approach to a more diverse array of the world's peoples and to a larger variety of folk biological categories. In so doing, other important regularities involving the relationship of people to plants and animals as mediated by language may also be discovered.

Acknowledgment

I am grateful to Eugene S. Hunn for commenting on an earlier oral presentation of this paper and to Pamela Brown for editorial help.

Endnotes

1. In this model it is also possible for aX, bX, and cX to emerge without prior development of X, through expansion of reference, as a generic label (encompassing several
   closely related species). Such a process accounts for the development of binomial labels
   involving "conceptional coordination" between classes at the same taxonomic level as
   described by Hunn and French (1984:86) and found, for example in Mixtepec Zapotec
   oak classification (see below).
2. As reflected in Table 7.1, Fleisher (1976: 52, 68) reports two SOTs for Clallam, a
   Salishan language of the northern Olympic Peninsula of western Washington State.
   These terms, *ča?ŋiłč* and *q!aput*, designate respectively *Q. kelloggii* and *Q. garryana*.
   This is surprising since only *Q. garryana* is known to occur natively in the region.
3. Perhaps the fact that languages of peoples practicing marginal agriculture show few
   binomial terms for oaks relates to the possibility that their folk botanical taxonomies are
   small relative to those of groups who are fully agricultural. This possibility needs
   investigating.
4. This is isomorphic with Ellen's (1999:110) proposal that ethnobiological inventories are
   likely to have a clinal distribution between the two hypothetical extremes of a pristine
   hunter-gatherer mode of subsistence and a fully developed agricultural way of life.

References Cited

Alcorn, Janis B., and C. Hernández V.
1983 Plants of the Huastecan region of Mexico with an analysis of their Huastec names. Journal of Mayan Linguistics 4:11-118.

Almstedt, Ruth F.
1968 Diegueño tree: an ecological approach to a linguistic problem. International Journal of American Linguistics 34:9-15.

Anderson, Jr., Eugene N.
1991 Chinese folk classification of food plants. Crossroads 1:51-67.

Anderson, E. Richard, and Hilario Concepción Roque
1983 Diccionario Cuicateco. México, D.F.: Instituto Lingüístico de Verano.

Applegate, Richard
1992 Ineseño Dictionary. Unpublished manuscript in the library of the Santa Barbara Museum of Natural History.

Atran, Scott
1990 Cognitive Foundations of Natural History. London: Cambridge University Press.

Baraga, R.R. Bishop
1878 A Dictionary of the Otchipwe Language. Minneapolis, Minnesota: Ross & Haines.

Barrows, David Prescott
1900 The Ethno-botany of the Coahuilla Indians of Southern California. Chicago: University of Chicago Press.

Bartlett, H. H.
1940 The concept of genus, I. History of the generic concept in botany. Bulletin of the Torrey Botanical Club 67:349-62.

Bean, John Lowell, and Katherine Siva Saubel
1972 Temalpakh: Cahuilla Indian Knowledge and Usage of Plants. Banning, California: Malki Museum.

Belmar, Francisco
1901 Idioma Amuzgo que se Habla en algunas Pueblos del Distrito de Jamiltepec. Oaxaca: Tipografía Particular.

Berlin, Brent
1972 Speculations on the growth of ethnobotanical nomenclature. Language in Society 1:51-86.
1986 Comment on "The Growth of Ethnobiological Nomenclature," by Cecil H. Brown. Current Anthropology 27:12-3.

1992 Ethnobiological Classification: Principles of Categorization of Plants and Animals in Traditional Societies. Princeton, New Jersey: Princeton University Press.

Berlin, Brent, Dennis E. Breedlove, and Peter H. Raven
1973 General principles of classification and nomenclature in folk biology. American Anthropologist 75:214-42.
1974 Principles of Tzeltal Plant Classification. New York: Academic Press.

Bonvillain, Nancy, and Beatrice Francis
1971 Mohawk-English Dictionary. Albany, New York: University of the State of New York.

Breedlove, Dennis E., and Robert M. Laughlin
1993 The Flowering of Man: A Tzotzil Botany of Zinacantán. Washington, D.C.: Smithsonian Institution Press.

Bright, William
1957 The Karok Language. Berkeley: University of California Press.
1968 A Luiseño Dictionary. Berkeley: University of California Press.

Brinton, Daniel G., and Albert Seqaqkind Anthony
1888 A Lenâpé-English Dictionary. The Pennsylvania Students' Series, Vol. 1. Philadelphia: The Historical Society of Pennsylvania.

Broadbent, Sylvia
1964 The Southern Sierra Miwok Language. Berkeley: University of California Press.

Brown, Cecil H.
1971 An Ordinary Language Approach to Transformational Grammar and to Formal Semantic Analysis of Huastec Terminological Systems. Doctoral dissertation. Tulane University.
1976 General principles of human anatomical partonomy and speculations on the growth of partonomic nomenclature. American Ethnologist 3:400-424.
1977 Folk botanical life-forms: their universality and growth. American Anthropologist 79:317-42.
1979 Folk zoological life-forms: their universality and growth. American Anthropologist 81:791-817
1983 Where do cardinal direction terms come from? Anthropological Linguistics 25:121-61.
1984 Language and Living Things: Uniformities in Folk Classification and Naming. New Brunswick, New Jersey: Rutgers University Press.
1985 Mode of subsistence and folk biological taxonomy. Current Anthropology 26:43-64.
1986 The growth of ethnobiological nomenclature. Current Anthropology 27:1-19.
1987 Polysémie, Attribution d'une Marque et le Concept 'Semaine'. Recherches Amérindiennes au Québec 17(4):37-50.
1989 Naming the days of the week: a cross-language study of lexical acculturation. Current Anthropology 30:436-550.
1990 Ethnozoological Nomenclature and Animal Salience. Proceedings of the First International Congress of Ethnobiology (Belém, 1988), edited by Darrell A. Posey et al., pp. 81-87. Belém, Brazil: Museu Paraense Emilio Goeldi.

1992 British Names for American Birds. Journal of Linguistic Anthropology 2:30-50.
1995 Lexical acculturation and ethnobiology: utilitarianism versus intellectualism. Journal of Linguistic Anthropology 5:51-64.
1996 A widespread marking reversal in languages of the Southeastern United States. Anthropological Linguistics 38:439-60.
1999 Lexical acculturation in Native American languages. New York: Oxford University Press.

Brown, Cecil H., and Stanley R. Witkowski
1981 Figurative language in a universalist perspective. American Ethnologist 8:596-615.

Byington, Cyrus
1915 A Dictionary of the Choctaw Language. Washington: Government Printing Office.

Callaghan, Catherine A.
1965 Lake Miwok Dictionary. Berkeley: University of California Press.
1984 Plains Miwok Dictionary. Berkeley: University of California Press.
1987 Northern Sierra Miwok Dictionary. Berkeley: University of California Press.

Camacho-Zamora, José A.
1983 Etnobotánica Cabécar. América Indígena 43:57-86.

Chafe, Wallace L.
1967 Seneca Morphology and Dictionary. Washington: Smithsonian Press.

Chamberlain, Alexander Francis
1892 The Language of the Mississaga Indians of Skūgog. Press of MacCalla and Company.

Chamberlain, Montague
1899 Maliseet Vocabulary. Cambridge, Massachusetts: Harvard Cooperative Society.

Conklin, Harold C.
1954 The Relation of Hanunóo Culture to the Plant World. Doctoral dissertation. Yale University.

Couro, Ted, and Christina Hutcheson
1973 Dictionary of Mesa Grande Diegueño. Banning, California: Malki Museum Press.

Day, Gordon M.
1994 Western Abenaki Dictionary. Abenaki-English, Vol. 1. Hull, Quebec: Canadian Museum of Civilization.
1995 Western Abenaki Dictionary. English-Abenaki, Vol. 2. Hull, Quebec: Canadian Museum of Civilization.

Delgaty, Alfa Hurley, and Agustín Ruíz Sánchez
1978 Diccionario Tzotzil de San Andrés. México, D.F.: Instituto Lingüístico de Verano.

Dixon, Roland B.
1910 The Chimariko Indians and Language. University of California Publications in American Archaeology and Ethnology 5:293-384.

Dorsey, James Owen, and John R. Swanton
1912 A Dictionary of the Biloxi and Ofo Languages. Washington: Government Printing Office.

Driver, Harold E.
1953 The Acorn in North American Indian Diet. Proceedings of the Indiana Academy of Science 62:56-62.

Duncan, John Whitfield
1963 Maidu Ethnobotany. Master's thesis. Sacramento State College.

Elias, Thomas S.
1987 The Complete Trees of North America: Field Guide and Natural History. New York: Gramercy Publishing Company.

Ellen, Roy
1999 Models of subsistence and ethnobiological knowledge: between extraction and cultivation in Southeast Asia. In: Folkbiology, edited by Douglas L. Medin and Scott Atran, pp. 91-117. Cambridge, Massachusetts: MIT Press.

Fernández de Miranda, María Teresa
1961 Diccionario Ixcateco. México, D.F.: Instituto Nacional de Antropología e Historia.

Fleisher, Mark Stewart
1976 Clallam: A Study in Coast Salish Ethnolinguistics. Doctoral dissertation. Washington State University.

Freeland, L.S., and Sylvia M. Broadbent
1960 Central Sierra Miwok Dictionary. Berkeley: University of California Press.

Gatschet, Albert Samuel
1890 The Klamath Indians of Southwestern Oregon. Washington: Government Printing Office.

Gatschet, Albert S., and John R. Swanton
1932 A Dictionary of the Atakapa Language. Washington: Government Printing Office.

Gilmore, Melvin R.
1977 Uses of Plants by the Indians of the Missouri River Region. Lincoln: University of Nebraska Press.

Goddard, Ives
1994 Leonard Bloomfield's Fox Lexicon: Critical Edition. Winnipeg, Manitoba: Algonquian and Iroquoian Linguistics. Winnipeg, Manitoba.

Grimes, Joseph E.
1980 Huichol life form classification II: plants. Anthropological Linguistics 22:264-74.

Haas, Mary R.
1953 Tunica Dictionary. Berkeley: University of California Press.
1988 Creek-English Index to Haas's Creek Vocabulary. Compiled by George A. Broadwell, David M. Cline, Abigail C. Cohn, Jack Martin, and Pamela Munro. Unpublished manuscript, UCLA.

Haeserijn V., Esteban
1979 Diccionario K'ekchi' Español. Guatemala: Editorial "Piedra Santa."

Harrington, John P.
1928 Vocabulary of the Kiowa Language. Washington: Government Printing Office.

Herbruger, Alfredo, Jr., and Eduardo Diaz Barrios
1956 Método para Aprender a Hablar, Leer y Escribir la Lengua Cakchiquel. Guatemala, C.A.: Tipografía Nacional Guatemala.

Hill, Jane H., and Rosinda Nolasques
1973 Mulu'wetam: The First People: Cupeño Oral History and Language. Banning, California: Malki Museum Press.

Hunn, Eugene S.
1998 Mixtepec Zapotec ethnobiological classification: a preliminary sketch and theoretical commentary. Anthropologica XL:35-48.

Hunn, Eugene S., and David H. French
1984 Alternatives to taxonomic hierarchy: the Sahaptin case. Journal of Ethnobiology 4:73-92.

Jordan, Julia Anne
1965 Ethnobotany of the Kiowa-Apache. Master's thesis. University of Oklahoma.

Kimball, Geoffrey D.
1994 Koasati Dictionary. Lincoln: University of Nebraska Press.

King, Duane Harold
1975 A Grammar and Dictionary of the Cherokee Language. Doctoral dissertation. University of Georgia.

La Flesche, Francis
1932 A Dictionary of the Osage Language. Washington: Government Printing Office.

Laughlin, Robert M.
1988 The Great Tzotzil Dictionary of Santo Domingo Zinacantán. Washington, D.C.: Smithsonian Institution Press.

Lemoine, Geo.
1911 Dictionnaire Français-Algonquin. Québec: Imp. L'action Sociale L'tée.

Loughridge, R.M., and David M. Hodge
1890 English and Muskokee Dictionary. St. Louis: Printing House of J.T. Smith.

Maracle, David Kanatawakhon
1992 One Thousand Useful Mohawk Words. Guilford, Connecticut: Audio-Forum.

Margery Peña, Enrique
1989 Diccionario Cabecar-Español Español-Cabecar. San José: Editorial de la Universidad de Costa Rica.

Martinez, Esther
1982 San Juan Pueblo Téwa Dictionary. San Juan Pueblo Bilingual Program. San Juan Pueblo, New Mexico.

Mendoza, Francisco Pérez, and Miguel Hernández Mendoza
1996 Diccionario Tz'utujil. Antigua Guatemala: Proyecto Lingüístico Francisco Marroquín.

Merriam, C. Hart
1979 Indian Names for Plants and Animals among Californian and other Western North American Tribes. Socorro, New Mexico: Ballena Press.

Messer, Ellen
1975 Zapotec Plant Knowledge: Classification, Uses, and Communication about Plants in Mitla, Oaxaca, Mexico. Doctoral dissertation, University of Michigan. Ann Arbor.

Michelson, Gunther
1973 A Thousand Words of Mohawk. National Museum of Man. Ottawa.

Mixco, Mauricio J.
1985 Kiliwa Dictionary. Salt Lake City: University of Utah.

Munro, Pamela, and Catherine Willmond
1994 Chickasaw: An Analytical Dictionary. Norman: University of Oklahoma Press.

Nellis, Neil, and Jane Goodner de Nellis
1983 Diccionario Zapoteco de Juárez. México, D.F.: Instituto Lingüístico de Verano.

Nixon, Kevin C.
1993 The Genus *Quercus* in Mexico. In: Biological Diversity of Mexico: Origins and Distribution, edited by T. P. Ramamoorthy, Robert Bye, Antonio Lot, and John Fa, pp. 447-58. New York: Oxford University Press.

Noordsy, Searle Hoogshagen, and Hilda Halloran de Hoogshagen
1993 Diccionario Mixe de Coatlán. México, D.F.: Instituto Lingüístico de Verano.

Olmsted, David L.
1966 Achumawi Dictionary. Berkeley: University of California Press.

Pennington, Campbell W.
1979 Vocabulario en la Lengua Nevome. The Pima Bajo of Central Sonora, Mexico, Vol. 2. Salt Lake City: University of Utah Press.
1980 The Material Culture. The Pima Bajo of Central Sonora, Mexico, Vol. 1. Salt Lake City: University of Utah Press.

Perry, Edgar, Canyon Z. Quintero, Sr., Catherine D. Davenport, and Corrine B. Perry
1972 Western Apache Dictionary. White Mountain Apache Culture Center. Fort Apache, Arizona.

Pinart, Alphonse
1952 The Mission Indian Vocabularies of Alphonse Pinart. Berkeley: University of California Press.

Pitkin, Harvey
1985 Wintu Dictionary. Berkeley: University of California Press.

Pyawasit, Wallace, Margaret Richmond, and Merceline Sanapaw
1975 Omǣqnomenēw-kīketwanan: An English-Menominee and Menominee-English Word List. Office of Equal Educational Opportunity. Milwaukee, Wisconsin.

Reeck, Roger
1991 A Trilingual Dictionary in Zapotec, English and Spanish. Master's thesis. Universidad de las Americas-Puebla (Mexico).

Rhodes, Richard A.
1993 Eastern Ojibwa-Chippewa-Ottawa Dictionary. Berlin: Mouton de Gruyter.

Riggs, Stephen Return
1992 A Dakota-English Dictionary. St Paul: Minnesota Historical Society Press.

Robbins, Wilfred William, John Peabody Harrington, and Barbara Freire-Marreco
1916 Ethnobotany of the Tewa Indians. Washington: Government Printing Office.

Robinson, Lila Wistrand, and James Armagost
1990 Comanche Dictionary and Grammar. Summer Institute of Linguistics. Dallas, Texas.

Rudes, Blair A.
1987 Tuscarora Roots, Stems, and Particles: Towards a Dictionary of Tuscarora. Algonquian and Iroquoian Linguistics. Winnipeg, Manitoba.

Ruyán Canú, Débora, Serapio Coyote Tum, and JoAnn Munson L.
1990 Glosario Español-Cakchiquel. Guatemala, C.A.: Instituto Lingüístico de Verano.

Sapir, Edward, and Morris Swadesh
1960 Yana Dictionary. Berkeley: University of California Press.

Sawyer, Jesse O.
1965 English-Wappo Vocabulary. Berkeley: University of California Press.

Sawyer, Jesse O., and Alice Schlicher
1984 Yuki Vocabulary. Berkeley: University of California Press.

Saxton, Dean, Lucille Saxton, and Susie Enos
1983 Dictionary Papago/Pima-English, English-Papago/Pima. Tucson, Arizona: The University of Arizona Press.

Schlichter, Alice
1981 Wintu Dictionary. Department of Linguistics. Berkeley, California.

Schoenhals, Alvin, and Louise C. Schoenhals
1965 Vocabulario Mixe de Totontepec. México, D.F.: Instituto Lingüístico de Verano.

Seiler, Hans Jakob, and Kojiro Hioki
1979 Cahuilla Dictionary. Banning, California: Malki Museum Press.

Shaul, David Leedom
1994 A Sketch of the structure of Oob No'ok (Mountain Pima). Anthropological Linguistics 36:277-365.

Shipley, William F.
1963 Maidu Texts and Dictionary. Berkeley: University of California Press.

Smith, Huron H.
1923 Ethnobotany of the Menomini Indians. Bulletin of the Public Museum of the City of Milwaukee 4:1-174.
1928 Ethnobotany of the Meskwaki Indians. Bulletin of the Public Museum of the City of Milwaukee 4:175-326.
1932 Ethnobotany of the Ojibwe Indians. Bulletin of the Public Museum of the City of Milwaukee 4:327-525.

Stairs Kreger, Glenn Albert, and Emily Florence Scharfe de Stairs
1981 Diccionario Huave de San Mateo del Mar. México, D.F.: Instituto Lingüístico de Verano.

Stubblefield, Morris, and Carol Miller de Stubblefield
1991 Diccionario Zapoteco de Mitla, Oaxaca. México, D.F.: Instituto Lingüístico de Verano.

Sturtevant, William C. (editor)
1978 Handbook of North American Indian. Washington: Smithsonian Institution.

Swanton, John R. (editor)
1946 The Indians of the Southeastern United States. Smithsonian Institution Bureau of American Ethnology Bulletin 137. Washington: Government Printing Office.

Sylestine, Cora, Heather K. Hardy, and Timothy Montler
1993 Dictionary of the Alabama Language. Austin: University of Texas Press.

Tapia, Fermín
1978 Etnobotánica de los Amuzgos: Parte 1: Los Árboles. México, D.F.: Cuadernos de la Casa Chata.

Thord-Gray, I.
1955 Tarahumara-English, English-Tarahumara Dictionary. Coral Gables, Florida: University of Miami Press.

Todt, Donn L., and Nan Hannon
1999 Preconditions for Acorn Intensification in California: A Landscape Ecology Approach. Unpublished paper in the files of the author.

Trumbull, James Hammond
1903 Natick Dictionary. Washington: Government Printing Office.

Turner, Paul, and Shirley Turner
1971 Chontal to Spanish-English Dictionary Spanish to Chontal. Tucson: The University of Arizona Press.

Tyler, Stephen A.
1969 Introduction. In: Cognitive Anthropology, edited by Stephen A. Tyler, pp. 1-23. New York: Holt, Rinehart and Winston, Inc.

Uldall, Hans Jørgen, and William Shipley
1966 Nisenan Texts and Dictionary. Berkeley: University of California Press.

Velásquez Gallardo, Pablo
1978 Diccionario de la Lengua Phorhépecha. México: Fondo de Cultura Económica.

Vestal, Paul A., and Richard Evans Schultes
1939 The Economic Botany of the Kiowa Indians as it Relates to the History of the Tribe. Botanical Museum. Cambridge, Massachusetts.

Voegelin, Erminie W.
1938 Tübatulabal ethnography. Anthropological Records 2:1- 90.

Watkins, Ben
1892 Complete Choctaw Definer, English with Choctaw Definition. Van Buren, Arkansas: J.W. Baldwin.

Waushope, Robert (editor)
1964 Handbook of Middle American Indians. Austin: University of Texas Press.

Whistler, Kenneth Wayne
1976 Patwin Folk-Taxonomic Structures. Master's thesis. University of California, Berkeley.

Williamson, John P.
1992 An English-Dakota Dictionary. St. Paul: Minnesota Historical Society Press.

Witkowski, Stanley R., and Cecil H. Brown
1977 An explanation of color nomenclature universals. American Anthropologist 79:50-57.

Witkowski, Stanley R., and Cecil H. Brown
1981 Lexical encoding sequences and language change: color terminology systems. American Anthropologist 83:13-27.
1983 Marking-reversals and cultural importance. Language 59:569-82.
1985 Climate, clothing, and body part nomenclature. Ethnology 24:197-214.

Witkowski, Stanley R., Cecil H. Brown, and Paul K. Chase
1981 Where do tree terms come from? Man (N.S.) 16:1-14.

Zeisberger, David
1887 Zeisberger's Indian Dictionary, English, German, Iroquois—the Onondaga and Algonquin—the Delaware. Cambridge: John Wilson and Son.

Zigmond, Maurice L.
1981 Kawaiisu Ethnobotany. Salt Lake City: University of Utah Press.

Zigmond, Maurice L., Curtis G. Booth, and Pamela Munro
1991 Kawaiisu: A Grammar and Dictionary with Texts. Berkeley: University of California Press.

Appendix

Language cases in alphabetical order with indication of (earliest known) location, genetic affiliation, and sources.

1. Achumawi: Northern California; Palaihnihan; Merriam 1979, Olmsted 1966.
2. Alabama: Alabama; Muskogean; Sylestine et al. 1993.
3. Algonquin: Southwestern Quebec; Algonquian; Lemoine 1911.
4. Amuzgo: Southeastern Guerrero (Mexico); Otomanguean; Belmar 1901, Tapia 1978.
5. Atakapa: Louisiana, Texas; isolate; Gatschet and Swanton 1932.
6. Biloxi: Southern Mississippi; Siouan; Dorsey and Swanton 1912.
7. Cabecar: Turrialba region (Costa Rica); Talamanca; Camacho-Zamora 1983, Margery Peña 1989.
8. Cahuilla: Southern California; Uto-Aztecan; Barrows 1900, Bean and Saubel 1972, Seiler and Hioki 1979.
9. Cakchiquel: Southern Guatemala; Mayan; Herbruger and Diaz Barrios 1956, Ruyán Canú et al. 1990.
10. Central Sierra Miwok: Central California; Utian; Freeland and Broadbent 1960.
11. Cherokee: Western North Carolina; Iroquoian; King 1975.
12. Chimariko: Northern California; isolate; Dixon 1910, Merriam 1979.
13. Chickasaw: Northern Mississippi, western Tennessee; Muskogean; Munro and Willmond 1994.
14. Choctaw: Central Mississippi; Muskogean; Byington 1915, Watkins 1892.
15. Chumash: Southern California; Chumashan; Applegate 1992, Merriam 1979, Pinart 1952.
16. Clallam: Northwestern Washington State; Salishan; Fleisher 1976.
17. Comanche: U.S. Plains; Uto-Aztecan; Robinson and Armagost 1990.
18. Creek: Alabama, Georgia, South Carolina; Muskogean; Haas 1988, Loughridge and Hodge 1890.
19. Cuicatec: Northwestern Oaxaca (Mexico); Otomanguean; Anderson and Roque 1983.
20. Cupeño: Southern California; Uto-Aztecan; Hill and Nolasquez 1973.
21. Dakota: Nebraska, Minnesota, North and South Dakota, Montana; Siouan; Riggs 1992, Williamson 1992.
22. Delaware: Pennsylvania, New York, New Jersey, and Delaware; Algonquian; Brinton and Anthony 1888, Zeisberger 1887.
23. Diegueño: Southern California; Yuman; Almstedt 1968, Couro and Hutcheson 1973, Merriam 1979.
24. Fox: Michigan (later Iowa); Algonquian; Goddard 1994, Smith 1928.

25. Huave: Southern Oaxaca (Mexico); isolate; Stairs and Stairs 1981.
26. Huichol: Northeastern Nayarit and northwestern Jalisco (Mexico); Uto-Aztecan; Grimes 1980.
27. Ixcatec: Oaxaca (Mexico); Otomanguean; Fernández de Miranda 1961.
28. Karok: Northwestern California; isolate; Bright 1957.
29. Kawaiisu: Southern California; Uto-Aztecan; Merriam 1979, Zigmond 1981, Zigmond et al. 1991.
30. Kekchi: Northern Alta Verapaz, southern Petén (Guatemala); Mayan; Haeserijn 1979.
31. Kiliwa: Baja California; Yuman; Mixco 1985.
32. Kiowa: West central Oklahoma; Tanoan; Harrington 1928, Vestal and Schultes 1939.
33. Kiowa-Apache: Western Oklahoma; Athapascan; Jordan 1965.
34. Klamath: South central Oregon; isolate; Gatschet 1890.
35. Koasati: Eastern Tennessee, central Alabama; Muskogean; Kimball 1994.
36. Lake Miwok: Northern California; Utian; Callaghan 1965; Merriam 1979.
37. Luiseño: Southern California; Uto-Aztecan; Bright 1968.
38. Maidu: Northern California; Maidun; Shipley 1963.
39. Maliseet: Maine; Algonquian; Chamberlain 1899.
40. Menominee: Northeastern Wisconsin; Algonquian; Pyawasit et al. 1975, Smith 1923.
41. Mississaga: Southern Ontario; Algonquian; Chamberlain 1892.
42. Mixe (Coatlán): East central Oaxaca (Mexico); Mixe-Zoque; Noordsy and Halloran de Hoogshagen 1993.
43. Mixe (Totontepec): Northeastern Oaxaca (Mexico); Mixe-Zoque; Schoenhals and Schoenhals 1965.
44. Mohawk: Northern New York; Iroquoian; Bonvillain and Francis 1971, Maracle 1992, Michelson 1973.
45. Mountain Pima: Chihuahua (Mexico); Uto-Aztecan; Shaul 1994.
46. Natick: Massachusetts; Algonquian; Trumbull 1903.
47. Nevome: Central Sonora (Mexico); Uto-Aztecan; Pennington 1979, 1980.
48. Nisenan: Northern California; Maidun; Duncan 1963, Merriam 1979, Uldall and Shipley 1966.
49. Northern Sierra Miwok: Central California; Utian; Callaghan 1987, Merriam 1979.
50. Ofo: Mississippi; Siouan; Dorsey and Swanton 1912.
51. Ojibwa: Wisconsin; Algonquian; Baraga 1878, Smith 1932.
52. Onondaga: Central New York; Iroquoian; Zeisberger 1887.
53. Osage: North central Oklahoma; Siouan; La Flesche 1932.
54. Ottawa: Southern Ontario; Algonquian; Rhodes 1993.
55. Papago-Pima (O'Odham): South central Arizona; Uto-Aztecan; Saxton et al. 1983.
56. Patwin: Northern California; Wintun; Whistler 1976.
57. Pawnee: North central Oklahoma; Caddoan; Gilmore 1977.
58. Plains Miwok: Central California; Utian; Callaghan 1984, Merriam 1979.
59. Seneca: Western New York; Iroquoian; Chafe 1967.
60. Southern Sierra Miwok: Central California; Utian; Broadbent 1964.
61. Tarahumara: Chihuahua (Mexico); Uto-Aztecan; Thord-Gray 1955.
62. Tarascan: Michoacán (Mexico); isolate; Velásquez Gallardo 1978.
63. Tequistlatec: Southern Oaxaca (Mexico); Tequistlatecan; Turner and Turner 1971.
64. Tewa: New Mexico; Tanoan; Martinez 1982, Robbins et al. 1916.
65. Tübatulabal: Central California; Uto-Aztecan; Merriam 1979, Voegelin 1938.
66. Tunica: Southern Mississippi; isolate; Haas 1953.
67. Tuscarora: North Carolina, Virginia; Iroquoian; Rudes 1987.

68. Tzeltal (Tenejapa): East central Chiapas (Mexico); Mayan; Berlin, Breedlove, and Raven 1974, Brent Berlin (personal communication).
69. Tzotzil (San Andrés): West central Chiapas (Mexico); Mayan; Delgaty and Ruíz Sánchez 1978.
70. Tzotzil (Zinacantán): West central Chiapas (Mexico); Mayan; Breedlove and Laughlin 1993, Laughlin 1975.
71. Tzutujil: Lake Atitlán (Guatemala); Mayan; Mendoza and Mendoza 1996.
72. Wappo: Northern California; Yukian; Sawyer 1965.
73. Western Abenaki: Southern Quebec; Algonquian; Day 1994, 1995.
74. Western Apache: East Central Arizona; Athapascan; Perry et al. 1972.
75. Wintu: Northern California; Wintun; Merriam 1979, Pitkin 1985, Schlichter 1981.
76. Yana: Northern California; Yanan; Merriam 1979, Sapir and Swadesh 1960.
77. Yuki: Northern California; Yukian; Sawyer and Schlichter 1984.
78. Zapotec (Juárez): Northern Oaxaca (Mexico); Otomanguean; Nellis and Nellis 1983.
79. Zapotec (Mitla): Oaxaca (Mexico); Otomanguean; Messer 1975, Stubblefield and Stubblefield 1991.
80. Zapotec (Mixtepec): Southern Oaxaca (Mexico); Otomanguean; Hunn 1998, Reeck 1991.

8

In the Field with People, Plants and Animals
A Look at Methods

Catherine S. Fowler, University of Nevada

In 1978, Richard Ford observed that ethnobotany, and by implication, the wider field of ethnobiology, lacked a unifying theory but did share a common discourse (Ford 1978). In other words, as particularly diverse fields of inquiry, embracing several subdisciplines in biology and anthropology, ethnobotany and ethnobiology were perhaps more consistent in their focus on a subject matter than they were in either how that subject matter was approached or how data were defined and gathered. Weber (1986) echoed the sentiment in his remarks before the Society of Ethnobiology in 1986, ten years after its founding, and Lipps (1995:53) has recently restated this position for ethnobotany as follows: "it should be clear that no single theoretical framework and methodology can encompass the diverse areas of study within the field of ethnobotany. Even a broadly based, ecologically oriented systems approach would be of limited use to, for example, linguists studying local plant names as a means of identifying the origins and movements of ancient peoples." Although Joyal (1998) has recently suggested some coming together around very broad theoretical themes (e.g., evolutionary theory) and two excellent manuals for ethnographic methods in ethnobotany now have been published (Martin 1995; Alexiades 1996), the discipline and its methods are still broadly focused and not easy to grasp. When I began work in the field some 35 years ago, there were very few places to learn much about how to do ethnobiology. There were some very good examples of what the results might be in specific studies, but very little on how to get there. In this paper, I will focus on data collection, or field methods in ethnobiology, particularly as they apply to ethnography and linguistics. My treatment will be historical and somewhat autobiographical and idiosyncratic, but I suspect not wholly different than would be that of other practitioners of my vintage and orientation.

As an anthropologist with a minor in biology and a strong theoretical and practical interest in hunters and gatherers in desert environments, I decided early that I ought to be able to catalog and describe what they knew best and probably interested them most: namely, plants and animals. At the time, in the early 1960s, what are now referred to as utilitarian approaches to ethnobiology were largely the models available, as exemplified by the work of Henderson and Harrington (1914), Robbins, Harrington and Freire-Marreco (1916), Gilmore (1919), Whiting (1939), Castetter (various), and others. But the cognitive/intellectualist tradition with its heavy dependence on linguistics was just emerging, exemplified by the work of Conklin (1954, 1957, 1962), Frake (1962a, 1962b), Goodenough (1956), and others. Anthropology had also just discovered ecology, so that what Cotton (1996) identifies as a third approach to ethnobiology, namely the ecological, was also about to step forward. For me, the latter was again exemplified by the work of Conklin (1954) and Frake (1962a), but also Rappaport (1963). Frake's call in 1962 for an emically based ecology, one that attempts to capture categories according to native ethnoscience, was particularly stimulating (Frake 1962a:55). But what of practical value did any of these approaches have to offer in the field?

Utilitarian Methods

Key and important utilitarian ethnobotanical studies in the past, and particularly works on Native North America, rarely had much to say about field methods or methods of analysis. For example, anthropologist David Prescott Barrows, who produced the first systematic work on the ethnobotany of an American Indian tribe, states simply: "The articles already published show how such a work may be conducted" (Barrows 1900:7). Of the articles he cites, only the bulletin by the botanist Coville (1895) titled "Directions for Collecting Specimens and Information Illustrating the Aboriginal Uses of Plants" offers a practical field guide. In it Coville stresses the importance of direct observation and direct questioning over hearsay evidence, and the necesssity of keeping careful field notes and making thorough step-by-step descriptions of plant preparations and uses. He also provides an outline of those areas of culture likely to have ethnobotanical correlates, and a guide to properly preparing herbarium specimens. Barrows seemingly followed Coville's blueprint, discussing Cahuilla uses of plants for a number of practical and a few esoteric purposes.

In 1911, botanist Ralph Chamberlin published his ethnobotany of the Gosiute of Utah, another monographic treatment of a single group. He devotes three sentences to methods, largely in the context of his discussion of native names. He notes that he has done his best to re-elicit names and uses from several individuals, in order "to determine the standard as distinguished from the occasional and extraneous" (Chamberlin 1911:358). He tells us he worked with the better-informed men and women of the tribe, singly and in groups, but that he was not always "able to test to an extent wholly satisfactory to myself" a certain number of species and names (Chamberlin 1911:358-59). He does not cite any references, but he likely consulted some early works, such as perhaps Coville.

During this decade, methodological discussions were expanded to several paragraphs. Melvin Gilmore (1919, 1977), another botanist, in his important work with tribes of the Upper Missouri, says the following:

> The information here collated has been obtained at first hand from intelligent and credible old persons, thoroughly conversant with the matters which they discussed. The various items have been rigorously checked by independent corroborative evidence from other individuals of the same tribe and of different tribes through a protracted period. The work of the interpreters employed has also been verified by comparison and by my own study of the languages of the various tribes interviewed.
>
> The information was obtained by bringing actual specimens of each plant to the observation and identification of many informants, and the names, uses, and preparation in each case were noted on the spot at the dictation of the informant. [Gilmore 1977:xvii]

In 1916, Robbins, Harrington and Freire-Marreco (1916:2-5) devoted a page and a half to methods in their Tewa ethnobotany, providing the first real discussion of the topic to date. They cover selection of consultants, the types of questions to ask, procedures for taking consultants to the field for on-site identification, and the keeping of adequate field notes. They also devote another page and a half to the collection and preparation of botanical specimens, something not covered by previous authors other than Coville (1895).

The multiple works by botanist Castetter and associates (1935; Castetter and Underhill 1935; Castetter and Opler 1936; Castetter and Bell 1937, 1951) Bell and Castetter 1937, 1941; Castetter, Bell and Grove 1938, 1942) in many ways shifted back to a minimal discussion of method, but significantly improved and thus exemplified in thoroughness the treatment of the plants in question. Several of these studies are in-depth treatments of individual taxa or a few related taxa, with distributional statements on their occurrence, and extensive comparative data for their uses among several tribes. These provided important data with implications as to how to conduct comparative field studies.

Whiting (1939) in his monograph on Hopi ethnobotany becomes the first to call for treatment of plants not used as well as used, not named and/or ignored, and some attempt at quantitative statements by use category. Whiting (1939:59) also cites the names and defines the expertise of each of his consultants. He states that all individuals were involved in direct observation of plants in the field, but that he also felt that the Hopi people were very adept at recognizing dried plant material, something that unnamed colleagues had told him was an ineffective method. He also provides the span of time he was in the field making observations, thus allowing the reader to further judge his thoroughness. Providing the names of consultants also allows contemporary Hopi people to judge the thoroughness and validity of the data.

Studies in ethnozoology during a roughly comparable period for Native North America provide similar hints as to how to proceed in the field, while noting some of the practical difficulties inherent in collecting animals vs. plants. For example, in order to avoid problems in field collecting, ornithologist Mearns (1896) took 200 study skins to Hopi in the summer of 1893 for his study of bird names. He was later faulted by Bradfield (1974:10) for taking some species that were nonlocal, which resulted in several Hopi descriptive terms rather than true names of taxa; but in reality, these data are extremely interesting for a broader study of Hopi ethnoscience.

Henderson and Harrington (1914) for their Tewa ethnozoology, first spent a month in the field collecting specimens, but note that this amount of time was far from satisfactory, as it did not provide an adequate sample, particularly of migratory species. They attempted to supplement their field collections with testimony from local ranchers and trappers, as well as data from the literature. They showed their mounts to Tewa consultants, but also attempted to do as much field observation of animal behavior with the people as possible. They supplemented these methods by showing consultants clear, high quality color plates from books. Henderson and Harrington stress that if ethnozoology is to remain scientific, it has to be rigorous in all of its identifications, and particularly by making sure whether and by what means people differentiate very similar species.

But perhaps the epitomy of rigor in one area of ethnozoology is Wyman and Bailey's (1964) work on Navajo ethnoentomology. For this they showed 801 individually mounted specimens of insects and other arthropods to 27 Navajo individuals for naming and further identification. They provide data on the background of each consultant, their judgment of his/her degree of acculturation, the number of specimens each named, and the degree of agreement among consultants. They also vouchered their collection at the Museum of Northern Arizona in case others wished to verify or follow up on their results.

Armed with this battery of suggestions, I did my first ethnobiological studies among the Southern Paiute people in southern Utah in the summer of 1962, when I was a senior at the University of Utah. I took older individuals to the field to collect plants, prepared a traveling herbarium of plants to show other elderly people who were house bound, and tried to keep careful notes. My herbarium sheets were barely adequate for identification. For animals, including insects, I depended almost entirely on pictures in local natural history field guides along with minor field observations—less than adequate. Overall the results were decidedly utilitarian, the data quite skimpy and the transcriptions poor. It was a bare beginning.

Cognitive/Intellectualist Approaches

While field workers who followed utilitarian approaches seemed to focus more on results than on methods, that was reversed in the 1960s with the advent of cognitive/intellectualist approaches. Infused by the probability of a high correlation between native linguistic categories and behavior (à la the Sapir-Whorf hypothesis), several now went to the field to study native classifications in ethnobiology as well as other domains as examples of how people think and organize their worlds. This orientation required fairly explicit training in linguistic methods, both in terms of the practicalities of accurate transcription, as well as the ability to properly segment and translate linguistic elements. This represented for some field workers a return to linguistics as a field tool, when it had been all but abandoned by many anthropologists who found work with interpreters and bilingual consultants increasingly adequate.

Practitioners of methods in the cognitive/intellectualist approach were most commonly anthropologists, including Bulmer (1965, 1967, 1968), Conklin (1954, 1967), Frake (1962a, 1962b), Goodenough (1957), Metzger and Williams (1966), Rappaport (1963), and others, although early Berlin worked with botanists Breedlove and Raven (Berlin, Breedlove and Raven 1966, 1968), and a few linguists such as Bright and Bright (1965) also explored the approach. The theoretical and methodological importance of "emic" vs. "etic" categories, an analogy from linguistic "phonemic" vs. "phonetic" categories (see Pike 1954-60), remained central for all, as did the development of field procedures that avoided as much as possible superimposing nonnative biases on the data, something that had always been of concern. The mid-1960s through the early 1970s saw a number of methodological statements, along with criticisms (Burling 1964; Berreman 1966; Harris 1968; Keesing 1973). It was not until the mid-1970s that more complete demonstrations of data began to emerge, with those in ethnobiology taking the lead (e.g., Berlin, Breedlove and Raven 1974; Hunn 1977). Broad-based comparative studies of the results of individual efforts in ethnobiology emerged even later (Brown 1984; Berlin 1992). Studies in other cultural areas, such as kinship, disease, architecture, material culture and metaphor, yielded less widely applicable results (D'Andrade 1995).

For most working with cognitive/intellectualist approaches, the focus of research now became how native categories were organized and discussed rather than the utilitarian data themselves. In essence, a thorough study in ethnobiology should now contain a careful and detailed study of native taxonomies or other methods of organization that some of the earlier authors had only briefly explored. Some of the new field methods advocated starting not at the bottom by carefully collecting data on individual specimens, or native names for things, but rather at the top, with the most general categories and systematically working down to the level of individual taxa. Others preferred methods that started with individual taxa and worked upward and outward in various ways. Methods proposed were all heavily based on native language elicitation, including what was called "formal frame analysis" (Metzger and Williams 1966), text-based "key word in context," eliciting folk definitions, slip/picture/specimen pile sorting and labeling, and having consultants draw tree diagrams or other schema that represented relationships (Perchonock and Werner 1969;

Fowler 1977). Yet others advocated using native elicitors to ask questions that they felt were pertinent and important to native contexts in which ethnobiological matters were naturally discussed. All texts in the native language needed to be transcribed, translated and analyzed for data on relationships, a labor-intensive task. Further questioning could then take place based on what was discovered. For data not organized hierarchically, alternative means of analysis such as through paradigms, keys, spheres of influence diagrams, and other structures, were proposed.

Armed with this new battery of techniques, Joy Leland and I began field studies with the Northern Paiute of western Nevada in the mid-1960s. Not only did we do what we could in the field to gather utilitarian data on plants and animals, but we now tried all of the new techniques to analyze the relationships among them. We gathered hours of tape recorded texts, using native elicitors as well as our own carefully constructed questions in the native language. We laboriously translated and analyzed them. We improved our transcription skills, and concentrated heavily on morphological and semantic analysis of the language. We had consultants sort slips, pictures and herbarium specimens; we took people to the Nevada State Museum to see and discuss bird and mammal study skins; and we joined in the national discussion of the practicality and utility of these methods (Fowler and Leland 1967).

As with the utilitarian methods, each of these techniques was of some use in practical field situations, but none was without at least some constraints and biases. We began to wonder whether we had unknowingly inserted our own categories into the work, or whether our consultants, all bilingual, were reflecting categories derived from English. Careful analysis of the semantics of the ethnobiological nomenclature became vital to the process, and seemed to indicate that what we were getting had some basis in reality. Only after the emergence of more data showing what appeared to be universals (Berlin 1972; Bulmer 1968) did we feel some confidence in the results. Brown (1984) and Berlin (1992) have both summarized what became a large literature in cognitive/intellectualist ethnobiology, an area that now has a firm place in theory and method in the discipline.

Based on the Northern Paiute experiences, I tackled a comparative topic of ethnobiological classifications in the Numic languages of Uto-Aztecan (Northern Paiute, Southern Paiute and Shoshone) for my dissertation (Fowler 1972a). I honed my historical linguistic skills, and proposed the possibility of homelands and migrations for these and other related Uto-Aztecan languages based on reconstructed plant and animal terminology. Although not a field method, that technique depends heavily on both highly accurate linguistic recording and on equally accurate binomial identifications of specimens. Just as Bye (1964) has called for vouchering ethnobotanical specimens, we need to think seriously about vouchering linguistic data to improve accuracy. I have continued to remain interested in use of ethnobiological data for linguistic prehistory since that time (Fowler 1972b, 1983, 1994).

Ecological Approaches

Although anthropology discovered ecology in the 1960s, and archaeologists as well as ethnographers applied the term variously to all types of field studies, it again appears that historically the methods associated with ethnoecology in ethnobiology are eclectic and only now beginning to take real shape. The advances being made in this direction are coming largely from biological ecologists and economic botanists rather than anthropologists, although a few of the latter are beginning to show that they have absorbed the literature in biological ecology. For many years, the field of "human ecology" or "cultural ecology" or even "ethnoecology" was more a stance that relationships of people to environments needed to be examined than an explicit method. People noted the obvious importance of indigenous burning as a land management technique (Lewis, 1993), as well as the primary effects of cultural practices such as agriculture, irrigation, selective cropping and harvesting, pruning and culling, but little systematic treatment was available. Both Martin (1995) and Peters (1996) have recently pulled together excellent treatments on methods in ecology and their application in ethnobiology. Martin (1995) divides the approaches into qualitative methods vs. quantitative methods, while Peters (1996:242f) provides treatment of quantitative methods of assessing species density vs. growth and yield studies. Under qualitative methods Martin (1995:138f) suggests that field workers make careful observations of how indigenous peoples define their landforms and apply toponymy, how they characterize their soils, climates, vegetative types and ecozones, how they see concepts of succession, overt and covert management techniques, and more. Each of these provides data on human/land relationships, and is instructive of overall adaptations. Quantitative approaches, most of which come more directly from biological ecology, include techniques for establishing study plots and/or transects, measuring the diversity and abundance of resources, estimating growth, fertility rates and recovery rates, gathering precise data on natural zone harvests vs. various plantings, and a host of other potential approaches. Tools such as Geographic Information Systems and other plotting techniques help immeasurably, but the studies for the most part involve long field hours, long-term observations and perhaps collaborative efforts with soil scientists and other experts. Peters' 1996 review focuses more on the quantitative techniques, but is equally informative.

My own experiences in this area have been modest, and largely qualitative. I have elicited ethnoecological concepts of ecological zones, communities and associations, and have focused some attention on indigenous systems of land management and toponymy in various parts of the Great Basin (Fowler 1972a, 1996, 1999). But I see a great need to add quantitative methods if the data are to become more than anecdotal. The beginnings of joint concerns with conservation biology in exploring biodiversity and other topics is pushing us all in the direction of quantitative methods. The work of Turner (e.g., 1999), Hunn (1990) and a few others in North America is in this direction, but there is even more coming out of work in tropical America and Southeast Asia where indigenous systems have been less altered (see, for example, Alcorn 1984; Balee 1996; Toledo et al. 1992; Lepovsky 1992; Nazarea 1999 and others). These are the areas for new and stimulating methodological developments, and ones all of us will look to in the future for new breakthroughs.

But in the meantime, new ethnobiologists will do well to learn all they can of the methods of the past as well as the present to move the discipline forward. As a marriage of biology and anthropology, the interplay within ethnobiology of the methods and theories from both has always been eclectic and likely will remain so. But this has served us well in the past, and likely will continue to do so in the future. Besides, where else but in the field with plants, animals and people can you have more fun?

References Cited

Alcorn, Janice B.
1984 Huastec Mayan Ethnobotany. Austin: University of Texas Press.

Alexiades, Miguel N. (editor)
1996 Selected Guidelines for Ethnobotanical Research: A Field Manual. The New York Botanical Garden. New York.

Balée, William
1996 Footprints of the Forest: Ka'apor Ethnobotany—The Historical Ecology of Plant Utilization by an Amazonian People. New York: Columbia University Press.

Barrows, David P.
1900 Ethno-Botany of the Coahuilla Indians of Southern California. Chicago: University of Chicago Press.

Bell, Willis H., and Edward F. Castetter
1937 The utilization of mesquite and screwbean by the aborigines in the American Southwest. Ethnobiological Studies in the American Southwest V. University of New Mexico Bulletin, Biological Series 5(2):1-55. Albuquerque.
1941 The utilization of yucca, sotol, and beargrass by the aborigines in the American Southwest. Ethnobiological Studies in the American Southwest VII. University of New Mexico Bulletin, Biological Series 5(5):1-74. Albuquerque.

Berlin, Brent
1972 Speculations on the growth of ethnobotanical nomenclature. Language in Society 1: 51-86.
1992 Ethnobiological Classification: Principles of Plant Classification of Plants and Animals in Traditional Societies. Princeton: Princeton University Press.

Berlin, Brent, Dennis E. Breedlove and Peter H. Raven
1966 Folk taxonomies and biological classification. Science 154:275-75.
1968 Covert categories and folk taxonomies. American Anthropologist 70:290-99.
1974 Principles of Tzeltal Plant Classification: An Introduction to the Botanical Ethnography of a Mayan-Speaking People of Highland Chiapas. New York: Academic Press.

Berreman, Gerald D.
1966 Anemic and emetic analyses in social anthropology. American Anthropologist 68(2, pt. 1):346-54.

Bradfield, Maitland
1974 Birds of the Hopi Region, Their Hopi Names, and Notes on Their Ecology. Musuem of Northern Arizona Bulletin No. 48. Flagstaff.

Bright, Jane O., and William Bright
1965 Semantic structures in northwestern California and the Sapir-Whorf hypothesis. In: Formal Semantic Analysis, edited by Eugene A. Hammel, pp. 249-58. Special Publication of the American Anthropologist 67(5, pt. 2).

Brown, Cecil H.
1984 Language and Living Things: Uniformities in Folk Classification and Naming. New Brunswick, N.J.: Rutgers University Press.

Bulmer, Ralph
1965 Beliefs concerning the propagation of new varieties of sweet potato in two New Guinea highlands societies. Journal of the Polynesian Society 74:237-39.
1967 Why is the cassowary not a bird? A problem of zoological taxonomy among the Karam of the New Guinea highlands. Man (n.s.) 2:5-25.
1968 Worms that croak and other mysteries of Karam natural history. Mankind 6:621-39.

Burling, Robbins
1964 Cognition and componential analysis: God's truth or hocus-pocus? American Anthropologist 66(1):20-28.

Bye, Robert A, Jr.
1986 Voucher specimens in ethnobiological studies and publications. Journal of Ethnobiology 6(1):1-8.

Castetter, Edward F.
1935 Uncultivated native plants used as sources of food. Ethnobiological Studies in the American Southwest I. University of New Mexico Bulletin, Biological Series 4(1):1-62. Albuquerque.

Castetter, Edward F., and Willis H. Bell
1937 The aboriginal utilization of the tall cacti in the American Southwest. Ethnobiological Studies in the American Southwest IV. University of New Mexico Bulletin, Biological Sciences 5(1):2-48. Albuquerque.

1951   Yuman Indian Agriculture: Primitive Subsistence on the Lower Colorado River and Gila Rivers. Albuquerque: University of New Mexico Press.

Castetter, Edward F., Willis H. Bell and Alvin R. Grove
1938   The early utilization and distribution of agave in the American Southwest. Ethnobiological Studies in the American Southwest VI. University of New Mexico Bulletin, Biological Series 5(4):1-92. Albuquerque.
1942 Pima and Papago Indian Agriculture. Albuquerque: University of New Mexico Press.

Castetter, Edward F., and M.E. Opler
1936   The ethnobiology of the Chiricahua and Mescalero Apache. A. The uses of plants for foods, beverages, and narcotics. Ethnobiological Studies in the American Southwest III. University of New Mexico Bulletin, Biological Series 4(5):1-63. Albuquerque.

Castetter, Edward F., and Ruth Underhill
1935   The ethnobiology of the Papago Indians. Ethnobiological Studies in the American Southwest II. University of New Mexico Bulletin, Biological Series 4(3):1-84. Albuquerque.

Chamberlin, Ralph V.
1911   Ethno-botany of the Gosiute Indians of Utah. Memoirs of the American Anthropological Association 2(5):329-405. Lancaster.

Conklin, Harold C.
1954   An ethnoecological approach to shifting agriculture. New York Academy of Sciences, Transactions 17(2):133-42.
1957   Hanunoo Agriculture: A Report on an Integral System of Shifting Cultivation in the Philippines. Food and Agriculture Organization, United Nations. Rome.
1962   Lexicographical treatment of folk taxonomies. In: Problems in Lexicography, edited by F. W. Household and S. Saporta, pp. 119-41. Publications of the Indiana University Research Center in Anthropology, Folklore and Linguistics No. 21. Bloomington.

Cotton, C. M.
1996   Ethnobotany: Principles and Applications. Chichester: John Wiley & Sons.

Coville, Fredrick V.
1895   Directions for Collecting Specimens and Infirmation Illustrating the Aboriginal Uses of Plants. Bulletin of the United States National Museum, No. 39 (pt. J). Washington.

D'Andrade, Roy
1995   The Development of Cognitive Anthropology. Cambridge: Cambridge University Press.

Ford, Richard I.
1978   Ethnobotany: historical diversity and synthesis. In: The Nature and Status of Ethnobotany, edited by R. I. Ford, pp. 33-49. Anthropological Papers, Museum of Anthropology, University of Michigan 67. Ann Arbor.

Fowler, Catherine S.
1972a Comparative Numic Ethnobiology. Doctoral Dissertation, University of Pittsburgh.
1972b Some ecological clues to proto-numic homelands. In: Great Basin Cultural Ecology, edited by Don D. Fowler, pp. 105-21. Desert Research Institute Publications in the Social Sciences No. 8. Reno.
1977 Ethnoecology. In: Ecological Anthropology, by Donald L. Hardesty, pp. 215-43. New York: John Wiley.
1983 Some lexical clues to Uto-Aztecan prehistory. International Journal of American Linguistics 49:224-57.
1994 Corn, beans and squash: some linguistic perspectives from Uto-Aztecan. In: Corn and Culture in the Prehistoric New World, edited by C. Hastorf and S. Johanneson, pp. 445-68. Boulder, Colorado: Westview Press.
1996 Historic perspectives on Timbisha Shoshone land management practices, Death Valley, California. In: Case Studies in Environmental Archaeology: Essays in Honor of Elizabeth Wing, edited by Elizabeth J. Reitz, Lee A. Newsom, and Sylvia J. Scudder, pp. 87-101. New York: Plenum Press.
1999 "We live by them": native knowledge of biodiversity in the Great Basin of western North America. In: Biodiversity in Native North America, edited by Paul Minnis and Wayne Elisens, pp. 99-122. Norman: University of Oklahoma Press.

Fowler, Catherine S., and Joy Leland
1967 Some Northern Paiute native categories. Ethnology 6:381-404.

Frake, Charles O.
1962a Cultural ecology and ethnography. American Anthropologist 64(pt. 1):53-59.
1962b The ethnographic study of cognitive systems. In: Anthropology and Human Behavior, edited by T. Gladwin and William C. Sturtevant, pp. 73-93. Anthropological Society of Washington. Washington, D.C.

Gilmore, Melvin R.
1977 Uses of Plants by the Indians of the Missouri River Region. Enlarged Edition. Lincoln: University of Nebraska Press. [Originally published, 1919, Thirty-Third Annual Report of the Bureau of American Ethnology, Washington, D.C.].

Goodenough, Ward H.
1956 Componential analysis and the study of meaning. Language 32:195-216.

Harris, Marvin
1968 The Rise of Anthropological Theory. New York: Thomas Y. Crowell.

Henderson, Junius, and John P. Harrington
1914 Ethnozoology of the Tewa Indians. Bureau of American Ethnology Bulletin 56. Washington.

Hunn, Eugene
1977 Tzeltal Folk Zoology: The Classification of Discontinuities in Nature. New York: Academic Press.

1990 Nch'i-Wana "The Big River": Columbia River Indians and Their Land. Seattle: University of Washington Press.

Joyal, Elaine
1998 Introduction to Results of Membership of Society of Ethnobiology and Society of Conservation Biology. Paper presented at Society of Ethnobiology Annual Meeting. Reno, Nevada.

Keesing, Roger M.
1973 Kwara?ae ethnoglottochronology: procedures used by Malaita cannibals for determining percentages of shared cognates. American Anthropologist 75:1282-89.

Lepovsky, D.
1992 Arboriculture in the Mussau Islands, Bismark Archipelago. Economic Botany 46:192-211.

Lewis, Henry T.
1993 Patterns of Indian burning in California: ecology and ethnohistory. In: Before the Wilderness: Environmental Management by Native Californians, edited by Thomas C. Blackburn and Kat Anderson, pp. 55-116. Ballena Press Anthropological Papers No. 40. Menlo Park.

Lipps, Frank J.
1995 Ethnobotanical method and fact: a case study. In: Ethnobotany: Evolution of a Discipline, Richard E. Schultes and Siri von Reis, pp. 52-59. Portland: Dioscorides Press.

Martin, Gary J.
1995 Ethnobotany: A Methods Manual. London: Chapman and Hall.

Mearns, E. A.
1896 Ornithological vocabulary of the Moki Indians. American Anthropologist (o.s.) 9:391-403.

Metzger, Duane, and G. Williams
1966 Some procedures and results in the study of native categories: Tzeltal "Firewood." American Anthropologist 68:389-407.

Nazarea, Virginia D. (editor)
1999 Ethnoecology: Situated Knowledge/Located Lives. Tucson: University of Arizona Press.

Perchonock, Nancy, and Oswald Werner
1969 Navaho systems of classification: some implications for ethnoscience. Ethnology 8:229-42.

Peters, C. M.
1996 Beyond nomenclature and use: a review of ecological methods for ethnobotanists. In: Selected Guidelines for Ethnobotanical Research: A Field Manual, pp. 241-76. New York Botanical Garden. New York.

Pike, Kenneth L.
1954-60 Language in Relation to a Unified Theory of the Structure of Human Behavior. Parts I (1954), II (1955) and III (1960). Summer Institute of Linguistics. Glendale, California.

Rappaport, Roy A.
1963 Aspects of man's influence on island ecosystems: alteration and control. In: Man's Place in the Island Ecosystem, edited by F. R. Fosberg, pp. 155-74. Honolulu: Bishop Museum Press.

Robbins, Wilfred W., John P. Harrington and Barbara Freire-Marreco
1916 Ethnobotany of the Tewa Indians. Bureau of American Ethnology Bulletin 55. Washington, D.C.

Toledo, Victor M., A. I. Batis, R. Recerra, E. Martinez and C. H. Ramos
1992 Products from the tropical rainforests of Mexico: an ethnoecological approach. In: Sustainable Harvest and Marketing Rain Forest Products, edited by Mark Plotkin and L. Famolare, pp. 99-109. Washington, D.C.: Island Press.

Turner, Nancy J.
1999 "Time to burn": traditional uses of fire to enhance resource production by aboriginal peoples in British Columbia. In: Indians, Fire and the Land in the Pacific Northwest, Robert Boyd, pp. 185-218. Corvallis: Oregon State University Press.

Weber, Steven
1986 The development of a society: an introduction to the special issue. Journal of Ethnobiology 6(1):iii-vi.

Whiting, Alfred F.
1939 Ethnobotany of the Hopi. Museum of Northern Arizona Bulletin 15. Flagstaff.

Wyman, Leland C., and F. L. Bailey
1964 Navajo Indian Ethnoentomology. University of New Mexico Publications in Anthropology, No. 12. Albuquerque: University of New Mexico Press.

9

Pieces into Patterns

Botany of British Columbia Cultures and Influences of
Society of Ethnobiology Members

Nancy J. Turner, University of Victoria

Introduction

When Dick Ford asked me to present a reflective paper on my particular subfield of ethnobotany for this Presidents' symposium, I decided to take this opportunity to look back over my own research in ethnobotany in British Columbia and try to figure out how it all came about, how it fits together with the general research in this field, and in what directions it might be going. Where did my ideas come from? Why did I undertake the lines of research that I did? Who put me up to it? Who inspired me?

I would like to start by acknowledging first and foremost my original teachers, the indigenous elders and plant specialists of British Columbia who have shared their knowledge—as well as their patience, their humor, their hospitality, their friendship and their trust—with me. I could name several dozen people here, but foremost I should recognize Christopher Paul, Elsie Claxton, Dr. Margaret Siwallace, Annie York, Sam Mitchell, John Thomas, Florence Davidson, Dr. Daisy Sewid-Smith, Chief Adam Dick, and Dr. Mary Thomas. I also had family influences in science, from my father and grandfather both of whom were entomologists, and from naturalists and members of the Victoria Natural History Society who were my mentors when I was growing up.

From the academic side, however, I realize that my research has paralleled in many ways the main developments in the discipline of ethnobotany as a whole, and this is largely because I have been so strongly influenced and inspired in my research directions by my colleagues, many of them founding and long-standing members of the Society of Ethnobiology. I can prove this in a very simple way: by going over the acknowledgments and references sections of my various publications over the years and seeing whose names and publications I've cited in each different area of research.

I would like to take this opportunity to trace some of these linkages between my research and that of my ethnobiology colleagues, many of whom attended our Millennium conference. I begin with a qualification and an apology. I write here only for myself and from my perspective; it might be seen quite differently by others working in the same region. The work of Dr. Dana Lepofsky, Dr. Sandra Peacock, Dr. Brian Compton, Dr. Leslie Johnson, Dr. Marianne Ignace and Chief Ron Ignace, Dr. Richard Hebda, among others, is not only of primary importance, but is ongoing, and I cannot begin to represent their perspectives. Nor can I adequately speak for or represent my indigenous colleagues and teachers in ethnobotany, although a number have been co-authors and co-presenters with me.

Early Beginnings

My first ventures into ethnobotany were strongly shaped by the "classic" modes of ethnobotanical research and inventory. The first ethnobotany studies I encountered as an undergraduate student in the 1960s were Erna Gunther's *Ethnobotany of Western Washington* (1945), Elsie Steedman's compilation of James Teit's field notes, *Ethnobotany of the Thompson Indians of British Columbia* (1930), and the ethnobotanical notes of Franz Boas (1909, 1921, 1930). These were rich descriptive treatments, mainly of aboriginal names and uses of botanically identified species arranged in categories and focused on a given cultural-linguistic group or groups. The early ethnobotanical research I undertook was essentially an extension of such works, compiling from intensive taped interviews and literature records as many names and uses of plant species as I could find (see Turner and Bell 1971, 1973; Turner 1973). This work was also largely inspired by Dr. Richard Schultes, then editor of *Economic Botany*, with whom I corresponded, and to whom my first two papers were submitted for publication. In these works, I made some attempts to sort the information into different subtopics: foods, medicines, and so forth. Although I was certainly aware of the cultural and linguistic aspects of plant knowledge, I would have to say that my work fit quite neatly into the "documenting names and uses of plants" category that Dick Ford discusses in his developmental "tree ring" model: the original type of ethnobotany defined by John Harshberger. I document plant names and cultural roles to this day, but my work and methods are now more richly informed.

My information includes greater depth and detail which in turn can be applied to develop more fully the theoretical aspects of ethnobotany. From the 1970s to the early 1980s, usually working with linguists, I undertook a number of ethnobotanical descriptions with various linguistic and cultural groups (e.g. Turner et al. 1983). Some of these descriptions and inventories (e.g. Squamish ethnobotany, with Randy Bouchard and Dorothy Kennedy) have never been published.

Folk Plant Classification

When I started graduate school at the University of British Columbia (UBC) in 1970, I proposed that we invite Richard Schultes as a visiting lecturer for the grad student symposium, so I finally got to meet the person who had been so inspirational and helpful to me in my initial academic interests in ethnobotany. At that time, too, I was introduced to one of the earlier theoretical debates touching ethnobiology, namely ethnoscience or folk classification systems. My doctoral supervisor, Roy Taylor, was a friend of Peter Raven, who had just co-authored, with Brent Berlin and Dennis Breedlove, some of the pioneering work on folk biological classification (see Berlin et al. 1966; Berlin 1972). Peter Raven also visited our university as a guest lecturer, and as a result of consultations with Taylor and Raven, my proposed graduate research was to focus on ethnobotany and folk plant classification of Haida, and later, Nuxalk (Bella Coola) and Stl'atl'imx (Lillooet) peoples of British Columbia, in a three-way ecological and linguistic comparison. I must note that one of the first and most inspiring reference works that I read at this time was Harold Conklin's doctoral dissertation, *The Relation of Hanunóo Culture to the Plant World* (1954). This and other works opened up a whole new area of fascination for me and provided some theoretical structure for my ethnobotanical research and analysis. Brent Berlin served as my external examiner for my doctoral dissertation, completed in 1974 (Turner 1974). My interest in folk classification has continued to the present time, and I have undertaken several papers in this area, inspired also by the work of Gene Hunn (1982), whom I met in the mid-1970s, Gene Anderson, and Cecil Brown (1984, 1985) among others. Much of this work, which requires exacting standards of linguistic analysis, has been aided and supported by collaboration with gifted linguists like Larry and Terry Thompson and others (see Turner 1987, 1988, 1989; Turner et al. 1998).

Plants in Traditional Food Systems

In 1980, the International Botanical Congress was held in Vancouver at UBC: "Botany 80." Just before the Congress, I had met Harriet Kuhnlein, who was then an ethnonutritionist at the School of Home Economics (later School of Family and Nutritional Sciences) at UBC. Harriet and I found much in common and she greatly stimulated my already existing interests in traditional food plants of British Columbia First Peoples. I also first met Tim Johns and Richard Hebda around this time. Then, at Botany 80, I met Dick Ford, Bob Bye, David French and other ethnobotanists who attended the Botany 80 Congress and co-presented in a plenary symposium on ethnobotany (published as a special issue of *Canadian Journal of Botany* in 1981). This was just when the Society of Ethnobiology was in its infancy, and Harriet, being one of the very early members, already knew Dick Ford, Bob Bye, Brent Berlin, Eugene Anderson, Amadeo Rea, and Gary Nabhan. In 1983, she encouraged me to come to the Society's meetings in Columbia, Missouri. From that time on, I was hooked. Listening to the wide range of papers presented at the conference opened the door to many new lines of thought for me in my own research. Until that time, I had barely heard about archaeobotany (or archaeozoology), for example. During the first few Society meetings, I was introduced to paleoethnobiology through the work of Liz Wing, Debby Pearsall, Paul Minnis, Steve Weber, Gail Wagner, Kristin Gremillion and later, Gayle Fritz, Mollie Toll, Karen Adams, Suzie Fish, Bruce Smith and others. I was also pleased to learn about the ongoing research being done in ethnoscience, ethnonutrition and other developing subfields of ethnobotany, as presented at these meetings.

Collaborating with Harriet Kuhnlein was one of the most stimulating and exciting times for me. It was at a time when I was working with a variety of First Nations, most particularly with John Thomas and other colleagues on a Nitinaht or Ditidaht ethnobotany (Turner et al. 1983). Harriet and John and I experimented with pit-cooking as a traditional cooking method during the course of Harriet's taking samples for nutrient analysis. Pit-cooking, as a highly effective and efficient method of large-scale food processing, is still an ongoing interest of mine, and it is gradually regaining popularity among British Columbia First Peoples. The Nuxalk Food and Nutrition Program, initiated and directed by Harriet is still held up as *the* example of an effective collaborative, community-based research program that has made a real difference to people's health and well-being (Nuxalk Food and Nutrition Program 1984; Kuhnlein and Moody 1989; Kuhnlein and Burgess 1997). Dick Ford made a site visit to Bella Coola during the course of this work, and saw first-hand what was being accomplished, including the development of a demonstration wild food plant garden at the health clinic. This program, too, gave me the first opportunity to work with Dana Lepofsky (see Lepofsky et al. 1985), then working on her master's degree, now an archaeobotany professor at Simon Fraser University and a leading light in British Columbia research on past human environments and relationships to land and resources.

During the decade from 1981 to 1991, Harriet Kuhnlein and I collaborated on many wild plant nutritional studies, and these were published in a variety of journals (Kuhnlein and Turner 1987; Turner and Kuhnlein 1982, 1983; Turner et al. 1985), culminating in a reference book, *Traditional Plant Foods of Canadian Indigenous Peoples* (Kuhnlein and Turner 1991). Of course, we were both inspired by the work of others like Gary Nabhan with his book *Gathering the Desert* (1985), and Timothy Johns with his research on chemical ecology and the origin of food and medicine (Johns 1990), not to mention Dick Ford's edited volumes, *The Nature and Status of Ethnobotany* (1978) and *Prehistoric Food Production* (1985). We still dream of further collaboration, although it is more difficult being at opposite ends of the country. Harriet's role in founding and developing CINE, the Centre for Indigenous Peoples' Nutrition and Environment at Macdonald College of McGill, later to be joined by Tim Johns, current director, is one of the major milestones in ethnobiological research development in Canada.

There are many others to acknowledge in the area of food and nutrition. For example, Paul Minnis raised my awareness of the significance of famine foods and other rarely but occasionally used foods in traditional diets (Minnis 1991; Turner and Davis 1993). My own interest in the role of plants in traditional diet, and in wild edible plants in general, continues to this day (see Turner 1995, 1998), and some of my graduate students like Sandra Peacock (1998), Dawn Loewen (1998), Kimberlee Chambers, and Brenda Beckwith, have continued and expanded this focus. Of course, I have to admit an interest in poisonous plants too, tied into my interest in food plants as well as in medicinal plants (Turner and Szczawinski·1991).

Plants in Traditional Healing

Medicines have always been a source of fascination for me, and have always been a part of my ethnobotanical research. Deep investigations in medicinal plants, however, require a knowledge of phytochemistry and analytical biochemistry, and this is not an area where I have any specialty. This is why the work of people like Tim Johns and his students and colleagues is so important. Tim Johns' work on chemical ecology is especially fascinating to me. My research in medicines is largely cultural and descriptive (Turner 1984; Turner and Hebda 1992). However, Kelly Bannister and others have taken this work further, undertaking antibiotic screening and more intensive analysis of medicinal plant compounds (Bannister 2000). This work has to be done with a high degree of sensitivity and recognition of primary issues like intellectual property rights, as well as safety issues, and conservation issues associated with overharvesting of medicinal plants by people who are not knowledgeable or qualified to use them. Kelly's work is exemplary in these areas. Here, I have to also acknowledge the contributions of Bob Bye and Edelmira Linares (see Linares et al. 1988) for their research on historical records of medicinal plant use in Mexico, as well as issues of marketing medicinal plants and sustainable harvesting of medicinal plants. I admire their work and that of their students very much; they have been role models for me. Trish Flaster's work in applied ethnobotany has also been an inspiration.

Plants in Technology

There have been many important references to the important material uses of plants in the work of Society of Ethnobiology members. Also, Dick Ford put me in touch with some of the original papers of Volney Jones and others who wrote long ago about this important area. Kay Fowler (1992), Elaine Joyal (1996a, 1996b), Kat Anderson (1993a), Michelle Stevens (1999) and others have all been working in areas of technology, and their work, especially experimental quantitative work, has inspired my thinking in this area (Turner 1996, 1998). I am particularly grateful to Marja Eloheimo, who was one of the key people to help provide a forum for the Northwest Native American Basketweavers Association's inaugural meeting, which I was privileged to attend in 1996. The importance of material plants, their management and conservation is of critical and ongoing interest. Some of these plants are also important in terms of sustainable harvesting as nontimber forest products.

"Pieces into Patterns":
Ethnoecology and Traditional Land Resource Management

All of the earlier work has culminated for me into an area of intense interest and importance, with direct relevance to both cultural and biological conservation. It started with the writings of Gary Nabhan, Amadeo Rea, Kay Fowler, Dick Ford, Gene Hunn (1990), Gary Martin, Gene Anderson (1996), Janis Alcorn (1994), Jan Timbrook (Timbrook et al. 1992), Kat Anderson (1993b, 1998), Bruce Smith, Virginia Nazarea (1998), Leslie Johnson Gottesfeld (1994a, 1994b), and Enrique Salmón (see Minnis and Elisens 2000)—more than I can even name or acknowledge, and is continuing through many areas of conservation biology and restoration right to the present time. I think it will consume and subsume much of my thinking and direct my future research. It is important to give critical consideration to the firm linkages that exist—and have existed for thousands of years—between indigenous peoples and their lands and environments, and the history of environmental and cultural change that has occurred in the colonial period and up to the present day. No matter what our areas of research focus are, the issues of loss of lands, loss of resources, loss of language, and loss of culture that threaten modern society throughout the world touch our work in innumerable ways. To me, this is a critical area of ethnobiological research, and as so many of members of the Society of Ethnobiology have already pointed out, this is going to remain the critical area for most of us in one way or another, far into the future.

Acknowledgments

Words cannot express my thanks and appreciation to the indigenous people of British Columbia who have been my teachers over the past thirty-plus years. Some of them are named in this short article; many others are not, but are acknowledged in various publications. Some have participated directly in the Society's meetings, particularly those held in Seattle and Victoria. I am indebted to my friends and colleagues in the Society of Ethnobiology for their research and insights. I have cited only a fraction of their work, just as examples. Many other individuals, and many other writings have provided me with ideas and information. In particular, I would like to acknowledge Dick Ford, whom I have named "Godfather of Canadian Ethnobotany" because of his constant and ongoing support of ethnobotanical researchers and research in Canada. Almost all of us studying ethnobotany in Canada have been touched by his wisdom and generosity.

References

Alcorn, Janis
1994 Huastec Mayan Ethnobotany. Austin: University of Texas Press.

Anderson, Eugene N.
1996 Ecologies of the Heart. New York: Oxford University Press.

Anderson, M. Kat
1993a Native Californians as ancient and contemporary cultivators. In: Before the Wilderness: Environmental Management by Native Californians, edited by T. C. Blackburn and M. K. Anderson, M. K., pp. 151-74. Menlo Park, California: Ballena Press.
1993b California Indian horticulture: management and use of redbud by the Southern Sierra Miwok. Journal of Ethnobiology 11(1):145-57.
1998 From tillage to table: the indigenous cultivation of geophytes for food in California. Journal of Ethnobiology 17(2):149-70.

Bannister, Kelly
2000 Chemistry Rooted in Cultural Knowledge: Unearthing the Links between Antimicrobial Properties and Traditional Knowledge in Food and Medicinal Plant Resources of the Secwepemc (Shuswap) First Nation. Doctoral dissertation, University of British Columbia. Vancouver, BC.

Berlin, Brent
1972 Speculations of the growth of ethnobotanical nomenclature. Language in Society 1:51-86.

Berlin, Brent, Dennis E. Breedlove, and Peter H. Raven
1966 Folk taxonomies and biological classification. Science 154:273-75.

Boas, Franz
1909 The Kwakiutl of Vancouver Island. American Museum of Natural History Memoir No. 8, pp. 307-515. New York.
1921 Ethnology of the Kwakiutl. Bureau of Ethnology Annual Report No. 35, 1913-1914. Smithsonian Institution, Washington, D.C.
1930 The Religion of the Kwakiutl Indians. New York: Columbia University Press.

Brown, Cecil H.
1984 Language and Living Things: Uniformities in Folk Classificaiton and Naming. New Brunswick, N.J.: Rutgers University Press.
1985 Mode of subsistence and folk biological taxonomy. Current Anthropology 26:43-62.

Conklin, Harold
1954 The Relation of Hanunóo Culture to the Plant World. Doctoral dissertation, Yale University.

Ford, Richard I. (editor)
1978 The Nature and Status of Ethnobotany. Anthropological Papers No. 67. University of Michigan Museum of Anthropology. Ann Arbor.
1985 Prehistoric Food Production in North America. Anthropological Papers No. 75. University of Michigan Museum of Anthropology. Ann Arbor.

Fowler, Catherine S.
1992 In the Shadow of Fox Peak: An Ethnography of the Cattail-Eater Northern Paiute People of Stillwater Marsh. Cultural Resource Series No. 5, U.S. Department of the Interior, Fish and wildlife Service, Region 1, Stillwater National Wildlife Reserve. Fallon, Nevada.

Gunther, Erna
1945 Ethnobotany of Western Washington. Seattle: University of Washington Press.

Hunn, Eugene S.
1982 The utilitarian factor in folk biological classification. American Anthropologist 84(4):830-47.
1990 Nch'i-Wana: "The Big River." Mid-Columbia Indians and Their Land. With James Selam and Family. Seattle: University of Washington Press.

Johns, Timothy
1990 With Bitter Herbs They Shall Eat It. Chemical Ecology and the Origins of Human Diet and Medicine. Tucson: The University of Arizona Press.

Johnson Gottesfeld, Leslie M.
1994a Aboriginal burning for vegetation managment in northwest British Columbia. Human Ecology 22(2):171-88.
1994b Conservation, territory, and traditional beliefs: an analysis of Gitksan and Wet'suwet'en subsistence, Northwest British Columbia, Canada. Human Ecology 22(4):443-65.

Joyal, Elaine E.
1995 An Ethnoecology of *Sabal uresana* Trelease (Arecaceae) in Sonora, Mexico. Doctoral dissertation, Arizona State University. Tempe, Arizona.
1996a The use of *Sabal uresana* (Arecaceae) and other palms in Sonora, Mexico. Economic Botany 50: 429-45.
1996b The palm has its time: an ethnoecology of *Sabal uresana* in Sonora, Mexico. Economic Botany 50: 446-62.

Kuhnlein, Harriet V.
1989a Change in use of traditional foods by the Nuxalk native people of British Columbia. Ecology of Food and Nutrition 27:259-82.

Kuhnlein, Harriet V., and Sandy Burgess
1997 Improved retinol, carotene, ferritin, and folate status in Nuxalk teenagers and adults after a health promotion program. Food and Nutrition Bulletin 18 (20): 202-10.

Kuhnlein, Harriet V., and Sandy A. Moody
1989 Evaluation of the Nuxalk Food and Nutrition Program: traditional food use by a Native Indian group in Canada. Report to the Society for Nutrition Education, pp. 127-132.

Kuhnlein, Harriet V., and Nancy J. Turner
1987 Cow-parsnip (*Heracleum lanatum* Michx.): an indigenous vegetable of Native People of northwestern North America. Journal of Ethnobiology 6(2):309-24.
1991 Traditional Plant Foods of Canadian Indigenous Peoples: Nutrition, Botany and Use. Vol. 8. In: Food and Nutrition in History and Anthropology, edited by Solomon Katz. Philadelphia, Penn.: Gordon and Breach Science Publishers.

Lepofsky, Dana, Nancy J. Turner, and Harriet V. Kuhnlein
1985 Determining the availability of traditional wild plant foods: an example of Nuxalk foods, Bella Coola, BC Ecology of Food and Nutrition 16:223-241.

Linares Mazari, Edelmira, Beatriz Flores Peñafiel, and Robert Bye
1988 Selección de Plantas Medicinales de México. México: Noriega Editores.

Loewen, Dawn L.
1998 Ecology, Ethnobotany, and Nutritional Aspects of Yellow Glacier Lily, *Erythronium grandiflorum* Pursh (Liliaceae) in Western University Canada. Master's thesis, Department of Biology, University of Victoria.

Minnis, Paul E.
1991 Famine foods of the Northern American desert borderlands in historical context. Journal of Ethnobiology 11(2):231-56.

Minnis, Paul E., and Wayne Elisens (editors)
2000 Biodiversity and Native North America. Norman: University of Oklahoma Press.

Nabhan, Gary Paul
1985 Gathering the Desert. Tucson: University of Arizona Press.

Nazarea, Virginia D. (editor)
1998 Ethnoecology: Situated Knowledge/Located Lives. Tucson: University of Arizona Press.

Nuxalk Food and Nutrition Program
1984 Nuxalk Food and Nutrition Handbook. Bella Coola, BC: Nuxalk Nation.

Peacock, Sandra
1998 "Putting Down Roots": Root Food Production in the Canadian Plateau. Doctoral dissertation, University of Victoria, BC

Rea, Amadeo
1997 At the Desert's Green Edge: An Ethnobotany of the Gila River Pima. Tucson: University of Arizona Press.

Salmón, Enrique
1996 Decolonizing our voices. Winds of Change, Summer 1996, pp. 70-72.

Steedman, Elsie V.
1930 Ethnobotany of the Thompson Indians of British Columbia. Based on James A. Teit's field notes. Bureau of American Ethnology 30th Annual Report. Smithsonian Institution. Washington, DC.

Stevens, Michelle L.
1999 The Ethnoecology and Autecology of White Root (*Carex barbarae* Dewey): Implications for Restoration. Doctoral dissertation, University of California, Davis.

Timbrook, Jan, John R. Johnson, and David D. Earle
1982 Vegetation burning by the Chumash. Journal of California and Great Basin Anthropology 4(2):163-86.

Turner, Nancy J.
1973 The ethnobotany of the Bella Coola Indians of British Columbia. Syesis 6:193-220.
1974 Plant Taxonomic Systems and Ethnobotany of Three Contemporary Indian Groups of the Pacific Northwest (Haida, Bella Coola, and Lillooet). Syesis, Vol. 7, Supplement 1.
1984 Counter-irritant and other medicinal uses of plants in Ranunculaceae by Native Peoples in British Columbia and neighbouring areas. Journal of Ethnopharmacology 11: 181-201.
1987 General plant categories in Thompson and Lillooet: two Interior Salish languages of British Columbia. Journal of Ethnobiology 7(1):55-82.
1988 "The importance of a rose"; evaluating the cultural significance of plants in Thompson and Lillooet Interior Salish. American Anthropologist 90(2):272-90.
1989 "All berries have relations": midlevel folk plant categories in Thompson and Lillooet Interior Salish. Journal of Ethnobiology 9(1):69-110.
1995 Food Plants of Coastal First Peoples. (Revised edition of Food Plants of British Columbia Indians. Part 1. Coastal Peoples. 1975.) Vancouver: University of British Columbia Press.

1996 "Dans une hotte": l'importance de la vannerie das l'économie des peuples chasseurs-pêcheurs-cueilleurs du nord-ouest de l'Amérique du Nord. Anthropologie et Sociétiés. Special Issue on Contemporary Ecological Anthropology: Theories, Methods and Research Fields. Montréal, Québec, 20 (3): 55-84.

1997 Food Plants of Interior First Peoples. (Revised and Reissued Handbook, orig. published in 1978 by British Columbia Provincial Museum.) Jointly published by University of British Columbia Press (Vancouver) and Royal British Columbia Museum (Victoria).

1998 Plant Technology of British Columbia First Peoples. (Revised Handbook, orig. published by BC Provincial Museum. 1979.) Vancouver: University of British Columbia Press.

Turner, Nancy J., and Marcus A.M. Bell
1973 The ethnobotany of the southern Kwakiutl Indians of British Columbia. Economic Botany 27(3):257-310.

Turner, Nancy J., and Alison Davis
1993 "When everything was scarce": the role of plants as famine foods in northwestern North America. Journal of Ethnobiology 13(2):1-28.

Turner, Nancy J., and Richard J. Hebda
1990 Contemporary use of bark for medicine by two Salishan Native elders of southeast Vancouver Island. Journal of Ethnopharmacology 229(1990):59-72.

Turner, Nancy J., Marianne Boelscher Ignace, and Brian D. Compton
1998 Secwepemc (Shuswap) tree names: key to the past? In: Salish Languages and Linguistics: Theoretical and Descriptive Perspectives. Trends in Linguistics, Studies and Monographs 107, edited by Ewa Czaykowska-Higgins and M. Dale Kinkade, pp. 387-417. New York: Hawthorn Books.

Turner, Nancy J., and Harriet V. Kuhnlein
1982 Two important "root" foods of the Northwest Coast Indians: springbank clover (*Trifolium wormskioldii*) and Pacific silverweed (*Potentilla anserina* ssp. *pacifica*). Economic Botany 36(4):411-32

1983 Camas (*Camassia* spp.) and riceroot (*Fritillaria* spp.): two liliaceous "root" foods of the Northwest Coast Indians. Ecology of Food and Nutrition 13:199-219.

Turner, Nancy J., Harriet V. Kuhnlein and Keith N. Egger
1985 The cottonwood mushroom (*Tricholoma populinum* Lange): a food resource of the Interior Salish Indian Peoples of British Columbia. Canadian Journal of Botany 65:921-27.

Turner, Nancy J., and Adam F. Szczawinski
1991 Common Poisonous Plants and Mushrooms of North America. Portland, Oregon: Timber Press.

Turner, Nancy J., John Thomas, Barry F. Carlson and Robert T. Ogilvie
1983 Ethnobotany of the Nitinaht Indians of Vancouver Island. Victoria: British Columbia Provincial Museum Occasional Paper No. 24.

-10-

Comments

Eugene N. Anderson
University of California, Riverside

The papers gathered here from the fields of archaeology and ethnography provide a mosaic of personal histories, and a set of visions for the future. Their common ground is an interest in ethnobiology as a field that records and analyzes data on traditional uses of plants and animals by particular ethnic groups. The papers agree that these data are collected not just out of interest, but for wider purposes—purposes that lie outside the field as narrowly defined. These wider agendas range from conservation to traditional land rights to reconstructing past cultures.

The archaeologists, in particular, clearly see their data as providing components of the data set needed to analyze sites and past cultures. The "plant remains" chapter and the "animal remains" chapter in the typical site report will eventually be folded into the synthesis made by the project director or equivalent authority. The more far-flung collections of archaeoethnobiological data will feed into studies of ancient Arizona agriculture, or of southeastern United States culture, or of mammal distribution in prehistory. One archaeologist in this collection adds an agenda for the future: a concern with conservation. Our knowledge of traditional resource management, from lost crops to fading agricultural techniques, can be useful to environmental managers, conservationists, and biologists.

The ethnographers are perhaps more conditioned to see learning about traditional biologies as an end in itself. Hunn and Brown have moved, during their careers, from a focus on general linguistics and cognition to a rather tight focus on how Native Americans see, understand, and classify biota. Nancy Turner has moved the other way, from botany to ethnology. (Our biologist readers might find it useful to be reminded that *ethnography* means the *description* of the cultures of particular ethnic groups; *ethnology* means the *comparison* and *analysis* of ethnographic materials. Ethnography yields data; ethnology generates theory or interpretation.)

Archaeologists

Karen Adams provides a superb and comprehensive introduction to paleo-ethnobotany in the Southwest. This is an article that should, and probably will, be mandatory reading for every student even slightly interested in that universe. It will be valuable for all paleoethnobotanists. She notes the value of paleoethnobotanical findings to ecologists and land managers, as well as to prehistorians. Interesting, to highlight one example, is her suggestion that we consider juniper not as "invading grassland," but as a plant as trying to reestablish itself in areas that were deforested by pre-Columbian peoples (see Chapter 5).[1] She documents a whole set of neat tricks for using plant remains as indicators of other matters: trade, status differences, medicine. *Ephedra* pollen in coprolites, for instance, indicates that the well-known uses of this plant as medicinal tea go back to prehistory.

Paul Minnis's paper (Chapter 4) is brief but to the point. He discusses the ways in which paleoethnobotany can and should be useful to biologists and environmentalists, and through them to conservation and land management. I will have more to say about these issues below.

Steven Weber (Chapter 3) provides a history of South Asian paleoethnobotany that serves as a valuable and exemplary case study. The trends he notes, from "grab it and bag it" to high specialization, are found throughout paleoethnobiology. Dr. Weber's contributions are among those (all too few) that are revolutionizing our understanding of prehistoric Indian agriculture. India is a meeting place of plants that has few equals in the ancient world; it not only innovated, but also borrowed, extensively and early, from the Near East, Africa, Southeast Asia, and probably China. Understanding this process will probably lead to striking reassessments of cultural development and exchange throughout Asia.

Elizabeth Wing covers the field of archaeoethnozoology in Chapter 2. Important to highlight are her and her colleagues' findings of local overexploitation of marine resources in prehistoric times and of the decline of clearwater mussels as early as the Archaic period because farming had so muddied the rivers by then. In California, too, we find overexploitation of marine resources (Erlandson and Glassow 1997), perhaps because local conditions periodically sharply and suddenly worsened, resulting in ruinous levels of exploitation of areas that had previously supported sustainable harvesting. She compares this with the depressing moa massacre by the first settlers of New Zealand, surely one of the sorriest blots on the hunting-history escutcheon. Fortunately, the Native Americans are not known to have exterminated any fish or shellfish species. But the next research project might change that.

Ethnographers

Cecil Brown (Chapter 7) provides his usual encyclopedic work, displaying an amazing knowledge of languages. He studies oak nomenclature, especially that of hunter-gatherers in areas where many species of oaks occur. He concludes that farmers have richer taxonomies, with more cases of folk generics broken into binomial folk specifics, than hunter-gatherers. This does not always hold. The Yucatec Maya have surprisingly few folk generics, though they do have more than many hunter-gatherer groups do. The Chinese, from the rather scrappy data available (to me, at least), started with a few oaks, each having a different name; as the Chinese people expanded, they encountered more oaks, and began to name them by giving them binomial specifics, assigning them to one or another of the formerly monolexemic classes they had. The Spanish seem to have done the same, as they expanded to Morocco and then to the Americas. The common native Spanish oaks all have their own monolexemic names: *roble, Quercus robur; encina, Q. ilex; coscoja, Q. coccifera; quejigo, Q. faginea; alcornoque, Q. suber.* In addition, *chaparra*, a Basque loanword, covers oak scrub in general. Rare oaks and non-native ones get the binomials, and this is evidently an extension since historic time. Brown has once again added to his encyclopedic study of plant and animal nomenclature around the world, a corpus that will be mined by scholars for decades.

Kay Fowler (Chapter 8) provides a useful quick overview of methods. Ethnobiology has been united more by methodology than by anything else. Working with ethnography, history, and archaeology, Fowler has combined all the methodologies in anthropology in her fieldwork among the Paiute. It is worth noting that excellent ethnobiology was being done right from the start of anthropology. Frank Cushing's fieldwork in Zuñi in the 1870s established a worthy benchmark. (He was the actual inventor of "participant observation," though Malinowski coined the phrase.) His research on maize was not published in book form until 1920 (Cushing 1920), but actually predates the earliest published ethnobotanies, having been initially published in 1884-85. It remains among the best studies ever done of a single food crop in a single culture. Cushing had the insight to bring production, consumption, religion, ritual, and myth together in one harmonious whole. Thus it foreshadowed the modern developments I shall discuss below. It is worth adding, also, that John P. Harrington brought to ethnobotany an insight into linguistics and cognition that was amplified by Barbara Freire-Marreco's insights into Native American culture, and the works Fowler cites therefore fully anticipate the cognitive revolution she discusses. Today, we have the many methodological guides that she reviews, and they form a very necessary part of the field kit. It should not be forgotten how well many early workers did in the course of actually inventing these methods.

In Chapter 6, Eugene Hunn notes that ethnozoology has been somewhat neglected by ethnobiologists, in spite of the fact that animals are so salient perceptually to people around the world. He segues into accounts of mythic animals, of animacy as a concept, and of Zapotec notions of animalness. He ends by saying that, since Berlin's early work, there has been a tendency to "loosen the grip of taxonomic structure, the better to appreciate the subtlety of peoples' understandings of the complex relationship among living things." Of course, the same thing has been happening among systematic biologists, who are now fighting over whether we should have scientific names and taxonomies at all. When I am among biologists, as I frequently am, I usually do not have to wait long before hearing an argument (or diatribe) on cladistics versus traditional approaches, on numbers versus Latin names, or on the current proposals to smash and regroup plant families. Formal structural-functional analyses have certainly seen challenges in recent years, and not just from postmodernism.

Nancy Turner (Chapter 9) gives us a delightful personal reminiscence of her days in ethnobotany. There is really little to add to her notes. Some of the happiest days of my life were those spent in the field with her and with her First Nations friends in Canada. The paper stresses the rich personal rewards of ethnobiological research, a matter that we all too rarely touch on in our presentations of data. But, again, she does not fail to make the point that ethnobotany is useful to conservation, to biology, and to Native Americans seeking support for recovering rights to their lands and resources.

We have learned to expect from Dr. Turner a deceptive simplicity covering a very rich and complex theoretical framework. In this paper, what appears to be a set of personal reminiscences soon reveals itself as a subtle series of comments on the human nature of ethnobiology. She supplies the full human element to this set of papers, describing both "outsider" and "insider" scholars as whole, living, breathing, feeling, and thinking persons. This is a point we must constantly recall to the foreground of our minds.

So we have archaeologists, cultural and linguistic anthropologists, and botanists. My own background and focus are still different. I am a cultural ecologist, primarily interested in biotic resource management. After switching from biology to anthropology, I was trained as an undergraduate in cultural ecology and ethnoscience, by Douglas Oliver and B. N. Colby, and I audited Richard Evans Schultes' ethnobotany course. As a graduate student I studied linguistic and cultural anthropology at Berkeley under Dell Hymes, George Foster, and others. Toward the end of my career, Brent Berlin came to Berkeley, and I wound up getting most of my final direction from him; he was not my "major professor" on paper, but he most certainly was my *doktorvater,* as the Germans say.

At that time, "ethnoscience" was a branch of cognitive studies, and was heavily influenced by linguistic concepts and methods. Some ethnoscientists were largely concerned with getting the exact usage of words (see Frake 1980). A wider interest, still cognitively focused, was displayed by Harold Conklin, whose superb paper at our meeting is unfortunately not available for publication here. When I discovered ethnoscience, he had just published his foundational work, *Hanunoo Agriculture* (1957)

"Ethnobotany," a term of older and wider use, was used more by botanists than by anthropologists. Schultes' famous researches in drug plants, and the work of his many students, were just beginning to revolutionize the field and to lead to far closer links between botanists and anthropologists (see Schultes and von Reis 1995).

Over the years, in addition to the trends toward specialization and technical sophistication noted above, ethnobiology has been characterized by two other trends: more cooperation between biologists and anthropologists, and increasing interest in how people relate through culture to the biotic world. From studies of economic botany (on the one hand) and word usage (on the other), we have moved to the present period, in which a good ethnobiological account will deal with religion, myth, prehistory, social relations of production, and all the other topics and subtopics dear to the ethnographer's heart. Pioneers like Schultes (and, before him, less well-known figures like Melvin Gilmore) pointed out the need for such holistic research long ago. We are now following their lead.

This is not just an academic matter. It has implications for that realm that academics condescendingly call "the real world." I will illustrate by telling my own story.

Most of my career was spent studying fisheries development, and, by later extension, the history and development of food systems. When Arturo Gomez-Pompa came to the University of California, Riverside, his charismatic presence led the Department of Anthropology to develop a major Maya focus. I was caught up in the excitement, and found myself moving from fisheries to Maya plant and animal knowledge and use. I have now spent twelve years doing research in Quintana Roo, mostly in the town of Chunhuhub, which (ironically in view of my fisheries past) has no permanent surface water.

I have been primarily concerned with the question of how we can achieve development without wiping out the planet. On the whole, the environmental movement has a simple answer: cut consumption. Many environmentalists spread this gospel by jetting to conferences around the world, staying in air-conditioned hotels, and consuming whole forests' worth of paper to produce memoranda and position papers.

I have spent most of my life among people who desperately need to consume more, not less. Three-fourths of the world's population still lives in want—cut off not only from the luxuries of modern civilization, but even from minimally adequate water, shelter, or services. Half the human race lives in poverty. Twenty percent of us—1.2 billion people—go to bed hungry every night or almost every night. Even in the affluent United States, 25% of our children live in poverty—only 14% did in 1970. In even less fortunate countries, I have seen children starving to death, and others dying of easily preventable diseases. I am thus not impressed with the adequacy of "cutting consumption" as a complete solution. The fortunate 10% of humanity who are truly affluent could redistribute their wealth, but that is a different question.

How can we provide adequate food, medical care, and education for the three billion poor of the world without destroying our resource base? It is all too true that we cannot sustain today's resource consumption, let alone a greater one.

There is only one way: to make far more efficient use of the resources we have (Smil 2000). Current agricultural and industrial practices waste the vast majority of the resources they consume (Smil gives truly astonishing figures). Only a tiny fraction of the world's plants and animals are utilized at all, and they are wastefully produced, processed, and utilized. Recent trends in agriculture have led to dependence on fewer and fewer species. We may soon be living entirely on wheat, maize, soybeans, rice, and four or five animal species. Thanks partly to this skewed system, we throw away enough food—in the garbage—to feed all those 1.2 billion malnourished people, and their pets into the bargain. This is neither sustainable nor morally tolerable.

The real question is: can we find efficient ways to use all the world's resources, thus escaping our current trap?

Ethnobiology provides the answer. Billions of people, throughout history and prehistory, have managed to have decent lives by using a far broader spectrum of resources, often using them more efficiently than we do.

The Maya of Quintana Roo survive by slash-and-burn agriculture, forest gathering and hunting, garden horticulture, and orchard-growing, supplemented today with stockrearing and wage work. My very preliminary list discloses 330 plants used for medicine and 122 for food. Many of these are wild plants that the Maya deliberately protect. Men cut little firebreaks around useful wild trees in the forest, and leave them uncut during milpa preparation. A dooryard garden can contain over 90 utilized species; the average is almost 40. There is a range from intensive raised-bed vegetable cultivation through open-field agriculture to managed weeds and then to slightly managed or protected wildlings. Traditional conservation measures carefully and rigorously protected wild trees. Traditions also controlled hunting, such that in old days game was abundant. Today the conservation measures have broken down and the game is rapidly disappearing.

Yields of maize agriculture in the area are about a ton per hectare, comparing favorably with the best that high-yield hybrid varieties can do under the Yucatan's harsh conditions. What matters, though, is the total yield of a milpa, which produces not only maize but also beans, squash, tomatoes, game, and wild plants.

By contrast, since the early sixteenth century, outsiders have always tried to manage the Yucatan Peninsula by monocropping, and they have always failed. Sugar, henequen, rice, sesame, cotton—all had their day and perished. Millions of acres are wasteland today because the forest will not reoccupy the worked-out soils that result. Currently, the big problem is attempted conversion of forest to cattle pasture. Cattle do well where there is natural grassland; otherwise they do poorly, or the pasture simply dies and the grows back to forest. Fruit culture is currently doing well, but only insofar as it is worked into the Maya polyculture system.

As most of us are aware, similar stories could be told almost anywhere in the world. In California, traditional use was less intensive and sophisticated than Maya agriculture, but we still have a great deal to learn from the Native Americans. They used the entire landscape, including a very large percentage of its plant and animal species. We do not exploit a single native plant for food or medicine on a significant scale, though we use several for industrial purposes, notably timber. We are thus shut out of using most of the state's area; less than 15% is suitable for our style of farming. Most of the rest offers some sort of grazing, but usually poor-quality and unsustainable.

This part of the story has often been told. Far better authors than I, such as Gary Nabhan (e.g. 1985), Mark Plotkin (1993), Victor Toledo, and Gene Wilken (1987), have made the case for using traditional resources and management methods. Here are some less well-known points to discuss.

First, we need to get traditional empirical knowledge accepted as science, not just "ethnoscience." Many scientists such as Lewis Wolpert (1993), as well as historians of science, tend to dismiss anything non-Western as not "real" science, and thus as unworthy of serious attention.[2] Yet, they are willing to follow the Ancient Greeks and the Renaissance theorists in referring to their activities as "science" (Greek *scientia*, from *scio*, to know)—though these sciences were based on very different principles from anything contemporary. Why, then, should we not use the term for empirical, practice-based knowledge of the world, so long as it generates general principles that systematize and extend observations? The case is being argued in a forthcoming book by Roberto Gonzalez, based on his thesis (Gonzalez 1998). Gonzalez points out that Zapotec agricultural science is based on "assumptions" that are sometimes clearly wrong by modern scientific standards, but on the other hand the Zapotecs have put together a vast amount of working knowledge that goes well beyond mere technology or traditional lore. This book will be a fine counter to the Wolperts of the world.

We are, thus, studying genuine science when we study Maya birdlore or Nuu-chah-nulth plant use. Moreover, the beliefs that are fundamental to Maya or Nuu-chah-nulth knowledge systems have to be seen as part of their science, no matter how odd those beliefs seem to modern agnostic academics (Gonzalez 1998). Ideas that certain animal species can turn into each other at will, or that trees are persons who need to be thanked when one takes their bark, are fundamental to these traditional sciences—just as humoral theories, phlogiston, and astrology were to the Western scientific tradition only a few generations ago. We cannot understand Maya science without understanding its transformation beliefs, any more than we can understand European medical science in the nineteenth century without knowing Galen's equally wrong but equally influential humoral theories.

Second, I have emphasized elsewhere (Anderson 1996) the value of traditional moral ideas. By and large, our biggest failure in the world today is in the moral area. Part of the reason is a flood of economic and pseudoevolutionary literature[3] that portrays

Man (mark the gender) as basically selfish and unable to defer gratification (see e.g. Wrangham and Peterson 1996). This almost writes off the possibility of morality, though some try to construct a Hobbesian social contract on that basis (e.g. Ridley 1996). Another problem lies with the ethical philosophers, who often seem to see ethics as "purely academic" in the worst sense of the word—a matter for arid debate, separated from real life.

A few welcome dissident voices occupy a middle ground, and argue for a practical morality that involves the environment and is based on the actual capacities and weaknesses of the human animal. It is significant that many of them (such as J. Baird Callicott 1994, and of course "our own" Arturo Gomez-Pompa and Gary Nabhan), are explicitly drawing on traditional ethical systems ranging from ancient Chinese to Native American.

In almost all societies except contemporary Westernized ones, environmental morality is usually, but not always, culturally constructed as what we usually call "religion."[4] Bringing it into the religious world gives it the emotional attraction, the powerfully compelling sanctions, and the social unity that properly belong to the religious sphere. Social scientists have known since Durkheim (1995/1912) that religion is a social phenomenon whose major purpose is to hold the group together and validate the group's social system, including its moral code. (Contrary to a widespread assumption, religion is *not* about explaining where things came from.) Durkheim showed that religion uses the carefully structured and managed emotions of ritual, ceremony, and festival to "sell" the moral messages. These moral messages include solidarity above all, but also other, more specific teachings. The Ten Commandments are a good example. Environmental ethics, too, fall into this pattern. The religious assumptions of the three "traditional" societies I know best—rural South China, the Northwest Coast, and the Mayan Yucatan—are quite different, but all work well at validating good environmental practice (Anderson 1996b). It should be noted that moral teachings by themselves are notoriously inadequate; so is economic rationality. Only when the two are combined, and socially constructed in some sort of political order, does anything get done in the real world (Anderson 1996b).

Third, science and religion in traditional societies are often associated with—and sometimes fused with—aesthetics. This requires further elucidation, but in the Northwest Coast (Anderson 1996a, 1996b), Aboriginal Australia (Johnson 1994; Morphy 1991, 1998), the American Southwest (see Ortiz 1969 for the Pueblos, Witherspoon 1977 for the Navaho) and many other indigenous societies, aesthetics is an inseparable and basic part of knowing the environment. It is impossible to imagine, envision, or teach such worldviews as the Navaho's without use of the arts. The feelings that we English speakers call "aesthetic emotions" are part of the basic way of interacting with the world. (Witherspoon's book on the Navaho gives the strongest and clearest statement of this, but the literature on Australia is perhaps, in total, more revealing.) John Muir, Sally Carrighar and many other "Western" environmentalists had the same general approach to the world, if I read them aright.[5]

In the end, I believe the most valuable lessons we can learn from traditional societies are lessons about how to implement conservation in the modern world. We can learn some biology from traditional peoples. We can learn a great deal about how people think. But, most of all, we modern world citizens have everything to learn about how to get conservation to work. The record of environmental protection in contemporary societies is not bright, and we are at an impasse to figure out what to do next. Traditional societies have the keys. This is not to say they were always successful, still less that they were "in harmony with nature"; they made their mistakes, as Dr. Wing points out. The point is that they were successful often enough to teach us something. We can, of course, learn from their mistakes as well. The Maori learned from theirs. By all accounts, they were excellent environmental managers when the English settlers came. Wiping out one's food supply and then having to say "What now?" must have been thought-provoking.

In short, we have to see ethnobiology as a science whose ultimate end is not just knowledge but knowledge applied to saving nature, and, as a part of that, to using resources more efficiently in order that humans and other creatures can live decent lives without wiping out the resource base. To do this, and even to understand adequately the actual uses and non-uses of plants and animals that we observe, we have to investigate entire worldviews: traditional science, religion, arts, stories, language, and society. This is a tall order, but books like Witherspoon's and Ortiz's show it is not an insurmountable difficulty. Indeed, over recent years, papers at our meetings by Leslie Johnson (1997 [this thesis includes material from several earlier papers]), Enrique Salmon (e.g. 1996), Marianne and Ron Ignace (e.g. M. Ignace 1994, 1996; M. Ignace et al. 1997; R. Ignace 1994), and many others have made the same general point, and illustrated it from their own observations. New works in ethnobiology, such as Amadeo Rea's *At the Desert's Green Edge* (1998), take account of this holistic view.

Obviously, no one paper can cover, or even deal with, all this ground. Papers like the ones in the present session, that treat particular specialties and methodologies within ethnobiology, are necessary and appropriate. What is needed is awareness of the total picture—awareness of the way the ground lies.

Endnotes

1. She says "pinyon/juniper," but pinyon is not invasive. I do not know of a single case of pinyon forest invading and taking over grassland. To the contrary: pinyon has been melting away with incredible rapidity in the last two centuries. Not only does it not invade new lands; it does not even reoccupy former pinyon lands cleared or burned in historic times (my observations, confirmed by frequent discussions with Richard Minnich, who has studied the matter). The areas deforested by mining in Nevada in the 1860s are still completely treeless. The myth of the invading pinyon has been perpetuated because of the wider myth of "pinyon-juniper forest," as if these trees were

somehow linked. They are not; they frequently occur in pure stands, especially at the lower margins (pure juniper) or upper margins (pure pinyon) of the semidesert woodland. I *have* noted pinyon invading small areas of yellow pine forests in recent years, no doubt as a by-product of the human-assisted warming and drying trend of the last few decades in the West.

2. Wolpert claims that "primitives" have some technology—which he equates with a chimpanzee's use of sticks—but not "science," because their knowledge of the environment is mere common-sense observation; it does not include counterintuitive or nonobvious inferences or principles. This is clearly wrong for all ethnoscience traditions so far studied in detail. The folk classifications that so many of us love to study require such inferences. So do the more complex and powerful cultural representations that lie behind actual behavior toward biota.

   Wolpert and his kin would have a case if they would restrict "science" to the specific inductive, experimental, and hypothetico-deductive traditions that were rather self-consciously begun by Bacon, Galileo, Descartes, Harvey, Boyle and others in the seventeenth century. This is indeed a very distinctive institution. Randall Collins (1998) calls it "rapid discovery science," a term I use with some reservations. However, by including the Ancient Greeks, Wolpert and his lineage privilege one traditional science (or ethnoscience) and invalidate their restrictive usage.

3. "Pseudo-evolutionary" because it draws on Darwinian theory to "prove" that humans cannot possibly do what they obviously do every day—live social lives characterized by the mutual restraint and mutual aid that is necessary to the maintenance of social systems. Hrdy (1999) has effectively challenged this literature from within the Darwinian camp. Humans are not alone; crows, wolves, most primates, and many other animals have evolved complex sociability. There are some evolutionary theories to account for this, based on the work of the late William Hamilton on kin selection; however, the whole field has weak theoretical underpinnings. See Cronk 1999, Sober and Wilson 1999 for reviews of recent and disparate views—none of them very convincing to the present author.

4. Unlike "science," "religion" really is a culture-bound term, and it is an unfortunate label for much of what goes on in non-Western cultures; there is, however, no good substitute word.

5. One might argue that Muir and Carrighar had enough Celtic heritage to absorb some late radiance from the very clearly aesthetic-religious view of nature that one finds in early Celtic literature, for example, the Irish epics. But, also, any reasonably sensitive person who spends years in more or less wild surroundings will understand without needing the heritage.

References

Anderson, E. N.
1996a Introduction. In: Bird of Paradox: The Unpublished Writings of Wilson Duff. Vancouver: Hancock House.
1996b Ecologies of the Heart. New York: Oxford University Press.

Callicott, J. Baird
1994 Earth's Insights. Berkeley: University of California Press.

Cushing, Frank
1920 Zuñi Breadstuff. Museum of the American Indian, Heye Foundation. New York.

Durkheim, Emile
1995 (1912) Elementary Forms of the Religious Life. Translated by Karen E. Fields. New York: Free Press.

Erlandson, Jon, and Michael Glassow (editors)
1997 Archaeology of the California Coast During the Middle Holocene. Institute of Archaeology, Perspectives in California Archaeology, 4. UCLA. Los Angeles.

Frake, Charles
1980 Language and Cultural Description. Stanford: Stanford University Press.

Gonzalez, Roberto
1998 Zapotec Science: Farming and Food in the Northern Sierra of Oaxaca, Mexico. Doctoral dissertation, University of California, Berkeley.

Hrdy, Sarah Blaffer
1999 Mother Nature: A History of Mothers, Infants, and Natural Selection. New York: Pantheon.

Ignace, Marianne
1994 More than the Sum of the Parts: Some Reflections on Secwepemc Discourse about Plants. Paper, Society of Ethnobiology, annual meeting. Vancouver.
1996 Salish Narrative Character Speech and Traditionl Ecological Knowledge. Paper, Society of Ethnobiology, annual meeting. Santa Barbara, California.

Ignace, Marianne, and Elders of the Cariboo Tribal Council
1997 Northern Secwepemc Ethnobotany: Teaching and Learning about Plants and Their Conext. Paper, Society of Ethnobiology, annual meeting. Athens, Georgia.

Ignace, Chief Ronald
1994 Traditional Land and Resource Relationships ot he Secwepemc People. Paper, Society of Ethnobiology, annual meeting. Vancouver.

Johnson, Leslie Main
1997 Health, Wholeness and the Land: Gitksan Traditional Plant Use and Healing. Doctoral dissertation, University of Alberta.

Johnson, Vivien
1994 The Art of Clifford Possum Tjapaltjarri. East Roseville, Australia: Gordon and Breach Arts International.

Morphy, Howard
1991 Ancestral Connections: Art and an Aboriginal System of Knowledge. Chicago: University of Chicago Press.
1998 Aboriginal Art. New York: Phaidon.

Nabhan, Gary
1985 Gathering the Desert. Tucson: University of Arizona Press.

Ortiz, Alfonso
1969 The Tewa World. Chicago: University of Chicago Press.

Plotkin, Mark
1993 Tales of a Shaman's Apprentice. New York: Penguin.

Rea, Amadeo
1998 At the Desert's Green Edge. Tucson: University of Arizona Press.

Ridley, Matt
1996 The Origins of Virtue. New York: Viking Penguin.

Salmon, Enrique
1996 A Model of Indigenous Botany. Paper, Society of Ethnobiology, annual meeting. Santa
      Barbara, California.

Schultes, Richard Evans, and Siri von Reis (editors)
1995 Ethnobotany: Evolution of a Discipline. Portland: Timber Press.

Smil, Vaclav
2000 Feeding the World. Cambridge, Mass.: MIT Press.

Wilken, Gene
1987 Good Managers. Berkeley: University of California Press.

Witherspoon, Gary
1977 Language and Art in the Navajo Univrse. Ann Arbor: University of Michigan Press.

Wolpert, Lewis
1993 The Unnatural Nature of Science. Cambridge, Mass.: Harvard University Press.

Wrangham, Richard, and Dale Peterson
1996 Demonic Males. Boston: Houghton Mifflin.